MARGARET
Countess of Jersey

MARGARET
Countess of Jersey

A BIOGRAPHY

Violet Powell

HEINEMANN : LONDON

William Heinemann Ltd
15 Queen Street, Mayfair, London W1X 8BE
LONDON   MELBOURNE   TORONTO
JOHANNESBURG   AUCKLAND

First published 1978

434 59956 5

Printed and bound in Great Britain by
Butler & Tanner Ltd, Frome and London

For
Georgia and Archie
great-great-grandchildren of M. E. Jersey

Contents

List of Illustrations		viii
Introduction and Acknowledgements		ix
Family Tree		x
1	Birth of a Head Girl	1
2	The Education of Margaret	11
3	The Road to Matrimony	26
4	Margaret's Predecessors	33
5	Introducing M. E. Jersey	43
6	Margaret as seen by Herself	50
7	'The joy of my life'	57
8	From Prussia to the Peloponnese	65
9	The Golden Jubilee	72
10	Through the Eyes of the Master	77
11	The Indian Experience	83
12	The Empress at Home: Two Countesses Abroad	96
13	Queen and Exile	105
14	Buried and Dug Up	113
15	An Island Night's Enchantment	119
16	Return to the Old World	132
17	The Children Grow Up	143
18	The Victorian Finale	151
19	The New Century	165
20	The End of an Old Song	175
21	Through the Eyes of a Granddaughter	180
Index		193

List of Illustrations

Between pages 20 and 21

1. The Honble Margaret Leigh, 1858
2. Stoneleigh Abbey, Warwickshire
3. Victor Albert George, 7th Earl of Jersey, as a child
4. Middleton Park, Oxfordshire

Between pages 52 and 53

5. Margaret, Countess of Jersey, 1878
6. Lady Galloway and her niece
7. Osterley Park, Middlesex

Between pages 84 and 85

8. Lady Jersey, 1880's
9. Lord Jersey, 1880's
10. Private View of the Exhibition of Old Masters, Burlington House, 1888
11. Arthur, Beatrice, Margaret and Mary Villiers, Osterley Park, 1890

Between pages 116 and 117

12. Government House, Sydney, *c.* 1890
13. The Governor General, his staff and family
14. Lady Jersey and Robert Louis Stevenson
15. Robert Louis Stevenson in Samoa

Between pages 132 and 133

16. Villiers, as an undergraduate, 1892
17. Margaret Villiers, *c.* 1895
18. Golden Wedding Party, August 22nd 1898
19. Lady Northcote and Lady Jersey

Between Pages 164 and 165

20. Middleton Park, Christmas 1904
21. The library, Middleton Park
22. Margaret, Countess of Jersey on her 90th birthday

Introduction and Acknowledgements

My grandmother, Margaret Elizabeth Jersey, was in her sixties when I was born. Consequently I can only remember with clarity the last twenty-five years of the ninety-six which she lived. I have, therefore, endeavoured to tell the story of her life as she saw it herself, and as it was seen by others, limiting my memories as a granddaughter to a final chapter. I should like to think that this is not only a portrait of a remarkable, even a brilliant, women, but of a particular aspect of the age in which she lived. Her travels, her years as a hostess, her friendship with influential men of four continents, had, as background, a family life of close affections and shared pleasures. I hope that I have done justice to both sides of M. E. J.'s career, and that this book is a tribute, not only of admiration, but of love and gratitude.

I must, in particular, thank my cousin, the present Lord Jersey, for access to his archives. I have reaped an immense benefit from my sister Lady Mary Clive's preservation of family photographs and from her reminiscences. I should like also to express my gratitude to Miss Janet Adam Smith, C.B.E., Mrs Cedric Barnett, O.B.E., Secretary of the Victoria League, Miss J. Coburn and the Staff of the Greater London Record Office (Middlesex Records), my cousin Lady Joan Colville, Mr Roland Gant, and my sister Lady Pansy Lamb. I owe much, once again, to my husband, Anthony Powell, for his help and advice.

FAMILY TREE *Chart A.*

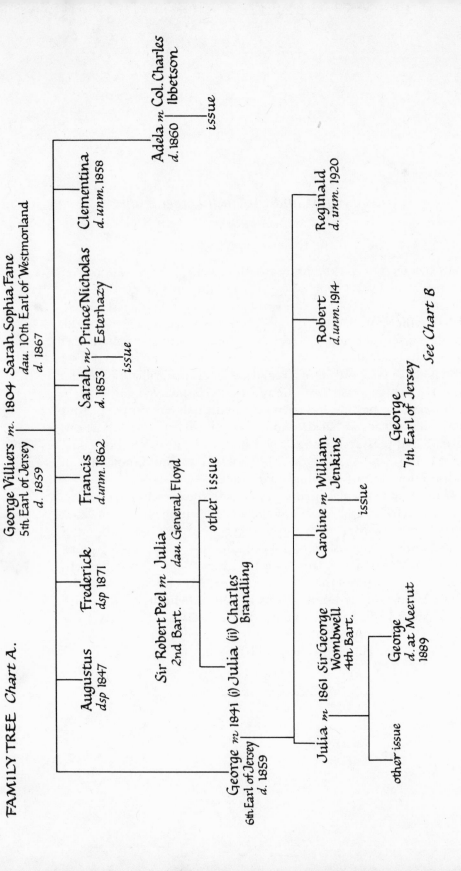

George Villiers *m.* 1804 Sarah Sophia Fane
5th Earl of Jersey   dau. 10th Earl of Westmorland
d. 1859   *d.* 1867

Augustus
dsp 1847

Frederick
dsp 1871

George *m.* 1841 (i) Julia (ii) Charles
6th Earl of Jersey   Brandling
d. 1859

Sir Robert Peel *m.* Julia
2nd Bart.   *dau.* General Floyd

other issue

Francis
d.unm. 1862

Sarah *m.* Prince Nicholas
d. 1853   Esterhazy

issue

Clementina
d.unm. 1858

Adela *m.* Col. Charles
d. 1860   Ibbetson

issue

Julia *m.* 1861 Sir George
        Wombwell
        4th Bart.

Caroline *m.* William
       Jenkins

issue

Robert
d.unm. 1914

Reginald
d.unm. 1920

other issue

George
d. at Meerut
1889

George
7th Earl of Jersey

See Chart B

FAMILY TREE *Chart B.*

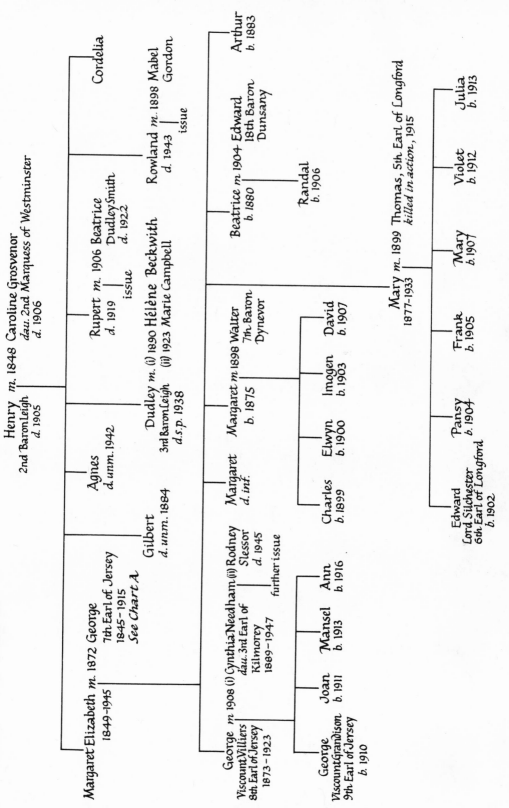

Henry *m.* 1848 Caroline Grosvenor
2nd Baron Leigh · *dau. 2nd Marquess of Westminster*
d. 1905 · *d.* 1906

Margaret Elizabeth *m.* 1872 George
1849–1945 · 7th Earl of Jersey
1845–1915
See Chart A

Agnes
d. unm. 1942

Gilbert
d. unm. 1884

Cordelia

Rupert *m.* 1906 Beatrice
d. 1919 · Dudley Smith
issue · *d.* 1922

Dudley *m.* (i) 1890 Hélène Beckwith
3rd Baron Leigh (ii) 1923 Marie Campbell
d.s.p. 1938

Rowland *m.* 1898 Mabel
d. 1943 · Gordon
issue

Beatrice *m.* 1904 Edward
b. 1880 · 18th Baron
Dunsany

Randal
b. 1906

Arthur
b. 1883

Margaret
d. inf.

Margaret *m.* 1898 Walter
b. 1875 · 7th Baron
Dynevor

Charles
b. 1899

Elwyn
b. 1900

Imogen
b. 1903

David
b. 1907

George *m.* 1908 (i) Cynthia Needham (ii) Rodney
Viscount Villiers · *dau. 3rd Earl of* · Slessor
8th Earl of Jersey · Kilmorey · *d.* 1945
1873–1923 · 1889–1947 · further issue

George
Viscount Grandison
9th Earl of Jersey
b. 1910

Joan
b. 1911

Mansel
b. 1913

Ann
b. 1916

Mary *m.* 1899 Thomas, 5th Earl of Longford
1877–1933 · *killed in action,* 1915

Edward
Lord Silchester
6th Earl of Longford
b. 1902

Pansy
b. 1904

Frank
b. 1905

Mary
b. 1907

Violet
b. 1912

Julia
b. 1913

Illustration Acknowledgements

The author is indebted to the following for permission to reproduce illustrations in this book: the National Portrait Gallery, London, for photograph no. 10, the New South Wales Government Printer for photograph no. 12 and the National Gallery of Scotland, Edinburgh, for photograph no. 14.

The majority of the photographs which appear in this biography are from the author's own private collection. Certain of the photographs used as illustrations are of unknown provenance and are believed not to be the subject of claimed copyright. If copyright is claimed in any of them the publishers will be pleased to correspond with the claimant and to make any arrangements which may prove to be appropriate.

1

Birth of a Head Girl

AT THE BEGINNING of the nineteenth century Stoneleigh Abbey, a great Warwickshire house with a wide estate, passed through a dramatic crisis of inheritance. This came about from the death of the Honble Mary Leigh, heir-at-law to her brother the last Lord Leigh of the first creation. The ennobled Leighs, who had commissioned Smith of Warwick to build a magnificent extension to the earlier Abbey buildings, came from a junior branch of the family. The head of the senior branch, the Revd. Thomas Leigh, lived less grandly at Adlestrop, forty miles away. It must have been clear that there would be a family scuffle at the death of Mary Leigh, for when this took place in 1806 Thomas Leigh had been warned to make haste and take possession of the Abbey, as the succession might well be disputed.

The new owner was a childless widower, but when he advanced upon his spectacular inheritance he had with him his cousin Cassandra, who had recently lost her husband the Revd. George Austen. With her two daughters in attendance, Mrs Austen had been staying at Adlestrop, and so it chanced that the complications of the Stoneleigh inheritance were exposed to the incomparably keen eye of Miss Jane Austen. At that date *Northanger Abbey* had been sold but remained unpublished in the hands of its purchaser. An Abbey in her mother's family may have been suggestive to the author, giving her the ideal background against which to ridicule the fashionable mock Gothic horrors, but Stoneleigh itself was to feature far more recognizably in *Mansfield Park*.

On an expedition that was to increase the emotional temperature of a complicated pattern of love-affairs, a party from Mansfield Park and the Vicarage drives to visit Sotherton Court. The scheme is ostensibly to advise Mr Rushworth, the unloved betrothed of Miss Bertram, as to the improvements that might be made to the grounds, should Humphrey Repton be engaged to remodel the landscape. In reality the day is spent in a sequence of flirtatious skirmishes. Jane Austen had seen the improvements Repton had made to the Revd. Thomas Leigh's grounds at Adlestrop. She knew the principles that were later to be applied to increasing the noble approach to Stoneleigh, and she gave to her heroine, Fanny Price, regrets that this would include the laying low of a wellgrown avenue. Indoors Fanny's romantic heart is disappointed by finding the chapel to be merely a handsome room, with plaster work, mahogany box pews and a family gallery. She had hoped in vain for signs that 'a Scottish monarch slept beneath', for Sotherton, like Stoneleigh, had been the home of Cavaliers. The chapel stands as it did. On the ledge of the family gallery there can still be seen the red velvet cushions, which to Fanny Price, standing below, seemed only part of a prosaic scheme of church furnishing.

For the Austen family Stoneleigh had a deeper concern than that of a cousin's inheritance, Mrs Austen's brother, James Leigh-Perrot, being one of those who had an interest in the estate. Mrs Austen herself regarded her family as likely beneficiaries under her childless brother's will, for her daughters were consistently kind to their lugubrious aunt, Mrs Leigh-Perrot. With these prospects, Jane Austen took a keen interest in the closer kin of the Revd. Thomas Leigh, even before he had inherited the Abbey.

She wrote from Bath in 1801 that she congratulated herself on having 'a very good eye for an adulteress', which had enabled her to identify a Miss Twisleton, a distant cousin, divorced by her husband, later Lord St Vincent, for crim. con. Instinct alone was not responsible for spotting the adulteress. Miss Twisleton's sister, Julia Judith, was known to the Austens as the wife of James Leigh, nephew, and eventual successor at Stoneleigh, of the Reverend Thomas Leigh.

Comparing the sisters, Jane Austen found the adulterous Miss Twisleton not so pretty as she had expected '... her face has the same defect of baldness [as Mrs James Leigh's], & her features are not so handsome'. The handsome, though bald-faced, lady was to be the great-grandmother of Margaret Elizabeth, the subject of this biography. Jane Austen saw Mrs Leigh with disapproval that went deeper than merely finding her to be lacking in eyebrows or eye-lashes.

When the Revd. Thomas Leigh died without issue in 1813, his

cousin Jane wrote with asperity that he died possessed of 'one of the finest estates in England and more worthless Nephews and Neices than any other private Man in the United Kingdom'. She also wrote that her aunt, Mrs Leigh-Perrot, must be pitied, as but for 'that vile compromise' she would now be mistress of Stoneleigh. The 'vile compromise' had resulted in James Leigh-Perrot receiving an income, and a lump sum from the Stoneleigh estate. Unhappily the hopes that their uncle's death in 1817 would result in immediate benefits to the Austen family were disappointed. Jane, struggling with the illness that was soon to kill her, was so distressed by the downcast state of those around her that she had a relapse.

There had, however, been a period of four years when Jane Austen must have observed that some of the worthless Nephews and Neices (her usual spelling) were having no easy time. Assuming that she regarded James Leigh and his wife Julia, the actual possessors of Stoneleigh, as among the most unworthy, it must have been difficult not to take a sardonic interest in the immediate threat to their inheritance. In fact these heirs were entering on a period of Gothic melodrama to delight Catherine Morland, whose every effort to raise horrid mysteries behind the walls of Northanger Abbey had met with a distressingly rational explanation.

The Leigh peerage, as already mentioned, had become extinct, but in 1813 the new owners of Stoneleigh were faced by a claimant not only to their inheritance but to the peerage itself. This claimant purported to be descended from a son of an earlier Lord Leigh, by a first marriage which, with its issue, had been recorded on a memorial in Stoneleigh church. A number of witnesses were produced who swore they recalled the monument, said to have been removed in 1811. However their recollection of the colour of the tablet varied so astonishingly that little credence could be given to their memory of what was written on it. Some swearing also took place that James Leigh had been seen supervising the removal of the memorial by night, his wife encouraging the dark deed by holding the candle, to light the disposal of the broken tablet into a convenient vault. The claimant was proved to come from a Lancashire family of Leigh, as had the Leighs of Stoneleigh originally, but not from a common ancestor. Those who thought this would settle matters were mistaken. As *The Complete Peerage* points out, the Leighs were assailed, legally and physically, on three subsequent occasions.

Educated privately, James Leigh made a more favourable impression on his tutor, the Revd. Isaac Hunt, than he did on Jane Austen, for the christian names of James Henry Leigh were given to the poet Leigh Hunt as a tribute to his father's pupil. James Leigh's own son was christened Chandos after his grandmother's brother, the Duke of Chandos, and there was a family legend that he had fagged for Byron at Harrow. They were certainly known to each other, for Byron, during one of his abortive efforts to sell Newstead Abbey, denied that 'Mr Leigh' was the real principal involved, but wished it had been so, because of Mr Leigh's readily available wealth. Why Mr Leigh, however rich, should contemplate bringing another abbey into the family was unexplained.

A frequenter of Holland House and London literary circles, Chandos Leigh was a prolific rather than an inspired poet, though there sounds to be some promise in a poem called *The Island of Love*. In 1839 the owner of Stoneleigh was made a baron at the instigation of Lord Melbourne. The staunchly Tory Vicary Gibbs, editor of *The Complete Peerage*, writes sharply of this elevation, as unsuitable, coming from a Liberal Prime Minister, for a supporter whose public life had been essentially local. Even in his own neighbourhood the new Lord Leigh was denied the quiet life that a sensible pamphlet, encouraging squires not to abandon themselves to despair at the Repeal of the Corn Laws, might have led him to deserve.

Rioting on behalf of a certain John Leigh, a mob stormed the Abbey, it being, apparently, a fixed idea locally that any Leigh had more right to the property than the Leigh actually in possession. Four years later, in 1848, there was an even more serious crisis, Lord Leigh being charged with the murder, thirty years before, of four workmen engaged on work at the Abbey. It is worth remarking that among the misadventures that dogged Chandos Leigh's school fellow, Lord Byron, his Abbey was never stormed by a mob, nor was he ever accused of quadruple murder. This last charge was proved to be a malicious fabrication, but the ordeal can have barely been over when Lord Leigh's heir, Henry, married Lady Caroline Grosvenor at St George's, Hanover Square. The birth of their first child, Margaret Elizabeth, inaugurated a new generation and a golden age of hospitality.

At the age of two days the infant Margaret, born on October 29th 1849, made the first of many public appearances. The North Warwickshire Hunt had met at Stoneleigh, as was the custom, for the opening meet of the season, and she was held up at a window for the followers of the Hunt to drink her health. When she came to write her memoirs she introduced herself in this picturesque incident. She also pointed out, with characteristic realism, that the Hunt's good wishes failed to turn her into a sportswoman in spite of a life spent among devotees of the chase. On the other hand public appearances became so much part of her life that she came to move from public to private life and back without self-consciousness or self-importance.

Although Margaret Leigh had been born at Stoneleigh, her parents had their first married home at Adlestrop, from whence Jane Austen had set out with her kindred to take possession of the Abbey. Among the Austens there continued to be concern as to the next presentation of the living of Adlestrop. This was held in trust by a cousin, of whom Jane Austen disapproved, until another cousin, a Twisleton, should return from Ceylon to claim it. Presentation of livings play an important part in the plots of *Sense and Sensibility*, *Pride and Prejudice*, *Mansfield Park* and *Persuasion*, but their author never attempted to paint such a turbid married life as that of Thomas Twisleton, first Archdeacon of Colombo and incumbent of Adlestrop. The wife he had married when only eighteen left him to go on the stage, her divorce by Act of Parliament not becoming absolute until she had given birth to a child by another man.

Besides being brother to the two Twisleton sisters stigmatized as bald-faced, the Archdeacon was brother and eventually heir to Lord Saye and Sele. His first wife's indiscretion brought about a legitimacy suit before the peerage could pass to the Archdeacon's son by a second marriage. This was after Jane Austen's death, but the Archdeacon himself came under the cloud of displeasure which blackened her view of the Twisleton family. She wrote with condemnation of the manœuvres by which the living of Adlestrop was passed to Thomas Twisleton. In fact, the living was to be held by connections of the Leigh family for more than a century.

Adlestrop achieved immortality when Edward Thomas's express train halted 'unwontedly' there on a July afternoon.

> And for that minute a blackbird sang
> Close by, and round him, mistier,
> Farther and farther, all the birds
> Of Oxfordshire and Gloucestershire.

In July a hundred years before Jane Austen had heard the ancestors of those birds of Oxfordshire and Gloucestershire singing. In 1915 the parish of Adlestrop was still in the care of one of the many clerical descendants of the worthless nephew, James Leigh, who, contrary to Jane Austen's gloomy prognostications, was the progenitor of a line of dedicated pastors.

Chandos, Lord Leigh, did not live long to enjoy the defeat of his enemies, dying in 1850 in his sixtieth year. Consequently Margaret's father and mother were only twenty-six and twenty-one when they came into their inheritance and moved from Adlestrop to Stoneleigh. It was a surprise to their daughter to realize how young they had been, when she came to write of her father's embarrassment at his daughter's cradle falling out of the back of his dog cart. On her first sight of William Henry Leigh, Lady Caroline Grosvenor had known at once that she could marry no one else. His reciprocation became obvious to bystanders when he paid £5 for a trifle at a charity bazaar at which this daughter of the Marquess of Westminster was selling.

It happened that another novelist, if only a minor one, was to hand, to leave word pictures of the 2nd Lord Leigh and his bride. The minor novelist was Mrs Archer Clive, wife of a landowning clergyman in Herefordshire, and a friend of Mary Russell Mitford. Caroline Clive's pen was sharp, but she obviously fancied good-looking men. In March 1847, she wrote, 'Mr Leigh is remarkably handsome-fair, with much colour, fine eyes, very fine mouth, and an open pleasant expression.' With these natural advantages it is sad that she found him 'a mere booby' conversationally, a man who had seen nothing to enjoy in Spain and, amazed at the Spaniards not understanding his bullying and swaggering, hated them and Frenchmen 'with true old stolidity'.

This turned out to be a misapprehension. Henry Leigh, as will be seen, thoroughly enjoyed setting the town of Mentone *en fête*, when spending a winter on the Riviera. Mrs Clive's interest in young Mr Leigh was intense as she understood that he had been refused by the only daughter and heiress of the friends with whom she was staying. On a visit to the National Gallery Mr Leigh was suddenly brought to Mrs Clive's mind by the sight of Correggio's *Christ Bound*, though she assured herself that the thought was unbidden. Next came the news of his marriage, indisputably a love-match, to Lady Caroline Grosvenor. Mrs Clive noted, 'She is very little, red-faced, plain, sensible, clever, amusing. He the hand-

somest dull but merry man in England.' So happy was this union
of Beauty and Brains that, a century later, their daughter Margaret
described her parents as having been lovers all their lives.

Small in size Caroline Leigh may have been – her husband
charmed the villagers at Stoneleigh by snatching up his bride and
carrying her over a puddle – but her personality was of the kind
known as towering. Throughout the fifty-seven years of her married life her dominion over her family was complete. As middle-
aged men and women her children laughed to find that 'Mama
said' was still quoted by them as the ultimate authority on any
debatable point. It should here be mentioned that the Leigh children addressed their parents as 'Mama' and 'Papa' with an intona-
tion that was presumably French in origin. This was passed on
to Margaret Leigh's own children, the accent deteriorating somewhat, so the names sounded perilously like 'Mummer' and 'Pup-
per'. Indeed the appellation 'Mummer' lingered on in the family
of one of Margaret's own daughters, not entirely appreciated as
a genuine, if eccentric, link with the speech of an earlier age.

Part of Lord Leigh's abounding hospitality was to entertain the
North Warwickshire Hunt annually at an opening meet, one of
which had been the occasion of his daughter's introduction to his
neighbours. Even his generosity faltered, however, when it was
rumoured that special trains were running from nearby Birmingham to take advantage of the bread, cheese and beer offered to
all comers. Lord Leigh was a fearless man to hounds, his falls out
hunting breeding a troop of applicants for his bounty from those
who claimed to have caught his horse or picked him out of a ditch.
Her father's merry nature, to quote Mrs Clive, was of special
pleasure to Margaret when, in 1922, she looked back on the
glowing happiness of her childhood in order to write *Fifty-One
Years of Victorian Life*, the memoirs of the first half-century of her
career.

Usually keeping an attitude of detachment, Margaret became
indignant when she contemplated the legends that Victorian children led cowed lives, with no luxuries and few treats, although she
acknowledged that her mother ruled with authority unquestioned. Margaret was regarded as a dangerous heretic by her
younger brothers and sisters when she allowed herself to express
a doubt that their mother might be able to make a watch. 'Vainly
did I hedge,' she wrote, 'by asserting that if she had learnt she could
make the most beautiful watch in the world – I had infringed the

first article of family faith by thinking that there was anything which she could not do by the uninstructed light of nature.'

This incident must have belonged to a time when the family had grown to five or six children, with Margaret as Vicereine, or, as the youngest child Cordelia called it 'Head Girl'. In earlier days when Margaret was four years old, she had rushed into the nursery shouting the exciting news, 'There is a country called France and I am going there!' The first journey in a lifetime of travelling also included her next brother and baby sister, both her parents being accustomed to travelling in family caravans. Chandos Leigh had travelled on the Continent for three years in hierarchic fashion, a coach each for parents, schoolroom and nursery. Meeting with this caravan on the Riviera the Grand Duke Constantine exclaimed, with reason, 'Toute l'Angleterre est en route.'

Lord Westminster, on the other hand, had sailed round the Mediterranean with his family in his yacht. Caroline Leigh could remember the sweetmeat seller in Constantinople who wiped his hands on the back of his cat between serving each customer, and the freedom with which, when at Rome, she and a sister, girls of twelve and thirteen, were allowed to ramble out by themselves onto the Campagna in the early morning. Both Margaret's parents came from families of nine or ten children, many of whom kept up the rate of reproduction. Margaret herself calculated that she had, at one moment, first cousins alive to the number of one hundred, seldom visiting any part of the world without finding a first cousin waiting to greet her. Naturally the spread of these families led to a confusion of generations, Margaret finally possessing first cousins younger than her own children, and nephews younger than her grandchildren.

Something of the exuberance of the Grosvenor family can be gathered from a conversation piece painted circa 1825, of Lord Westminster seated amid a dozen of his kindred, two of whom play the harp and spinet so that a pair of little girls can dance before their elders. Margaret cherished a copy of this picture, the background being the Long Gallery of Grosvenor House, one of the victims in what might be called the massacre of Mayfair mansions which took place in the nineteen-twenties. The picture had been painted before Caroline Leigh's birth, but in the copy made for her husband an extra little bonneted head was added to the toddlers playing on the floor.

An affectionate family, the Grosvenors grieved deeply if a child was snatched from them by accident, or by the killer diseases of the period. Although when her fourth daughter died she had seven surviving, Lady Westminster welcomed the ninth as a gift from God and christened her Theodora. Grandchildren swarmed in the Long Gallery at Grosvenor House and it was here that Margaret, aged less than three years old, was introduced to the most famous man alive in Europe, the first Duke of Wellington. Lord Leigh said the hero kissed his daughter, Lady Leigh that he shook hands, but Margaret was herself determinedly honest in saying that the incident was before the dawn of her memory, phenomenal as this turned out to be. Had any additional reason been needed for bringing her great-grandchildren to see her, it would have been to keep alive this historic contact until the latest possible moment.

Queen Victoria's visit to Stoneleigh was, on the other hand, totally recalled by Margaret, now aged eight. So packed was the house that the younger children were farmed out, but Margaret and her six-year-old brother Gilbert, called Gilly, were stowed away with some of the maids and allowed to join in the revels. The object of the Queen's visit in July 1858 was to open Aston Hall and Park for the benefit of the people of Birmingham. Lord Leigh was Her Majesty's Lord Lieutenant for Warwickshire, and consequently it was his duty to entertain her for the two nights she would be spending in that county, an obligation to him entirely congenial.

Had the Queen been settling at Stoneleigh for a month, preparations could hardly have been more magnificent. The main block of the house and the gatehouse, which bore the arms of Henry II, were outlined with 22,000 fairy lights. Long afterwards one of Margaret's sons was told further details by a former coach painter, who recalled with nostalgia that even the pigsties were painted. It was improbable that the Queen would carry her inspection to such extremes, but equal efforts were made to please her indoors. On the understanding that her preference was for white and gold furniture, the Chippendale fittings in her bedroom were so painted. If such a decorative scheme was far from the cabinet maker's intention, the result, hallowed by association, was prettily baroque in effect. The royal suite was blocked off by a temporary wall, and in later years children would delight in displaying the water-closet, which had been installed in a cupboard in the Queen's dressing-room.

Although Queen Victoria was apt to keep even the most loved of her own children at arm's length, on this visit she was charming to the children of her host. Her kindness engendered a respect and love in Margaret, which was never to falter in the ninety years that followed the great day at Stoneleigh. The Prince Consort did not, however, win the same loyal approval. Accustomed to kindly notice from visitors, Margaret and Gilly found his reserve to be repellent. He lost any chance of winning their hearts by sweeping them aside when they were running forward to see the Queen plant a commemorative tree. As in later years the name of Lytton Strachey, to her an iconoclastic traitor, could hardly be breathed in Margaret's presence, the Prince Consort's behaviour must have been exceptionally rough to have remained so long unforgiven. At the age of eight Margaret's position of leadership in her family was already established, her education soon making it un-challenged.

2

The Education of Margaret

FIRST TO CARE for Margaret was her wet nurse, who, when her charge was about four years old, married the coachman. Although the author was usually quick to deal with any question of moral ambiguity, *Fifty-One Years of Victorian Life* offers no clue as to whether the nurse had been previously widowed, or whether the need for a wet nurse had over-ruled objection to a lapse from virtue. Luckily for the children, her successor, Mrs Gailey, was a stimulating companion as well as a kind nurse. Round her the nursery and schoolroom children clustered, while she told them her own versions of fairy tales, novels and, on Sundays, the *Pilgrim's Progress*.

Mrs Gailey had come to Stoneleigh from the household of Lady Leigh's first cousin, the Duke of Norfolk, whose eldest son was the most beloved of her nurslings. That she was a disciple of Spurgeon may seem an anomaly for the nurse in the family of the leading English Roman Catholic, but at that date the Duchess of Norfolk was an Anglican, her daughters following their mother's faith. The Duchess's conversion made Mrs Gailey's position impossible, and so she came to Stoneleigh. Hearing about the distress of the eldest Norfolk daughter, a child of twelve, at the uprooting of her faith influenced Margaret in a life-long distaste for the Roman Church. She would refer, in later years, to those 'wicked Anglo-Catholics', regarding them as having emerged from a Trojan Horse, wilily insinuated by the Pope into the Church of England.

Although doing her best to topple legends of the suppression of Victorian children, Margaret did admit that religious instruction was more intensive than a later generation would have tolerated. It was, however, conducted at home, and not by the local clergyman. Descended from many clerical forbears and with many kinsmen in Holy Orders, the Leighs did not see this as a reason for seeking spiritual direction from those to whom they were frequently in the position of patrons. This attitude was summed up by Lady Westminster when she remarked to her daughter Lady Leigh: 'My dear, you and I spend much of our lives in rectifying the errors of the clergy.'

Morning prayers were read in the chapel by Lord Leigh, in the dramatic manner characteristic of his family. As well as being disappointed in the appearance of the chapel at Sotherton, Fanny Price was pained by Miss Crawford's cynical comment that no sensible person could regret that family prayers were no longer said there. If this was true when Jane Austen first knew Stoneleigh, later generations made up for the years of lost devotion. The children of the house were sat on rep stools, their backs to the ledge which ran along the gallery, while Lady Leigh bustled in, drawing on the long suede gloves which she kept on for breakfast. This took place when the menservants, segregated on one side of the chapel from the maidservants, had returned to their domestic duties.

On Sundays the Leighs went to two church services, and the children had extra scripture lessons to learn. Besides learning her own, Margaret was expected to oversee the lessons of her brothers and sisters. Born with a memory of rare tenacity, this practice caused a vast amount of scripture to be imprinted on her mind. Eventually there was a problem as to what possible holy lessons could be set for her to learn, and the solution brought about a unique gesture of rebellion towards her mother. Ordered to learn extracts from Thomas à Kempis' *Imitation of Christ*, Margaret did not refuse, but repeated her task in such lugubrious tones that this scheme for her spiritual advancement was allowed to lapse.

With a religious faith that withstood, unshaken, the buffets of life for nearly a century, Margaret had always a sharp apprehension as to when enthusiasm degenerated into the ridiculous. Somewhat surprisingly, she passed through a period when she worshipped at High Church altars, but this was in her youth, and she returned to the Evangelical tradition of the Church of England in which she had been brought up. In her autobiography she took the opportunity of quizzing what she called 'the New Oxford School' on matters of ecclesiastical apparel. She could just recollect the Vicar of Stoneleigh preaching in a black silk Geneva gown, regarded as an essentially Low Church robe, but, incidentally, the most Popish garment in the Reformed Church, being none other than the monk's frock. Earlier the Geneva gown had been abandoned by a cousin, Charles Twisleton, son of the Archdeacon of Colombo of whom Jane Austen disapproved. When Mr Twisleton astonished his cousins at the Abbey by following the 'new Oxford School's' innovation of preaching in a surplice, he denied that he had become an adherent of the High Church Doctor Pusey. ' "No, my dears" [he said] "but black silk gowns are very expensive and mine was worn out." '

Readers of the novels of Charlotte M. Yonge, a staunch supporter of High Anglicanism, will be surprised to find that there was a reason of economy for following Doctor Pusey's innovations. These novels contain wonderful pictures of the details of Victorian life and religious practice, and, as they were often written for a public of growing girls, Confirmation frequently plays a part in their plots. For instance *The Castle Builders* has *The Deferred Confirmation* as its second title, and it is the continued postponement of the ceremony that gives the story its tension. Miss Yonge's readers were by no means limited to girls of an age to be prepared for Confirmation. During a walking tour Mr Gladstone was reported to have been absorbed, late at night, in a book by Charlotte M. Yonge, putting it down, at last, with the relieved remark, 'I see daylight. Mr—— is going to be confirmed.' Margaret Leigh's account of her own preparation for Confirmation is so remote from that of Miss Yonge's candidates that her own words may be quoted.

'In 1867 I was confirmed. The church which we attended was in Park Street. It has since been pulled down, but was then regarded as specially the church of the Westminster family. One Sunday . . . the clergyman gave out notice of a Confirmation, with the usual intimation that Candidates should give in their names in the Vestry. My mother told me to do this accompanied by my younger brother (Gilbert) as chaperon. The clergyman seemed a good deal surprised, and I rather fancy that I was the only Candidate. He was an old man who had been there for a long time. He said that he would come and see me at my parents' house and duly arrived at 37 Portman Square.

'I was sent in to my father's sitting-room for the interview, and I believe that he was more embarrassed than I was, for I had long been led to regard Confirmation as the proper sequence to learning my

Catechism and a fitting step in religious life. The clergyman somewhat uneasily remarked that he had to ascertain that I knew my
Catechism, and asked me to say it. This I could have done in my
sleep, as it had for years formed part of my Sunday instruction.
When I had ended he asked me after a pause whether I knew why
the Nicene Creed was so called. This was an unexpected pleasure.
I had lately read Milman's *Latin Christianity* to my mother, and
should have enjoyed nothing better than delivering to my pastor
a short lecture on the Arian and Athanasian doctrines. When I
began it, however, he hastily cut me short, saying that he saw that
I knew all about it – how old was I? "Seventeen and a half." "Quite
old enough," said he, and he told me that he would send me my
ticket, and when I went to the church someone would show me
where to sit. This ended my preparation as far as he was concerned.
I believe he intimated to my parents that he would see Miss Leigh
again, but in practice he took care to keep clear of the theological
enfant terrible.'

This passage is valuable both for the picture it gives of Margaret's background, and as an example of the narrative skill which
enabled her to set the scene before the reader; the arrival of Miss
Leigh, grand-daughter of the Vicar's patron, in the Vestry, the
embarrassed interview, the flight from the theological lecture,
which it might have been considered should have been delivered
by the Vicar. The succeeding incidents, and the detachment which
enabled Margaret to enjoy her own bumptiousness, stand out as
freshly as if she was not writing sixty years later. The grammar
and punctuation are undeniably somewhat rough, probably from
lack of instruction in parsing and analysis. English grammar was
a study which Margaret declared, throughout her life, to be superfluous to those who had, like herself, studied modern and ancient
languages. In later years, granddaughters set to translate their
grandmother's fairy stories into French found this theory to be
distinctly suspect.

Margaret's literary career began in childhood, an early work
being dedicated, touchingly, 'to Papa because he is so kind'.
Chandos Leigh may have been a serious poet, though fecund
rather than inspired, but to the next generation of Leighs the
writing of prose and verse seemed no more than a natural celebration of any event, public or private, providing entertainment
both for performers and audience. Chandos Lord Leigh's
second son, Edward Chandos, had particularly the knack of

writing what he called 'business' for his nephews and nieces to act. A bachelor in middle life, he had no closer family claim than his brother's children, until Margaret was a grown-up young lady.

Uncle Eddie, his niece wrote, was charmingly unaware that his own affairs might be of less interest to others than to himself. Impressed by a play, *The Detective*, written by Margaret at the age of twenty, he promised to leave the young dramatist a thousand pounds in his will. The legacy was, however, to depend on his final rejection by the handsome Liverpool heiress he was then courting. Details of the courtship had been confided to all the family, and its prospects had even been referred to the planchette board for an augury. Margaret, therefore, knew better than to build much hope on her prospects. Indeed the following morning Uncle Eddie came roaring along the corridor where the young people slept, with the news that the lady had relented and that Margaret had lost her thousand pounds.

Among the children of Uncle Eddie's marriage was a daughter, Violet, who married Sir Bertram Hardy and lived to be ninety-five. In her eighties she wrote a book of memoirs, *As It Was*, which gives a picture of life at Stoneleigh, seen by a child of a younger generation. To her Lady Leigh was not omniscient Mama, but Aunt Car, whose dicta on diet and decorum roused rebellion in the breast of her niece. Lively and talented, Violet Leigh might have been expected to have been congenial to her aunt, but the gifts they shared for music and water-colour painting did not bring them together. Down the years Lady Leigh and her husband remained devoted, but she increasingly tended to rule her kingdom through the agency of her unmarried daughters.

In earlier days it was Lady Leigh who wrote plays for her children. She also wrote verse to release her feelings on occasions of joy and sorrow. There is a convincing bleat in the last lines of a poem written during a holiday in the Highlands, when all day the mountains had echoed with the cries of ewes whose lambs had been taken from them, woolly Rachels who would not be comforted.

> Past the sweet peril! and gone the sweet pleasure!
> Well might the echoes tell sadly that day
> The plaint of the mothers that cried at Kingairloch
>   The day that the lambs were taken away.

At the time of her wedding Lady Leigh had been said to have a red face, but by the time Violet Leigh remembered her this had been replaced by sallowness. When Violet's mother tried to force green vegetables on her, because her Aunt Car said they were essential for a good complexion, the child shouted that she did not want to be like Aunt Car who she thought was hideous. Such an emanation of rude disloyalty could never have been uttered in the presence of Margaret and her brothers and sisters. In her general admiration for her mother, Margaret singled out her water-colours as charming, adding that she was also a true musician. The gift for painting was scarcely hereditary, Margaret's sketches were no more than the products of a lively eye and unskilled hand. Musical feeling was even more intransmissible. Miss Custarde, the family governess, was musically accomplished, but failed totally to develop her pupil's ear. Even God Save the Queen (or King) gained, in after life, no recognition, as Margaret walked out of an auditorium, embarrassed descendants at her heels.

Miss Custarde, a name for some reason brilliantly appropriate for a governess, was remembered with gratitude by her pupil. Her manner of teaching encouraged children to look up things for themselves, a habit which suited Markie's inquisitive mind and which remained with her for life. Miss Custarde also encouraged the girl to write stories based on the characters of her own admirers, of whom she seems to have had a surprising number, if stories of oppressed Victorian governesses are recollected. This practice in writing left Margaret with the confidence that she could construct a tale whenever one was required. Miss Custarde married one of her admirers when Margaret was fourteen, and the chief criticism of her pupil was that the governess bore too hard on her conscience, giving trivial offences the weight of sins. Probably Miss Custarde left at a fortunate moment, before she had either cramped Margaret's conscience permanently, or led her into an adolescent rebellion. In any case the treats and presents that Lord Leigh enjoyed giving to his family were an antidote to repression.

It does not seem as if architects were required to design special quarters for the children of their patrons when building the mighty rural palaces of the eighteenth century. With the servants who tended them, children were stowed away at the top of the house, it being axiomatic, as Ivy Compton-Burnett has pointed out, that those with the shortest legs should have to climb the most stairs. At Stoneleigh benefits, probably unforseen by Francis Smith, its architect, included corridors many yards in length along which the children could race. The housekeeper's room was a favourite goal. There Mrs Wallace, the Scotch housekeeper, compounded cakes, ices and home-made wines, feeding two generations of greedy children with chocolate from a special marble box.

Mrs Wallace was said to sleep with a menagerie of birds and animals, belonging to the children, in her room. She also taught Margaret a practical piece of domestic economy, the making of shortbread, which Lady Jersey was able long afterwards to turn out in an Indian jungle, using a block of marble from a ruined temple as a slab on which to roll out the pastry. Only once did Mrs Wallace fail to come up to expectations. Informed that the housekeeper had had an uncle who fought at Waterloo, the children rushed to her room to ask for details. Questioned, Mrs Wallace made what Margaret called 'a cautious and rather chilling reply'. She believed that her uncle, like Stendhal's Fabrice in his unawareness of the historical importance of the occasion, had hidden behind his horse.

By the time her youngest sister, Cordelia, was born Margaret was sixteen years old and in total command of her brothers and sisters. An infant brother had died at eighteen months old, and Cordelia was welcomed as a replacement. An impression remains that the eldest son, Gilly, was the only one of the family to have parity with the Head Girl. Agnes was notoriously unable to stand up for herself. Dudley and Rupert (Duddy and Rupy) were handed over to their eldest sister's supervision in the holidays, because Lord Leigh thought it right that his wife's vague state of ill-health (she lived to be seventy-eight) should be respected by her children's daily routine being taken out of her hands. Margaret ruled with a self-confidence worthy of Miss Custarde herself, making Rupy, the most obstreperous of the boys, repeat a calendar of forbidden activities before releasing him from his lessons. Rowland, the fourth son, was a pet of both his mother and sister. The condition of being doted on may well have affected his grown-up personality, which was that of a particularly inscrutable poker-player.

Greatest glory of winter at Stoneleigh was the Festival of Christmas, which lasted nearly a month, and set a standard imported by Margaret into her own married home. There it was preserved until war and widowhood struck their cruel blows. Among the Christmas rituals was one which, if not unique to the Leigh family, is not commonly mentioned in nineteenth century Christmas celebrations. A Bullet Pudding was brought to the table, a small hillock of flour on top of which was perched a bullet. Each diner had to cut a slice, and whoever caused the bullet to fall was required to get it out with their mouth.

Violet Leigh wrote that 'Aunt Car [Lady Leigh] always cut first, and very carefully, a slice about the size of a small visiting card, always with a hysterical little giggle.' Although conquering her awe of her long dead aunt, and able to complain of her shrivelled size, her sallowness and her insistence on children eating cabbage, even this tough niece had not the temerity to visualize what would have happened had the bullet fallen among the flour when the châtelaine was cutting the pudding. Although Violet Leigh's brother Chandos was prepared, for a consideration, to strip to his shirtsleeves and retrieve the bullet on behalf of whoever had let it fall, such a gesture of rebellion by even an inanimate object would have caused confusion and distress to Lady Leigh's family.

When Margaret was thirteen, Christmas was not celebrated at Stoneleigh. Her mother had been ordered to spend the winter in the South, at that date a panacea recommended for almost any frailty to those who had the means to afford it. Those who might be called the second class children were left at home, but Margaret travelled with her parents. It appears that she did not pine for her juniors, cherishing ever after the happiest memory of sunlit days in the Midi. Originally the intention had been to pass the winter in Rome, but the party came to a halt at Mentone, the doctors having decreed that Rome, particularly its galleries, would be too cold for Lady Leigh. Medical recommendations of earlier times frequently sound peculiar, and it seems to have struck nobody that Lady Leigh could have compromised by leaving the galleries unvisited.

A peaceful life was led, Lady Leigh sketching among the olive trees, while Margaret composed stories of imaginary kingdoms, into which, on her return, her brothers and sisters were to be initiated as dutiful subjects. Their travelling library was limited to two small volumes, one of Dryden and one of Milton's *Paradise Regained*, through which Margaret happily read her way. She was at the age when a bookish child can read indiscriminately and

retentively, before adolescent melancholy brings criticism, with
ennui at its heels. She even added to the family's library by, as
she wrote, perpetrating an Epic in Six Cantos on the subject of
Rienzi. Margaret was fond of the word 'perpetrated' when writing
of her literary efforts, but this reiterated lowly opinion of the end
product never caused her to hesitate in its manufacture.

An interest in Roman history of the 14th century did not lead
her to take much notice of a remarkable link with the recent past
of her own country. Lord Brougham, at eighty-five, was still alive
and receiving visitors at Cannes. This survivor from a coarser age
of English politics had arrived at the small port one golden morning and decided that this was the place on the Golfe de la Napoule
where he would ever wish to be. When the Leighs paid their re-
spects to the former Lord Chancellor, who had manipulated the
fortunes of Queen Caroline to his own advantage, Margaret could
only recall that he was very voluble. She was entirely absorbed
in the fascination of a little house built at the bottom of the garden
for a Brougham great-nephew.

Only the year before Mentone had been ceded by Italy to
France, leaving the largely Italianate population boiling with
resentment. Surprisingly for someone renowned for her good
judgement, Lady Leigh helped to keep the pot boiling by playing
the forbidden 'Inno Garibaldi' on the hotel piano, to the obvious
delight of any listening waiter. Margaret added her own provoca-
tion by wearing a scarlet flannel jacket, being greeted as 'petite
Garibaldi' by the women working in the fields. There was one
gala to interrupt the pastoral existence, when the English and Dan-
ish visitors united to feast the inhabitants of Mentone in celebration
of the wedding of Princess Alexandra of Denmark to the Prince
of Wales.

Nothing could have delighted Lord Leigh more than the organization of this *fête*. First of all he had to get a dispensation from
M. le Curé to allow his flock to eat meat during Lent, a dispensation granted provided fish was not eaten at the same meal. Then
there was a social problem, orange carriers being considered inferior by orange packers when it came to sitting down at a banquet, while women were thought to be too inferior to share the
meal by all the males concerned. Finally, in the garden of the Hotel
Victoria, three hundred workmen sat down, but not even Lord
Leigh's charm could conquer the custom of female segregation,
the women standing laughing behind while the food was passed

back to them by the seated men. This Breughelesque scene was followed by a boat race and a finale of fireworks and illuminations.

Thirty years later, in Samoa, Margaret discovered that these fireworks had been watched by Robert Louis Stevenson, a boy of her own age. Like the Leighs, the Stevensons had come from Edinburgh in pursuit of the will o' the wisp of health, but in their son's case the chase was to lead him far from Mentone to a grave in the South Seas.

In later days Margaret's daughters were agreed that their mother's attitude to illness was bracing, if not Spartan. It is something of a surprise to find that, as a girl, her eyes in a weak state after chicken pox, she should have been sent to recuperate in the Isle of Arran. Alone with a maid she found the only disadvantage was the devotion of a child-niece of her landlady's. This follower could, however, be evaded by going into the mountains of Arran, where the child feared to follow, knowing that giants dwelt there. The affection of the eyes gave Margaret a lifelong excuse for avoiding needlework. Daughters and grand-daughters might present models of industry, socks and embroidery forever growing under their busy fingers, but it was only when old age made reading difficult that the matriarch took up a crochet hook to create woollen strips that could be sewn into cot covers for great-grandchildren. Otherwise she cheerfully declared that her attack of chicken pox had disqualified her from giving an opinion on such a rudimentary exercise as buying a reel of cotton.

The Princess of Wales, whose wedding had been celebrated by the festival at Mentone, had been given Lady Leigh's sister as a lady of the bedchamber. Lady Macclesfield had fifteen children of her own, but was prepared to take on extra work. When Margaret, with her mother, visited her aunt the Princess had just given birth to her second son. The baby was put into Margaret's arms, enabling her to boast ever after that she had nursed the future King George V.

Lady Macclesfield also passed on a story of a contretemps at the wedding itself. The Princess Royal, Crown Princess of Prussia and eldest daughter of Queen Victoria, had been largely responsible for arranging the marriage of her eldest brother, and brought her own eldest son William, later the last German Emperor, to attend this triumph of his mother's matrimonial diplomacy. Her diplomacy in her own Court circle was less happy. Her Prussian ladies-in-waiting protested when Prince William, aged four, appeared

Honble Margaret Leigh, 1858, by Richard Rothwell

Stoneleigh Abbey, Warwickshire

Victor Albert George, 7th Earl of Jersey, as a child

Middleton Park, Oxfordshire

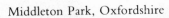

in Highland dress, instead of the miniature Prussian uniform that it had been agreed he should wear. With the tactlessness that made her life in Germany even more difficult than it was already, the Princess explained that a hasty search for an outgrown Highland dress belonging to one of the little Prince's many uncles had had to be made. When dressed in the Prussian uniform Prince Leopold and Princess Beatrice, an uncle and aunt of ten and five, decided that their nephew looked so preposterous in a tail coat that they prevented him from appearing in it by cutting off the tails.

When Margaret was of an age to be presented the pall of the Queen's mourning still hung over the Court. Consequently it was to Princess Christian, deputy for the Queen, that Margaret made the curtsey that was required for girls who were to 'come out' in Society. A season of London balls was followed by house-parties among her own vast clan and the friends of her parents. Still determined to stamp on the legend that Victorian girls lived so dragooned by their mothers that they dared not enjoy themselves, Margaret insisted that mixed parties of young people were encouraged rather than forbidden. A few girls were limited to square dances and not allowed to waltz, but the latter dance had long ceased to be a source of such scandal that Byron could forbid Lady Caroline Lamb to join in this wicked whirl. Sitting-out, on the other hand, was not permitted. Girls were supposed to be returned to their chaperones between dances. In practice little walks to admire conservatories or illuminations were allowed, which in due course was to be the way that Margaret achieved her life match.

Variety of circumstance among a multitude of kinsfolk gave Margaret an experience of contrasting styles of life without leaving her own family circle. At one end of the scale was her mother's father, the Marquess of Westminster. The owner of immensely valuable estates, rural and urban, he left an impression on his granddaughter of carpet slippers and a diffident manner, attributed by her to the oppression of his great wealth. This, with a 'saving disposition', led him to feel that he was never justified in spending much money on himself or his family. In his last days his frugality intensified, and he would only take the pills he was ordered if his wife cut them in two and took half herself. Even this measure of economy he found to be inadequate, for after his death his halves of the pills were discovered 'intact and done up with red tape'.

Great-uncle Charles Willes, brother of Lord Leigh's mother, lived in complete contrast to the atmosphere of diffidence and carpet slippers that hung about Lord Westminster. He had married a Miss Polly Wise, nearly as plump as himself, and in their manor house near Banbury an old-fashioned country style of life prevailed. There was nothing 'saving' about Great-aunt Polly, who was said to keep a book in which the names of a hundred nephews and nieces were recorded, a pig being sold to buy a present whenever one of them married. It was with this genial pair that Margaret and her brother Gilly had the good fortune to stay for a New Year's Eve party on the last day of 1868.

Even then the revels belonged to an earlier age. At dinner, between six and seven in the evening, there was a clutch of great-aunts, great-uncles and cousins. Turkey and beef were decked in holly and the plum pudding came in flaming with brandy, Aunt Polly beaming from one end of the table, and portly Uncle Charles needing two chairs to accommodate him at the other. After dinner the dining-room was cleared for dancing to music from two fiddlers and a 'blowing man,' a trio for whom a table served as bandstand. Musically incurious, Margaret could not recollect what a 'blowing man' might have been, so it can never be known if he blew *à bec* or *traversière*. However she kept a vivid memory of Aunt Polly trying to dance everyone down in a perpetual jig.

Just before midnight the dancing stopped, so that the company could listen to the muffled bells ringing out the Old Year from the belfry of King's Sutton church. At twelve o'clock the muffles were taken off and the Year of Our Lord 1869 was rung in with a joy peal that must have rocked that church's delicate spire. Punch in great silver goblets was brought in, and everyone kissed with good wishes for a Happy New Year.

Margaret's diary gives a glimpse of the charm of her brother Gilly, who was to die early in a tragic accident. 'After many attempts,' she wrote, 'Gilly succeeded in catching Aunt Polly under the mistletoe and kissing her.' With the New Year welcomed in, quadrille, lancers, jig, reel and valse were danced until nearly two in the morning. Jane Austen, a disapprover of romping at dances, and of plumpness, might have found Aunt Polly's exuberance offensive to her sense of decorum. Had she, however, been able to excuse these inelegant high spirits in a hostess who would have been, after all, only a connection by marriage, she might have found the impromptu ball little different from the ones at which she had herself danced and flirted seventy years before.

At Stoneleigh, in this December of 1868, the Leighs had had the excitement of entertaining Jefferson Davis, the Confederate President, who was visiting Europe on parole. Although a Liberal, Lord Leigh was apparently among those Radicals about whom Henry Adams complained. On arriving in England after the end of the Civil War Adams had, he wrote, expected to find Conservatives on the side of the Southern States, but found it depressing that Liberals should take the same attitude. The Leigh boys, told that the former President had been in prison, speculated as to whether the marks of chains would still be visible. Informed of the expected guest's incarceration the old housemaid, preparing his room, decided that he would not be wanting the silver candlesticks, though whether she thought him unworthy of them or liable to steal them was not clear. On Margaret and her girl cousins Jefferson Davis made his most lasting impression by addressing them indiscriminately as 'Daughter'.

Two years later, in 1871, another Southerner was to arrive at Stoneleigh, but this was the bride of Lord Leigh's brother James, a newcomer who quickly became Margaret's confidante. James Leigh, Uncle Jimmy, was a clergyman, gifted histrionically. Dressed in a white sheet as a ghost, his rendering of the ballad of 'Alonzo the Brave and the fair Imogene' caused the Christmas party at Stoneleigh to quake in delicious terror. As he presided in the same costume over the flaming dish of snapdragon, the fate of the faithless Imogene, snatched from her wedding by the ghost of Alonzo, was appropriately mixed-up with the flames from the spirits of wine in which the raisins of the snapdragon wallowed.

To Margaret her new aunt, only ten years older than herself, was a delightful acquisition, passionately interested in her niece's thoughts and feelings. Uncle Jimmy had found his bride, Frances Butler, on a plantation in Georgia, where her father, Pierce Butler, descended from an Irish family, had owned cotton plantations worked by slave labour. Her mother, Fanny Kemble, the actress daughter of Charles Kemble, and niece of Mrs Siddons, was violently anti-slavery, which made Aunt Fanny's parents an incompatible couple, doomed to divorce. Although Margaret, writing in the nineteen-twenties, claimed to have liked Mrs Kemble, she still picked her words when dealing with a woman whose profession as an actress, and position as a *feme-sole*, would have been regarded as morally suspect by Victorian standards.

Mrs Kemble had only gone on the stage with reluctance, in a hazardous but successful attempt to save her father's management of Covent Garden from financial collapse. She had already begun a career as a writer, and enjoyed literary society more than the chancy life of the theatre. In her day she attracted homage from Macaulay, Samuel Rogers, Sydney Smith and Edward Fitzgerald, adding Longfellow and Henry James to her admirers when she crossed the Atlantic. Describing Mrs Kemble's course through life as 'somewhat erratic', Margaret could not refrain from pointing out that, when she married Pierce Butler, she must have known that anti-slavery views would not be found congenial in Georgia, least of all by her husband. Concerning the divorce, Margaret wrote that there had been 'no wrong-doing; only incompatibility', a view not shared by *The Oxford Companion to American Literature*, which calls the case 'notorious'. Female matrimonial losers found little sympathy in mid-Victorian times, and to Margaret the gloom left with Mrs Kemble by her unhappy life as Mrs Pierce Butler was distinctly comic.

Meanwhile Mrs James Leigh was startled when her praise of Stoneleigh Abbey got an unexpected reaction. With intensity the eldest daughter of the beautiful house replied that to her it was a prison. Perhaps in consequence of this expressed restlessness, the James Leighs took Margaret with them on their first continental trip after their marriage, the convention dictating that the newly married should be left in a private grapple not being so cast-iron as it later became. During this tour of the Netherlands, Margaret wrote, they came across a copyist in the Antwerp Gallery who, being armless, painted with his toes, 'an amusement, as much to my uncle, who loved freaks, as to myself'. To the Leigh family there seemed nothing morbid or patronising in a love of freaks, which continued into the next generation. Margaret's brother Dudley was for many years a popular figure behind the scenes at circuses, where dwarfs and midgets greeted him on terms of affectionate equality.

The last journey that Margaret took with her parents before her marriage was a tour of Ireland. Much as she may have wanted to spread her wings, she remembered this journey with a nostalgic sentiment as the last time that her only duties were those of head girl in her family. The rare but splendid Irish sunshine gave a brilliance to land and water which Margaret only saw surpassed when she found herself among the coral islands of the South Seas. Always a keen collector of legends whether pagan or Christian, she found the story of St Kevin pushing the importunate Kathleen into the lake at Glendalough difficult to understand. (Margaret's religious education appears to have stopped short at the recognition that saints should resist the temptations of the flesh.) Her bafflement embarrassed the guide who was taking the party round the Seven Churches. He side-stepped the question by glibly advising the young lady not to push a suitor, chosen by her parents but not to her taste, into any lake. Fortunately the suitor who soon presented himself was one who she felt no hesitation in accepting, and no temptation to push into any sheet of water.

3

The Road to Matrimony

AT EDGEHILL IN Warwickshire there is an ancient inn called The Sunrising, standing at the top of the bluff down which, in 1643, Prince Rupert launched his cavalry and increased his reputation for tactical impetuosity. Casualties from the battle lie buried roundabout, and the scene can have changed little when, two hundred years later, Margaret and her brother Gilly happened to be playing round the door of The Sunrising. Why the two children were playing there, Margaret did not mention, but she remembered a fair-haired boy, older than herself, who came to the inn door and smilingly flicked his whip at the younger children. He had ridden over from Upton House nearby, putting up his pony at The Sunrising while he did lessons with a neighbouring clergyman. He might well have done so at the time of Prince Rupert, in the manner of John Aubrey, 'not as the vulgar boys, carrying a satchell on his back but riding a delicate little horse'. This fair-haired boy was the Honble George Villiers eldest son of Lord Villiers, who was himself the eldest son of the Earl of Jersey. He was unconscious at the time that this was his first salutation to his future wife. Their paths did not cross again until they were grown-up.

It is hard not to imagine that, during the three or four years in which she danced at balls, a girl so attractive as Margaret did not have particular admirers, nor that her own heart did not beat quicker on occasion. To quote Nancy Mitford, 'The back of a head, seen at a ball, can have a most agitating effect on a young girl, so different from other heads that it might be surrounded by a halo.' On this subject Margaret was consistently reticent, only allowing that her 'great friend' was her cousin Hughie Shaw-Stewart. He was five years younger than herself, too young to be considered as anything more than a troubadour, for he was the earliest of the many bards in her life to celebrate her doings in verse.

Herself born of a love match, Margaret had cooler blood than either of her parents, and her account of the marriage of her first cousin Carry Lawley was sardonic as well as sympathetic. This daughter of Lord and Lady Wenlock was a brilliant creature, with a charm that remained undimmed when Margaret's grandchildren knew her as Mrs Molyneux. At the age of eleven she had won the heart of Caryl Molyneux, the younger brother of Lord Sefton. Her age was uncertain but still juvenile when he made his declaration, but she quickly learnt to love him in return. Far from having planned this sort of marriage for their fascinating daughter, the Wenlocks refused consent to a union with a young man whose prospects and fortune were unpromising. Carry was not daunted, beating down opposition by setting up a cough which hinted at decline.

In contrast to this triumph of love over prudence was the marriage of Margaret's second cousin Gwendolen Howard. A niece of the Duke of Norfolk, this girl's Roman Catholicism was a grave handicap in the matrimonial stakes. Additionally she suffered from an unsympathetic stepmother, but opportunities to escape to a home of her own appeared restricted in circles that regarded the Church of Rome as a sinister alien force. There was, however, one fabulously wealthy *parti*, a recent convert to Roman Catholicism. Miss Howard was brought to his notice, and Margaret liked to quote the letter this Cinderella wrote to say that 'she had never known a moment's happiness, until she suddenly, and most unexpectedly, found herself engaged to Lord Bute'. Though rejoicing at her friend's transposition from pumpkin-and-mice to coach-and-four, Margaret also enjoyed giving an example of the Marquess of Bute's isolation from everyday problems. A visitor in the same country house, she found him, envelope in hand, baffled as to how to expedite the letter he had just written. Tactfully she made him understand that not only was it necessary to affix a stamp, but also to inquire how the household's letters were conveyed to the post office.

It was at the Wenlocks' house that Margaret happened to sit next to Lord Jersey, as George Villiers had now become. Introductions, except between those paired to go into dinner, were not then the fashion. Only when the ladies had retired to the drawing-room did she discover who he was. Then she was teased for having distracted this notoriously shy young man's attention away from his dinner partner. She met him no more that summer, nor the following winter when some congestion of the lungs sent her to stay in Wiltshire, with her aunt and uncle Lady Octavia and Sir Michael Shaw-Stewart.

Lord Westminster had built a house at Fonthill so that his daughter and her husband might have a home in the south. Like her sister, Lady Leigh, Lady Octavia was labelled as delicate, though this was no handicap to producing eight or nine children in either case. Cosseted though women might be from the cold winds of Stoneleigh, Warwickshire, or the even colder winds of Ardgowan, Renfrewshire, child-bearing for that generation was considered as an unavoidable hazard of existence. At Fonthill, under the shadow of Beckford's ruined abbey, Margaret shared her intellectual pre-occupations, sketching and the composition of Latin verse, with her friend, Hughie Shaw-Stuart, the son of the house. He was also suffering from a complaint for which the chest took the blame, but that was no handicap to an affectionate cousinly association. Margaret had no idea in how few months she was to return to Fonthill as a bride, with a husband she had, at that date only met once at dinner.

Restored by Wiltshire air, painting and Latin poetical composition, Margaret began what was to be her last London Season as an unmarried girl. Dining at Lord Camperdown's, Lord Jersey and Miss Leigh saw each other again, but each thought the other would have forgotten their previous meeting and did not speak. Lord Leigh, as a young man, had been looked on favourably by the formidable Sarah, Countess of Jersey. She had been given to saying 'Go and dance with Clemmy', in the hope that he would be a husband for her beautiful daughter Clementina. Both mother and daughter were now dead, but Lord Leigh, happening to meet the young Lord Jersey, had sufficiently pleasant memories of his grandmother to tell Lady Leigh to ask him to dinner. Margaret remarked to her mother that it was no good, in arranging the table, to reckon Lord Jersey as a young man, for he wasted no conversation on girls. However, at the end of the evening, Lord Jersey did make the effort to cross the drawing-room and say a few words to his host's daughter, advancing a pawn on the chess board of courtship.

Jersey then began to appear at the balls given in the great private houses of London, functions he had previously shunned. This change of behaviour did not go unnoticed, particularly as he did not dance and could only develop his acquaintance with Miss Leigh by means of little walks. Admiring illuminations was the best excuse for these strolls. Margaret remembered that on one occasion a helpful chaperone had physically barred the way to the ballroom, insisting that the fairy lamps at the other end of the garden were something not to be missed.

Lady Leigh's eldest sister, Eleanor, had married the Duke of Northumberland, who besides his castle, Alnwick, owned Syon House with lawns romantically rolling down to the River Thames. At the time of Margaret's engagement, Duchess Eleanor was already a widow, but her niece, not easily cowed, wrote of her with something approaching awe, 'a very great lady' who was regarded as almost royal in her own neighbourhood. When Cordelia Leigh, in middle life, was staying with Duchess Eleanor a policeman, shaking with fright, appeared with a summons for the riding of a tricycle without a lamp. The delinquent niece, usually a paragon of good behaviour, had to settle the fine without the offence coming to her aunt's knowledge. It was at a Syon garden party that Margaret found herself under the family microscope, when she was returning from a little walk with Lord Jersey. Although Duchess Eleanor was no longer the hostess, she was presumably part of a gallery of aunts, sitting with Lady Leigh, a gallery alert to see if Car's daughter was on the point of bringing off a matrimonial coup. At one of the last balls of the season, Lord Jersey realized that Miss Leigh would be leaving London, and that the little walks would cease. He presented himself to Lord Leigh as a suitor, and on July 18th 1872 the engagement was settled.

Among the most eager of Aunts on the side lines was Mrs James Leigh. 'Laid up', a period euphemism for troubles connected with pregnancy, she had been visited daily by Margaret, with reports of what the racing world would call the form, the speculation being as to whether Lord Jersey would jib at the last fence. Immediately after his proposal, Margaret hurried to her confidante. She found Mrs Kemble in her daughter's bedroom, and the scene is best described by the new fiancée.

'One word was enough to enlighten my aunt, who then said, "May I tell my mother?" I assented, and she said, "This child has come to tell me of her engagement." Whereupon Mrs Kemble demanded, with a tragical air worthy of her aunt Mrs Siddons,

"And are you very happy, young lady?" I cheerfully answered "Oh yes" – and she looked as if she were going to cry. My aunt said afterwards that any marriage reminded her of her own unfortunate venture.'

It is frustrating not to know what the one word which enlightened Mrs James Leigh could have been, but that lady's rejoicing at the engagement seems to have been tempered by the fear that the bridal outfit might be unworthy of Margaret's new position. Lady Leigh's taste in dress for her daughters was, to put it mildly, undeveloped. Violet Leigh wrote that her own dressmaker mutinied when Aunt Car persisted in ordering the white muslin and blue sash suitable for a *jeune fille* for Cordelia Leigh, long past her girlhood and totally uninterested in clothes.

Experience of her sister-in-law's unenterprising attitude towards clothes may have led Aunt Fanny to urge on Margaret the importance of ordering a trousseau from Paris. Although lending samples from her own trousseau, she was not able to make her point. A slightly frosty note has survived asking that, if Lady Leigh was not convinced by Aunt Fanny's own clothes that Margaret's should be ordered by Aunt Fanny in Paris, could the nightdresses be returned? Being 'laid up', they were, at the moment, her most acute need.

Probably Margaret kept this letter because on the back there was a note of farewell to 'Cousin Markey', signed with what looks like 'Dan', but is in fact 'Owen'. This was Fanny's sister's son, Owen Wister, a boy of twelve who was returning to America. Although obviously charmed by his honorary 'Cousin Markey' his congratulations on her marriage are touched with the melancholy suitable to his age, speculating that they might never meet again. Owen Wister grew up to write *The Virginian*, a novel sometimes credited not only with the parentage of a myriad cowboys and Indians, but with the entire Western Industry in book and film. His anxiety at parting was unnecessary. In the nineteen-twenties he was still seeing Lady Jersey on his visits to London, and in his many letters to her the signature still seemed to be 'Dan'.

On the night following her engagement, Margaret found that the turmoil of her feelings needed a sedative, so she set herself to work out the longest sum she could find in Colenso's *Arithmetic*. To find sleep elusive remained for her a circumstance so unusual that she reflected on its rarity in her old age. At any symptom of undue wakefulness, she had, she said, always been able to lull herself by a few repetitions of 'Je vais dormir, je vais dormir'. Colenso was never again invoked as a sleep inducer, but the incident was an early example of the stability of Margaret's character and the steadiness of her head.

Besides Mrs Kemble's uncheerful reaction, there were mixed feelings among the bride's brothers and sisters. Cordelia, aged six, burst into tears when the news reached her nursery at Stoneleigh, declaring that she would not allow Lord Jersey to take her big sister away. On meeting him, she relented, and even went so far as to suggest that, if her sister Agnes 'would only marry or die', she would herself become 'head girl and hear the boys their lessons'. Woman's supremacy, as has been seen, was well established among the Leighs, but as the youngest of the boys was six years older than Cordelia, her claim might, as Margaret wrote, be considered exceptional even in that family.

September, chosen for the wedding, was also the month in which Gilbert Leigh came of age, a double event that Lady Leigh said could never happen to her again. For someone professing ill-health she stood the strain well, only deputing the launching of a life-boat, to be called 'Lady Leigh', to her daughter Agnes. At Stoneleigh the gatehouse was illuminated with fairy lamps as it had been for the Queen's visit, although the ivy had thickened with the years and an iron frame was necessary. Against this background, the bride and her brother shared in presentations from the tenantry. Aunt Polly Willes had died, so was unable to kill a pig, but the wedding gifts were diverse and splendid.

Lord Camperdown, who had entertained the young couple when each thought the other had forgotten their first meeting, gave a gold bracelet set with pearls and blue enamel. It opened to reveal a row of five tiny picture frames, space, as the giver pointed out prophetically, for the portraits of five children. Lady Leigh's eldest brother, who had become the first Duke of Westminster, caused the artificer of the family jewellers to copy what was then called the Venus de Milo necklace. The original, a circle of delicately chased urn-shaped gold beads, is to be seen in the British Museum, but it is now dated from the 3rd century B.C., two hundred years before the Venus de Milo was cut free from her marble prison. Had the pleasing legend that it had been found round her neck been true, the Venus de Milo must have inherited the necklace.

In a last-minute whirl settlements were signed, the bride, she said, gaily unaware of their implications. At a moment of frustration Margaret may have called Stoneleigh a prison, but on the evening before her wedding she shed many bitter tears at the realization that she was leaving her home and her family. She did not weep alone, her distress being increased by floods of tears from her tender-hearted brother Dudley.

Next morning, September 19th 1872, the family had composed themselves sufficiently for the ceremony, conducted by Uncle James Leigh, to pass off without too much emotion. The service was not at the parish church, but St Thomas', Orchard Street, (later to become the car-park of Selfridges). Consequently a special licence was necessary, a point that would have been appreciated by Jane Austen. It will be remembered that, in *Pride and Prejudice*, Mrs Bennet's reaction to the delirious news that her daughter Elizabeth is to marry rich Mr Darcy is to insist that only a special licence could do justice to the glory of the wedding.

Amid all the glory of her own wedding there were two counsellors, her Aunt Fanny and her mother, who gave advice that Margaret cherished ever after. Aunt Fanny wrote a letter which gives more evidence that, loved and valued in her home, the young girl had felt a power in herself that craved a wider scope. That, in the new course, before her, she might be protected from the rocks in the sea of life was Aunt Fanny's prayer. Lady Leigh's attitude was more practical. 'Do not think [she said] that because you have seen things done in a particular way that is the only right one.' Good advice for any bride, but particularly for one marrying into a family very different in tradition from the affectionate, play-acting, poetry-writing circle at Stoneleigh.

4

Margaret's Predecessors

ON MARCH 24th 1845, Queen Victoria wrote to Sir Robert Peel
from Windsor Castle. Her letter's tone of perfect confidence in
her Prime Minister showed how far in the past was the young
Queen who had taken a malicious pleasure in thwarting the disliked supplanter of Lord Melbourne. The Queen began by
approving Sir Robert's submission of various ecclesiastical
appointments, only stipulating that, as they might cause a stall at
Winchester to become vacant, she would like to see that stall filled
by 'a person decidedly averse to Puseyism'. She ended on a note
that was positively affectionate. 'It would give the Queen much
pleasure to stand sponsor to Sir Robert Peel's little grandson, and
perhaps Sir Robert would communicate this to Lady Villiers.'

Lady Villiers was the daughter of Sir Robert Peel. His wife, born
at Fort St George, Madras, was christened Julia by Schwartz,
the most famous of eighteenth century missionaries in India. This
Julia was the daughter of the distinguished General Sir John Floyd.
The General brought his family back to England, where his
daughter married Sir Robert Peel, the second baronet and future
Prime Minister. Sir Robert's devotion to his wife lasted until the
day he mounted his horse for a morning ride, only to be brought
home to die after a fall. Called Julia after her mother, this daughter,
as will be seen, had a distinctly unamiable disposition. Fortunately
the Julias of the next three generations inherited the character of
Lady Peel, rather than that of Lady Villiers, and were much loved
throughout their lives.

The Queen's godson later, as Lord Jersey, to marry Margaret
Leigh, was christened Victor Albert, with the addition of George,
a name which had belonged to the founder of the Villiers fortunes.
Queen Victoria, who insisted that she had held the baby at the

font, had the mistaken idea that his name was Victor Alexander. She went so far as to inscribe books to him in this style, and it was not considered loyal behaviour to argue the point. Her christening cup, however, was cherished without any embarrassment as to what the Queen thought her godson was called.

The first George Villiers to appear in royal circles had caught the roving eye of James I. The year was 1614, and the occasion one of careful stage management. Groomed for the part of favourite by a Court party which included the Queen, George Villiers ousted Robert Carr, an unpopular and unpleasant young man. King James, entranced by Villiers' beauty, gave him the pet name of Steenie, comparing him to St Stephen, who was said to have had the face of an angel. When, in 1628, Villiers was stabbed to death by a disgruntled assassin, he had, for fourteen years, been the most powerful subject in the kingdom. He had charmed not only the admittedly homosexual King James, but also the assuredly normal King Charles. According to the practice of the day, a splendid heiress had been found for Villiers to marry, and he died as a Duke, with a load of other honours and a collection of profitable offices. He also left his family, including the children of his father's first marriage, securely moored in the upper reaches of the English peerage. Not only had peerages been created for them, their marriages were arranged to confirm the position to which their brother's meteoric ascent had guided them.

The majority of the Villiers creations have become items in Burke's *Extinct and Dormant Peerages*, but the descents by female lines have been striking in the number of famous men and women who have flowered on the branches. Maynard Keynes, in *Essays in Biography*, gave a list of these descendants. To quote only a few names, the list included the first Duke of Marlborough (and consequently Winston Churchill) both the Pitts, Lady Hester Stanhope, and Henry Fielding the novelist. Keynes went so far as to call the Villiers Connection 'the real Blood Royal of England'. It is certainly undeniable that the Stuart Blood Royal tended to find the Villiers family hard to resist.

Barbara Villiers, Duchess of Cleveland, has been famous as one of the liveliest and most rapacious of Charles II's mistresses. Her notoriety has somewhat overshadowed the career of her cousin Arabella Churchill, whose children by James II included the Duke of Berwick, a general in the wars of Louis XIV. William of Orange, nephew of these two kings, had a taste for male

favourites, recalling James I from whom he was descended. However, after the Glorious Revolution of 1688 when he had become
William III, he chose an English mistress. She, it seems inevitably,
was a Villiers, Elizabeth, descended from Edward, elder half-
brother of the first Duke of Buckingham. The *Complete Peerage*
demurely suggests that the King ceased to consort with the Countess of Orkney (as his mistress was created) after the death of his
wife Queen Mary. If historically correct, this seems something of
a moral non sequitur.

William, brother of the Countess of Orkney, was created Earl
of Jersey, and so came into being the first of the Countessess of
Jersey, of which Margaret Leigh was to be the seventh. This first
countess was Barbara, daughter of William Chiffinch, Keeper of
the Closet to Charles II, a man whose job was no sinecure. Contemporary plans of the Palace of Whitehall show accommodation
marked for Mr Chiffinch next to the King's private apartments,
he having the sole right of access, unannounced to the King's
presence. Besides her *louche*, if interesting, background Barbara
Chiffinch, appears to have had a stormy temperament. The poet
Matthew Prior, who was Lord Jersey's secretary on diplomatic
missions to The Hague and to Paris, mentioned, in passing, that the
day's events had included an attempt by My Lady to stab My Lord.

Another result of the marriage seems to have been a particular
cast of countenance, inherited for at least seven generations. The
portrait in the Dulwich Gallery of William Chiffinch by Gerard
Soest might, allowing for the open neck then fashionable, pass for
Victor Albert George, seventh in descent from the Royal Closet
Keeper. There is the same foxy colouring and the same shape of
face, together with the eyes set in a slant which recalls a cat. This
last characteristic continued to appear in the generations which
followed the marriage of Margaret Leigh and the seventh Lord
Jersey, overcoming a variety of powerful physical differences.

Becoming a widow by natural means rather than by stabbing,
Barbara Lady Jersey, with her son William, the 2nd Earl, retired
to Paris where she paid court to the titular King James III. Debts,
according to the *Complete Peerage* sent her to live in Paris, but she
made herself ridiculed by her desire to be important, and to dine
constantly with 'the top people', an interestingly early date for
this expression. Her son was less ardently Jacobite than his mother.
His troubles were domestic rather than political. His wife, Judith
Hearne, daughter of a London merchant, had such a formidable

attachment to her own property that Lord Jersey left her only the sum of one shilling in his will. This was to express his condemnation of his wife's refusal to settle her lands on her children.

In the next generation matters improved financially and domestically. William, 3rd Earl of Jersey married Anne, widow of the Duke of Bedford, and granddaughter of the first Duke of Marlborough. Her grandmother, Sarah Duchess of Marlborough, wrote scathingly that Lord Jersey's public show of affection for his bride was due to the size of her jointure, rather than a measure of his love. This spiteful comment seems to have been untrue, and typical of Sarah Duchess of Marlborough, who was uninhibited in venting her evil temper on her grandchildren. Lord Jersey left letters of deep affection, calling his wife 'My dst Soul', 'My dst Angel'. This was the first generation to settle at Middleton Stoney near Bicester, in Oxfordshire, where the family was to remain for two hundred years.

It was at Middleton Stoney that George, the 4th Earl, built a new house with a particularly large pillared porch, satisfactorily filling the eye at the end of a mile-long avenue. His home life was, however, less well-balanced than the improvements to his property. He married Frances, the posthumous daughter of the Right Reverend Philip Twysden, Bishop of Raphoe in Ireland. The legend that the Bishop augmented the income from his benefice by standing in with a gang of highwaymen can be believed or not according to taste, but his daughter's career is well-documented. It was for Frances Lady Jersey that George Prince of Wales deserted Mrs Fitzherbert, with whom he had gone through a form of marriage, a ceremony illegal under the Royal Marriage Act.

Queen Charlotte, mother of the Prince of Wales, who had every reason to regard Lady Jersey as a menace, admitted her charm, calling her Lord Jersey's 'bewitching little wife'. As Prince and King, George IV has sometimes been abused, not only for his seduction of the wives of his own, or his father's subjects, but for the fact that he found these wives most irresistible in later middle-age. In fact Lady Jersey, nine years older than himself, was the only one of his more famous mistresses who was separated from him by a gap of years. He seems to have had a liking for his own age group. With the advance of years this taste caused him to settle like an elderly cuckoo in the domestic nests of Lord Hertford and Lord Conyngham.

Lord Jersey had held positions at Court, Master of the Buck-hounds and Master of Horse, which led to ribald caricatures in Continental newspapers on the subject of his wife's liaison. She did not display the diplomacy which had marked the behaviour of the Royal favourites among her husband's ancestors. Both Mrs Fitzherbert and Caroline, the incompatible wife of the Prince of Wales, made complaints about Lady Jersey's evil influence on the man who wished to be the husband of one and had been obliged to become the husband of the other. Lady Jersey, when her reign was over, did not willingly accept her congé. After hints had failed, the Prince's secretary brought a message to request that she would refrain from speaking to his master, when she and he happened both to be present on a public occasion.

Although it was said that the Prince had been the father of Lady Sarah Villiers, there was no question about the paternity of Frances Lady Jersey's eldest son, George, 5th Earl of Jersey, he having been born when the Prince was about twelve years old. He was famous on the turf as the breeder of three Derby winners, the huge fortune of his wife giving him the means to develop his stud at Middleton Stoney. By his marriage he acquired a wife who, without indulging in a royal adultery, brought fame not unmixed with notoriety to the name of Jersey. She also brought a splendid inheritance which had come to her as a result of the elopement of her mother, Sarah Child with John, 10th Earl of Westmorland.

So often has the story of this elopement been told, that it need only be briefly recapitulated. Robert Child, of Child's Bank under the shadow of Temple Bar, was anxious that his only child should marry a suitable successor in the business and not a fortune-hungry nobleman. Lord Westmorland trapped Mr Child, by putting the hypothetical question as to what a man should do if the parents of the girl he loved refused their consent to the marriage. Unguardedly, Robert Child recommended elopement, only to find himself, soon afterwards, in pursuit of Lord Westmorland and his own daughter as they made a dash for Gretna Green. This was the first stop over the Scottish border, where the law then allowed that a declaration of marriage before two witnesses was valid. Most accounts agree that when Miss Child saw her father's grooms in pursuit, and realised that she might be snatched back from her handsome lover, she cried, 'Shoot, my lord, shoot.' Lord Westmorland then halted the pursuit by shooting a groom's horse from under him.

The story ended rather sadly, for she only lived ten years to enjoy Lord Westmorland's society, dying in Dublin where he was serving a term as Lord Lieutenant. Robert Child himself died two months after the elopement. He left the Bank and Osterley Park, inherited from his brother and further embellished by himself, to the second son, or failing that, to the eldest daughter of Lady Westmorland. This act of unforgiveness towards his son-in-law's senior male heir resulted in Lady Sarah Sophia Fane inheriting not only a fortune but Osterley, called by Horace Walpole 'the palace of Palaces'.

In her early days as a political hostess, and Lady Patroness of Almacks where the fashionable world assembled, Sarah Lady Jersey was far from generally admired or even liked. Princess Lieven, wife of the Russian ambassador, and Lady Palmerston, wife of the statesman, exchanged letters complaining about her ebullience and coarseness of tone, which others also found wearisome. She did, however, display moral integrity in her friendship with Lord Byron, who found Middleton Park a peculiarly agreeable house in which to stay. Among the worldly ladies who had fawned on the poet, Lady Jersey was alone in refusing to cut him when rumours of incest began to run through London drawing-rooms. It was to her that he wrote from Missolonghi, introducing John Zaimes, who came to London to raise a loan for the Greeks. By this time Lady Jersey was senior partner in her own right of Child's Bank, so the introduction would have been for business rather than social reasons.

For Margaret Leigh, when she married, the earlier Countesses of Jersey were figures of historical interest, with the exception of Sarah Lady Jersey whose posthumous influence was considerable. As a child, driving with her mother, Margaret's attention had been drawn to an old lady, sitting upright in a grand yellow chariot. That, said Lady Leigh, was 'poor Lady Jersey', so called because she had outlived her husband and six of her seven children. All unaware, Margaret was looking at the matriarch into whose shoes she was one day to step.

Benjamin Disraeli was among the close friends of Sarah Lady Jersey, and when A. E. Chalon painted the three Ladies Villiers, Disraeli wrote a poem prognosticating their future. Unhappily his prophecy, that their lot should be as brilliant as their birth, was far from being fulfilled. Princess Lieven and Lady Palmerston watched with unkind amusement as Lady Jersey stalked Prince

Nicholas Esterhazy, son of the Austrian Ambassador, as a husband for her daughter Sarah. The hunt was long, the quarry sometimes disappearing into the wide plains of Hungary, but the match was at last achieved. Like her grandmother, the eloping Miss Child, Sarah Villiers only lived to enjoy her grand marriage for ten years. In her lifetime the Court of Vienna took a stiffer view of the brilliance of the Villiers birth than had Disraeli, causing embarrassment by demanding the possession of more quarterings than the descendant of Robert Child could supply.

If Lady Jersey managed to catch a Prince for her eldest daughter, she had no success when it came to marrying Clementina, the second and most beautiful. It was true a Prince did present himself, Prince Louis Napoleon, the future Napoleon III, but Lady Jersey disapproved of the Bonaparte in exile, and his suit was not encouraged. Clementina died a spinster, leaving a memorial of her beauty in a portrait of herself as Undine, pearls in her long hair and a wreath of water lilies on her head. Supposedly she had only loved one man, the poet Matthew Arnold. Whether or not her passion was a fact is hard to say, but dates disprove the family legend that Arnold wrote *Requiescat*, 'Strew on her roses, roses', in memory of Clementina. The poem was published six years before the beauty faded into 'the vasty halls of death'. It was, however, generally agreed that the lines, 'Her life was turning, turning/ In mazes of heat and sound', were a fair description of Lady Jersey's social methods, of which her attack on Henry Leigh was an example.

The disappointment over Clementina was nothing to her mother's shock when the youngest daughter, Adela, aged seventeen, disappeared from her parent's house at Brighton. For three days, Lady Palmerston cheerfully wrote to Princess Lieven, they were distraught, not knowing with whom she had eloped. Making the mistake of not choosing a nobleman, and failing to realize that the gesture was somewhat outmoded, Adela had run off to Gretna Green with Captain Charles Ibbetson of the 11th Hussars. It was long before her mother forgave her child sufficiently to stop her carriage outside the Ibbetson's house and allow her daughter to come and sit with her.

Lady Jersey's eldest son, the father of Margaret's future husband, was thought to have grown up oppressed by his father's great reputation on the Turf, and his mother's even greater reputation throughout Europe. He manifested his taste for concealing his private affairs by never drawing a cheque except to himself. His next two brothers led lives that were unremarkable, but the career of Francis, the youngest, was a gigantic disaster. Starting life, like his brother-in-law, in the 11th Hussars he served abroad, and returned to England and a seat in Parliament. His good looks were worthy of a grandson of Lord Westmorland, but he behaved with a breathtaking lack of financial morality, both in politics and on the Turf. By Admiral Rous, the dictator of the racing world, he was objurgated for the running of 'the Clementina colt', presumably son of a mare named after his sister, and as a 'notorious levanter'. The diarist Greville mentioned Francis Villiers' involvement with 'Mrs Edmunds bawd, whore and usurer'. Finally it needed the loyal friendship of Disraeli to cover the delinquent's retreat abroad. It was through Disraeli that his mother sent her son's annual remittance of £300. She had had to pay up formidable sums for him, and when he ventured as near home as the Channel Islands she, understandably, had a heart attack.

By the time Francis Villiers died in exile, at San Sebastian in 1862, death had already taken his three sisters, his father and his eldest brother. This last had died after only three weeks as Earl of Jersey. The little boy who had put up his pony at The Sunrising was now at Eton. Summoned home at his grandfather's death, he returned to school as Viscount Grandison. As, only three weeks later, he again went home for his father's funeral to return to Eton as Earl of Jersey, it was complained that each time he came back to school he bore a different name.

Julia, the widowed mother of the new earl, had only been a countess for three weeks, but she stuck to the title even through a second marriage. A harsh light has fallen on her character and behaviour from a collection of letters published within the last twenty years. Except for Frederick, Sarah Lady Jersey's surviving son, there were few males in the Villiers family. The most distinguished was the Earl of Clarendon, a statesman descended from a son of the Lord Jersey who had cut his wife off with a shilling. In the crisis of two successive deaths, family feeling induced Lord Clarendon to take on the task of keeping the peace between the two so recently widowed countesses. The letters in which the reluctant umpire gave rein to his feelings were written to the stunningly beautiful Duchess of Manchester. Having, more than once, insisted that his letters should be burnt by the Duchess, Lord Clarendon felt free to repeat gossip and scandal, unaware that his letters were being relentlessly hoarded by the young woman whom he persistently praised for her charm and discretion.

It might be expected that Sarah, accustomed to ruling by the force of her character and the power of her fortune, would be the most awkward customer. On the contrary, Lord Clarendon was touched by her willingness to overlook the insults of her daughter-in-law. Taking the precaution of assuring the Duchess that he could see no charm in Julia Lady Jersey, Lord Clarendon complained that the name of her lovers was said to be legion. He also deplored that, to promote an impression of her mother's youthfulness, Julia Villiers, at seventeen, was kept in short skirts and pantalettes as worn by little girls.

Lord Cardigan, who led the Charge of the Light Brigade, appears to have been among the lovers named legion. His widow, shunned by society except by those of her husband's family who hoped for financial benefits, wrote vindictively of Julia, still Viscountess Villiers. Lady Cardigan classed her among the discarded mistresses when Lord Cardigan was struck by a *coup de foudre* for herself.

As it happened, among the six hundred to follow Lord Cardigan into the mouth of Hell had been Sir George Wombwell, a Yorkshire baronet. He was one of the few to ride back again, after being taken prisoner and escaping on a loose horse. In 1861 he married Julia Villiers, now presumably out of short frocks and pantalettes. Once again Lord Clarendon was called upon to wrestle not only with Julia Lady Jersey, but with the gallant Sir George Wombwell, whose attitude towards settlements was unheroic not to say niggardly. Of the bride's mother, Lord Clarendon wrote that it had never been his misfortune to meet such an incarnate devil. Among other offensive actions she had fixed the wedding-day on the first anniversary of the death of poor Lady Adela, whose elopement had been so unappreciated.

Sarah Lady Jersey died in 1867, having been Senior Partner of Child's Bank for more than half a century. Her eldest son's eldest son was her heir, to the Bank, to the contents of Middleton Park, to Osterley Park and to an estate in South Wales with a romantic view across the Bristol Channel. It was upon these properties that the marriage settlements were based when Margaret Leigh married Lord Jersey. She herself wrote that she signed them uncomprehendingly, and it seems unlikely that the trustees drew her attention to the financial gale through which her husband had passed only four years earlier. Ominously it had then seemed that irresponsibility over money matters might have descended to the nephew of Francis Villiers.

As the obvious heir to a large inheritance, Lord Jersey found it easy to set up a racing establishment at an age when he was not legally liable for his debts. His grandfather's gift for breeding Derby winners was not, unhappily, hereditary. According to Roger Mortimer's *History of the Derby Stakes*, Jersey fled the country owing the Ring £50,000, compounded for £25. He being now of age, the crisis was resolved, in 1868, by an undertaking to abandon the Turf, where he naturally was unpopular with the Ring. It was agreed that Jersey's uncle Frederick Villiers and his cousin Charles Fane, partners of Child's Bank, should handle his affairs, and that in return the Bank should advance the impressive sum of £90,000 in a rescue operation. Jersey's own children remembered that he consistently spoke as if the family were on the edge of destitution, a morbid tendency that can, perhaps, be explained by a bad fright in early life.

Matters must have been on an even keel by the time the young Jerseys arrived at Middleton. If Margaret then knew of the storms in the recent history of her new family she was undaunted. The neighbourhood hurried to welcome her. Only from Blenheim Palace, nine miles away, was there a sound of disapproval. With six Ladies Churchill for whom to find husbands the Duchess of Marlborough had her eye on Lord Jersey. Her reported comment, 'that little dowdy', on hearing of the engagement did not endear this new neighbour to Margaret, though it gives some justification for Mrs James Leigh's concern about her niece's trousseau. There was more cause for umbrage when the Duchess wrote recommending a lady's maid, with the depressing qualification that she would be unsuitable for anyone who aspired to smartness in dress. Otherwise there was nothing to undermine Margaret's self-confidence in the career of usefulness opening before her. It was soon to be clear that her husband's judgement, if faulty on the racecourse, was impeccable when it came to picking a wife.

5

Introducing M. E. Jersey

WITH HER MARRIAGE Margaret acquired the initials M.E.J., which soon became so much part of her personality that her descendants could not imagine them to have belonged to anyone except Margaret Elizabeth, Countess of Jersey. The husband who had given her this name must be included among the strangers she had to get to know in her new life. Before he proposed, she told her grandchildren, she had only met him on twelve separate occasions, and, as has been seen, their private exchanges had been limited to little walks at balls and garden parties. Until their engagement, it does not appear that they had even stayed in the same house. Their wedding journey was limited to a few days at Fonthill, where so recently Margaret had practised Latin verse and painting in watercolours. From there they went to Middleton, where Margaret was faced with arranging the hand of cards dealt to her by fate.

Her early experience showed her that she had inherited the position of her husband's grandmother, rather than that of her own mother-in-law. Sarah Lady Jersey had died five years before her grandson married, but her fortune had given her the control of the estate, her daughter-in-law, Julia, only visiting Middleton occasionally. Letters and bits of needlework belonging to Sarah were lying undisturbed in drawers, even the china boxes on the bride's dressing-table were as her grandmother-in-law had left them. These relics gave the new Lady Jersey the feeling that she was following not only an historical personage but a powerful personality.

Nowhere were the traces of the late Lady Jersey's personality more apparent than among the dwellers on the Middleton estate. Instructed by her mother's example, Margaret was aware that the wife of a landowner had the duty of caring for his tenants and seeing to the schooling of their children. She found Sarah Lady Jersey's desire that the tenants' children should be educated had caused rules to be made which the awe she inspired left unquestioned, in spite of the inconvenience caused by her mandates. Two years old was the age ordained for the village children to begin to attend the Infant School, which now might be considered somewhat premature for initiation into a play-group.

For the big girls, Lady Jersey had instituted a training school for domestic servants, where not only was a demand for labour satisfied but the pupils were qualified to get far better situations than if they had been fresh caught from the village school. Margaret thought it slightly comic to have inherited the position of dictator of this school, when, in the domestic hierarchy of those days, she would have been considered young for a second housemaid. The school, incidentally, was still, in the early nineteen-twenties, training the girls of Middleton Stoney, and from it a nursery-maid was engaged to care for the great-great-granddaughters of the foundress. Flora Thompson in *Larkrise to Candleford* has immortalized her own village whose real, beautiful, name was Juniper, a hamlet only four miles from Middleton Stoney. In this book she goes into detail as to the openings for the young girls in her village when they reached an age, as their mothers said, 'to get their legs under other folks' tables'. From Flora Thompson's account it can be seen that Lady Jersey's training school must have been of benefit to a girl, who might otherwise start life as a servant in a farmhouse and stay there for ever. Flora Thompson would have understood one of the school mistresses who, Margaret found, had never troubled her rheumaticky limbs by putting on a gown, unless she had word that her patroness was at home and might make a snap inspection.

If the cottages were filled with young families, the new Lady Jersey often found herself alone in the big house at the end of the avenue. An unusual note of acerbity crept into her description of the early days of her marriage when her husband was out hunting, 'a sport to which he was much addicted in those days'. The loneliness was depressing without a train of brothers and sisters to direct and entertain. To return to Stoneleigh for Christmas was a particular joy. Afterwards consideration for her weak chest, an idea strange to those who knew her in later life, sent the Jerseys to Cannes, which, in Margaret's opinion, did as much good to her husband as herself. Not even a European war was to stop her taking him there in the last months of his life. Now, however, it was the beginning of their own family that preoccupied the young couple. In June 1874 their eldest son was born, a son and heir who always remained to Margaret a person as much in advance of her younger children as she herself had been in her own family circle. Christened George, but always called Villiers from his courtesy title, this little boy grew up to be renowned in the racing world. His father's undertaking to give up the sport seems to have had as little influence on the child's future as the wishes of the North Warwickshire Hunt that his mother would become a hunting woman.

During the winter that Margaret spent with her parents in the South of France, Lady Leigh's sister Agnes had joined them, with her husband Sir Archibald Campbell of Garscube. Margaret remembered provoking her uncle by a bumptious, but accurate, prediction that the Kingdom of Italy would expand to include both Venice and Rome. As it happened Sir Archibald died before the prediction was fulfilled, and his widow, another delicate Grosvenor, fell into a state of heartbroken ill-health. Roused by pity for the wounded in the Franco-Prussian War, she made plans to go abroad to nurse in a hospital, arrangements to be made by a Doctor Frank, a popular medical man of German-Jewish descent.

Among the vast Grosvenor clan, family pressure was a powerful element, and on this occasion its full force was turned on Lady Agnes to prevent her going on her mission of mercy. Lord Leigh was the emissary chosen to dissuade her, but congratulations were premature, for though she yielded, she hit back by marrying Doctor Frank. However the Grosvenors were soon placated by the obvious happiness of the marriage. Settled at Cannes, it was the Franks who found a charming, newly-built house, Isola Bella for the Jerseys, who came there for a second winter. Margaret was again pregnant, and for company the Jerseys brought with them Jersey's second sister, Caroline, married to William Jenkins, famous for his skill with horses and their training.

Daughter of a Liberal peer, Margaret had already become the strong Tory that she was to remain for the rest of her life. Sitting on the terrace in the sunshine, it was pleasant to wait for the postman to bring news of the Conservative successes in a General Election. Mr Jenkins smoked, but Jersey, 'no smoker' wrote his wife, occupied himself with crochet. Her uninterest in needlework was too great, apparently, to record what her husband was making.

If the story of Doctor Frank and Lady Agnes had the quality of a romance with a happy ending, the genial William Jenkins had, some years before, been involved in a drama of revenge positively mediaeval in its thoroughness. His sister had married a Mr Powell and the couple had been murdered while travelling in Abyssinia. With Mr Powell's brother, Jenkins had gone to Egypt and raised an armed force. The brothers of the victims then advanced on the village where the murderers were sheltering. They burnt the village, handing over the guilty men to the Abyssinian authorities for execution. It would be futile, though fascinating, to speculate what, a century later, would be the local and global reaction to such a proceeding. At the time this demonstration of fraternal vengeance was considered to have made a deeper impression locally than the whole of Lord Napier's expedition, in which Magdala was captured and King Theodore killed.

It was ten years since Margaret, in her red jacket, had been hailed as 'la petite Garibaldi', but her wish for knowledge and her interest in Italian affairs were unabated. With her husband and her sister-in-law, she took Italian lessons from one of the fiery Italian patriots who abounded in her travels. This particular tutor produced a gruesome story of his mother refusing to make further confessions, after one of her family had been arrested, perhaps even executed, by reason of a priest's betrayal of something confided in the confessional. Mr Jenkins does not seem to have shared the Italian lessons, though he might have been able to suggest a practical reprisal for such a sinister breach of faith.

The journey home ended sadly, for Margaret gave birth, prematurely, to a daughter who lived only one day, the birth taking place in the Lord Warden Hotel, Dover. Here Margaret spent a dreary month of convalesence, following the medical practice of the period, which, among the rich, treated post-natal recovery as only to be achieved if the patient was first turned into an invalid. In October 1875 the short-lived infant Margaret was replaced by a second daughter, also called Margaret. This child was always known as Markie, an old-fashioned diminutive favoured by the Leigh family. As it was the name by which Lady Jersey was herself known to her parents, brothers and sisters, only the Victorian habit of using Papa and Mama before the children can have averted confusion.

Two more daughters followed, Mary in 1877 and Beatrice, a romantic name popular at that period, in 1880. Finally the last frame in Lord Camperdown's bracelet was filled by Arthur born in 1883. A life-long pattern of relationships among the children had already begun to form itself, Arthur, by his late arrival, becoming the pet of all his sisters. Herself the eldest child in a happy home, Margaret seems not to have reflected that the father of her children had grown up against a stormier background, with terrors and stresses transmitted to the next generation.

The gloomy three weeks which had seen the funerals of his grandfather and his father, had left Lord Jersey poised between a grandmother and a mother intensely out of sympathy with each other. Fortunately for him, Sarah Lady Jersey was attached to her grandson, and, when Julia Lady Jersey remarried, her second husband, Charles Brandling, does not appear to have had Murdstonian characteristics. With a guarded lack of enthusiasm, his step-daughter-in-law wrote that Mr Brandling had a long beard, a loud voice and a habit of throwing open the dining-room door when he came down to breakfast in the morning, 'but otherwise left little mark in the world'. Observing that he was fond of reading, Margaret suggested, more than once, that he might occupy himself by reviewing books, a practical suggestion that met with no response. She admired her mother-in-law's handling of Mr Brandling's uncertain temper, particularly in evidence at the whist table, but being no player Margaret was, herself, unconcerned. Unhappily, whether from imitation of his step-father, or from natural testiness, Lord Jersey's own snappiness at the card table became a hazard which caused his daughters to quake.

Although in the early voyages of their married life the Jerseys followed the example of the Leighs in taking their children with them, the habit died away as the family increased. Anyway delight in the South of France with its palm trees and mimosa was not shared by little Mary Villiers who pined for her English nursery, and only relished a visit to the crystallised fruit factory at Grasse. Mary was, perhaps the most emotionally sensitive of her family, loving intensely her home and her younger sister and brother, while suffering from nervous apprehension of the moral disapproval of her parents. As a very small child she had been detected in lying. She had denied that the miniature orange she held in her hand had been picked off the tree in the conservatory at Middleton, the children being allowed only to take the shrivelled fruit that had fallen from the tree. Betrayal came from the bright skin of the fruit, and the reproof for trying to lie her way out of her predicament, made a permanent impression. Right as Mary admitted her parents were in teaching her to shun untruth, she later felt that their treatment of a child of three was somewhat uncompromising.

The impression of this incident on an infant mind must have been unusually vivid for its background soon disappeared, the conservatory being transformed into a ballroom where three generations were to dance with their assorted loves. Villiers' first words, his mother recorded, were 'Hammer, hammer', picked up from hearing the work on the new tower to supply the house with water. Forty years earlier, in the time of Sarah Lady Jersey, an unhappy maidservant had drowned herself and her new-born child in the tank that then supplied the household, so perhaps a separate system had more than convenience to recommend it. Balancing the new ballroom, the nurseries were extended by adding to the wing on the opposite side of the house. When the children descended to spend an evening hour with their parents they were allowed to use the front staircase, where the portrait of Anne Lady Jersey, granddaughter of the Duke of Marlborough, in panniers and with a page holding an open umbrella over her head, hung among a collection of Chinese dragons embroidered on silk.

In the daytime the nursery establishment were required to use a flight of wooden stairs, leading to a side door and cut off from the front hall. It was on this well-scrubbed wooden flight that Margaret was faced by a sudden manifestation of rebellion from her little daughters. One evening Villiers alone joined his parents, who, when they inquired as to what his sisters were doing, were startled to receive the answer, 'Running away.' At the top of the wooden stairs the girls were found, dressed in their boots and ulsters. They carried with them a basket of scraps, hoarded in their toy cupboard for days beforehand, and chiefly extracted from Mrs Bourne, the children's nurse, as bribes to stop teasing the baby.

Presumably the idea for this escapade had come from a story book, but when Mary Villiers told the story to her own children she admitted that, beyond the initial provisioning, the plan was hazy. They had had an idea of heading for Malvern, because they knew the spring water, drunk at their parents' table, to be whole-some. Possibly they planned to push on into Wales, where their father owned Baglan House in Glamorgan, a holiday home loved by all the children. Mary remembered the surprise she felt at her parents' concern over the runaways, who had intended no personal reproach, merely an exciting excursion into story-book behaviour. Conceding that her parents were right to be distressed that so little reflection had been given to the anxiety that would be caused, Mary, it seemed to her children, cherished a certain nostalgia for the days when she had lived so dangerously.

Opening out of the new ballroom was a room decorated in the Chinese style and appropriated to Margaret as her sitting-room. It was here that she read to her children and told them the tales created by her own imagination. Undoubtedly the children appreciated the stories, but this pleasure ranked below the happy birthdays which were celebrated by a tea party consisting of the Draper family. Two years after Margaret had arrived at Middleton Park as a bride, Mr Draper had arrived as Rector of All Saints Church, Middleton Stoney. He outlasted her reign, for when she as Dowager, came to write her memoirs forty years later, he was still the incumbent. As the Draper family were eleven strong, a team that might have emerged from the novels of Charlotte M. Yonge, there were contemporary companions for all the Villiers children.

One evening at dinner, Margaret wrote, Lord Strathnairn, a famous general in the Indian Mutiny but now old and deaf, had lagged behind in the conversation. The topic, rather unappetisingly, had been leprosy, but the subject had changed, and the hostess happened to remark that the Rector's wife had eleven children. His mind still on leprosy and its perils, Lord Strathnairn said courteously, 'It is not catching, I believe?'

It was other things about the Drapers that the Jerseys, knowing how swiftly little girls turned into marriageable young ladies, thought might be catching among the Drapers. They believed it was never too soon to start discouraging penniless young men. When the birthday on which, traditionally, the Drapers had been entertained approached, Margaret raised the question of a change in the style of celebration. Would it not be nice, this year, she suggested, to have tea with her in her sitting-room, after which she would entertain her children with stories? Reaction was swift, not to say devastating, the children bursting collectively into such floods of tears that their mother made haste to withdraw her proposal. For that year, at any rate, the Drapers came to a birthday tea party.

6

Margaret as seen by Herself

IT WAS IN 1875 that Disraeli, then Prime Minister, wrote to offer Lord Jersey an appointment as Lord-in-Waiting. With a choice of words that might be called dead-pan, he added that he thought the appointment would be pleasing to Her Majesty, many members of Lord Jersey's family having been connected with the Court. The Queen was pleased with her godson's appointment, and certainly the respectability of his behaviour contrasted with the raffish Court record of earlier Villiers's. It thus became Jersey's duty to answer for local government in the House of Lords. Fortunately his wife found even the most humdrum aspects of politics interesting. Additionally her assiduity in attending the House of Lords debates was made more enjoyable by the company of a new friend with whom her sympathy was complete.

This new friend had been born Mary Cecil, a half-sister of that Marquess of Salisbury who was to become Prime Minister in 1886. She had married the Earl of Galloway, but, like all her family, remained closely devoted to her mother, *en secondes noces* the wife of another statesman, the Earl of Derby. Lord Derby was charmed by Margaret, and became her valued adviser and correspondent. About Lady Derby she had reservations, feeling that Lady Derby's adoring children might have had easier lives had their mother been less intensely all-pervasive.

An example of Lady Derby's over-anxious kindness occurred when the Jerseys paid their first visit to Knowsley. With the idea that a woman as young as Margaret might feel abashed at confronting a vast house where the host and many of the guests were unknown to her, Lady Derby came down to the front door to meet the young couple. Margaret said that her heart was won by this kind attention, which was also a lesson to her on the importance to a stranger of an initial welcome. She could not, however, refrain from adding that she thought she would have survived the shock of meeting the house-party unprotected by her hostess. This assessment of her own character would not have been contradicted by Margaret's family and friends.

It is from a period when her friendship with Lady Galloway was at its closest that a journal of Margaret's has survived. She was not a consistent diarist, except that when she travelled, her letters to her mother sometimes took this form. The diary opens in January 1880 with the speculation as to how long the enterprise would be sustained, but in spite of lapses of time it does give a picture of Margaret painted by herself.

For four years she used the locked volume intermittently, the entries varying from detailed accounts of certain occasions to a summary of events after several months had passed. She had known Lady Galloway since 1875 and referred to her as 'my twin', a period phrase for friendship with an identical soul. In the same year, Edith Somerville, future literary collaborator with Martin Ross, possessed a 'twin' in a favourite cousin. Edith Somerville's diary recorded the sickening wrench when 'that unprincipled woman, the Twin' marched on the arm of her bridegroom down the sail walk laid by the coastguards from the church at Castletownshend, Co. Cork.

Not having met until they were both married, such a separation was no threat to the twinship between Margaret Jersey and Mary Galloway. Every pleasure was doubled if they shared it. Together they drove from Middleton to luncheon with Doctor Jowett, Master of Balliol. On the drive they passed through a fairyland of trees hung with hoar frost. Of their host Margaret wrote, rather ambiguously, 'that he was a little man with a little manner, accustomed to receive attention'. About a Sunday soon afterwards, she had no reservations, calling it one of the happy days when she and her twin could go to Holy Communion together.

From her diary it is obvious that Margaret had become all-presiding in the neighbourhood of Middleton, in succession to her predecessor Sarah, Lady Jersey. Her afternoons in the first week of March were a sequence of local duties, 'Tuesday, Inspected Caulcut Infant School; Wednesday, Mother's Meeting, Middleton Stoney; Thursday, Mother's Meeting, Caulcut; Friday, Meeting at Bicester about the Nursing Fund; Saturday, Prize Giving at Somerton School'. Bicester was the local market town, and a famous fox-hunting centre, but the other villages were still unsophisticated. At the Mother's Meeting there was an opportunity to make tactful suggestions for the better care of the babies, who suckled at the breast while an improving reading was given.

On the subject of breast-feeding of babies Margaret seems to have shared Queen Victoria's distaste, though, unlike the Queen, she had no cause to complain that her daughters made cows of themselves. Nursed herself by a wet nurse, and obliged to procure one for her own small and premature eldest baby, Margaret regarded it as impossible that her daughters would be able to nurse their children. Her propaganda was so effective that this natural function was only resumed by her granddaughters. Now, in the spring of 1880, she entered on her fifth pregnancy, and noted that she had had her first visit from Doctor Matheson, presumably a specialist new to her, ' . . . had to conjure up maladies for him to cure. Like him.'

This comment was typical of Margaret's attitude to medical practitioners, and indeed to illness in general. Throughout her life she regarded doctors as social callers rather than advisers, and naturally preferred those who made agreeable conversation. At intervals she wrote of measures taken by her husband to improve his health, of a trip to Switzerland not being the success that had been hoped, but she never specified from what he was thought to be suffering. His children believed that his troubles were probably digestive, and that a more suitable diet might have mitigated his pains and mollified his uncertain temper. His daughter Markie recalled that her father thought it correct to eat eggs for breakfast, though he disliked them and they did not agree with him. The only restraint in diet practised by the Jerseys was to ban soup from the menu when the family dined alone, but it was not clear if this was from distaste or a regard for digestion.

Her pregnancy did not prevent Margaret from moving briskly from Middleton to Jersey's Welsh property, and to London as need arose. Although railway stations had to be reached by horse-drawn vehicles and the trains themselves may have been slower, an age that has seen the attrition of the railway service can have little conception of its past excellence. Trains ran frequently by day, and, as milk and mail depended on steam, throughout the night. After attending the beginning of a mother's meeting, Margaret was able to catch a train from Heyford Station which would bring her to Paddington in time to go down to the House of Lords with Lady Galloway to listen to a debate.

Margaret, Countess of Jersey, 1878, by L. Desanges

Lady Galloway and her niece, Cumloden, Kirkcudbrightshire, 1890

Osterley Park, Middlesex, Garden front

An even greater pleasure for Margaret was to shun the heat of political squabbles, and spend 'a very happy evening' with her twin, never failing to write in her diary of her enjoyment of these tête-à-têtes. Married for eight years, Margaret had not yet, as she herself noted, cast off the feeling that her doings still needed the imprimatur of her mother's approval. She recorded her relief and pleasure that her mother, meeting Lady Galloway at a house-party, had had the opportunity of getting to know and like this dear friend of her daughter's.

It was not only Lady Jersey who took part in village meetings. Her husband was a performer at the Penny Readings, organized for intellectual improvement in the Boys School at Middleton Stoney. Margaret recorded that, 'George read William of Wykeham. He and I read Hubert and Arthur's scene from *King John*.' She did not say if the horror and pathos of the scene produced a strong reaction from the audience, only that she found herself more nervous in reading Prince Arthur's harrowing appeal to spare his sight than she did, when acting in a play. It is to be presumed that the earlier scene in *King John*, when the Bastard of Fauconbridge cross-examines his mother on his paternity, rejoicing to hear that his father was Richard Coeur de Lion, would have been judged less suitable for the ears of the village.

When the London season was over, Lady Galloway came to Middleton. The two friends lay in garden chairs in their favourite angle of the house, while Lady Galloway read aloud Tennyson's *Lotus Eaters*, and they wondered if that was what they might call themselves. In fact moments of lotus-eating were rare in their lives, for if Lady Galloway had no children, she was continually travelling up and down from London to Scotland, where her husband was sorting out a financial tangle concerning his property. Commenting on her other activities, Lady Galloway once said that 'She Opened Bazaars', would be the suitable epitaph for her tombstone. Margaret, on the other hand, thought 'She Gave Away Prizes' would be more appropriate for herself, claiming in later years that she doubted if there was a child in Middlesex who had not received a prize from her hands. Middlesex was the county in which stood Osterley Park, soon to become the most loved of Margaret's homes.

Beatrice, the Jerseys' fourth daughter, but the third to survive, was born at Folkestone in October 1880. Her mother did not record

why Folkestone was chosen as a birthplace, but she made an unself-
consciously devout note in her diary, praying that as God had sent
her this gift, so might the child, in her time, return to God. Judging
by Beatrice's character and the conduct of her life, the mother's
prayer was duly answered. Mary, for three years 'Baby' in her
family, was at first displeased by her new sister. Then her mother
noticed that she showed resentment if not addressed as Mary. Having passed through the phase of 'I used to be the baby till the other
baby came', Mary became devoted to Beatrice, whose nursery pet
name was Puss, and to whom she sent a calendar every Christmas,
specially chosen with a picture of the softest of kittens. Beatrice
reciprocated this devotion, and when Mary became a widow in
World War I she offered a kind of consolation that none other
of the family could give.

With an increasing family even Margaret's impatience with illness could not keep the infectious fevers of childhood from disrupting her plans. Villiers she nursed through scarlet fever, taking
an evening bath in Condy's fluid before joining her husband at
dinner. Less acute measures were taken when the little girls were
dispatched from London to Middleton in quarantine for measles,
which they promptly developed. Their mother did not, however,
arrive until they were convalescent. 'Markie had some delirium,'
wrote Margaret, 'but was well enough to go out in the carriage
to-day.' On another occasion she wrote that, 'Mary and Baby
(Beatrice) had chicken-pox at Baglan'. This attack failed to register
with Mary herself, it being almost before her memory. It was an
unlucky omission, as Mary grew up to be a great stickler for
quarantine in her own family. When one of her daughters infected
five other members of the household with chicken-pox Mary kept
herself at arm's length from the sufferers, a precaution she did not
know to be superfluous.

In the nursery at Middleton, Mrs Bourne reigned. ('Mrs' was
an honorary title, given in large households to the unmarrried
female heads of departments.) Certain cares Margaret did, however, take upon herself. She noted when she cut her two eldest
daughters' hair into fringes, for the first time, perhaps she would
have been surprised to know that Mary retained this style for her
own children, fringes and a bow on top, until fashion became too
strong for her. As well as trimming the fringes on her daughters'
foreheads, Margaret also trimmed the fringes of their sashes when
these began to ravel, sashes worn round white muslin dresses being

uniform wear for little girls who came down to the drawing-room after tea.

This was not the only time when the children saw the visitors who grown-up whim had invited to the house. There was also a meeting in the morning for the assembled household to join in family prayers. Villiers was six years old when Thomas Hughes, author of *Tom Brown's Schooldays*, came to stay, and old enough to appear to be reading the Psalms for himself. Margaret wrote that she liked Mr Hughes immensely, and he returned her regard by giving her the poems of James Russell Lowell, marking his own preferences. Just as Thomas Hughes was leaving he was concerned by a protest from Villiers that he had never, as promised, told Villiers the story of the King of the Cats.

On the same day, back in London, Hughes wrote to his hostess, telling her that he had been in the habit of recounting old fairy stories to a son who had died, long ago, as a little boy. Villiers was the first child for whom he had felt able to attempt the same practice. To Villiers he wrote that he had been taught never to 'run word', by parents who never 'ran word', that is broke a promise, with him. He thought that, though Villiers had put up a good show of reading the Psalms at prayers that morning, his mother reading them over his shoulder might have been a help. She should be appealed to if Villiers found Mr Hughes's writing, although carefully large, too difficult. Faithfully written out, the story was that in which a cat, hearing the grand funeral of one of his race described, exclaimed, 'Then I am the King of the Cats', and vanished up the chimney.

With Lord Galloway's valet, brought to Middleton by his employer, Thomas Hughes was less of a success. Initially the valet had been so much attracted by Hughes' enthusiasm for founding a town to be called 'New Rugby', in the State of Tennessee, that he had offered to accompany the founder as his body servant. The town was to be run on Christian Socialist and teetotal principles, but proved to be a financial disaster for Thomas Hughes. American resistance to the prohibition of alcohol was already energetic, traders coming to bury bottles on the perimeter of 'New Rugby', which the inhabitants then dug up in secret. Waving aside any question of valeting, Hughes told Lord Galloway's servant that he would be glad to accept him as a comrade. In his turn, the valet retreated before such an unsuitable idea, telling his fellows that Mr Hughes had no idea of real English aristocracy.

Margaret's spiritual affinity with Lady Galloway continued throughout the period in which she kept this particular journal. Together they went to Holy Communion at All Saints, Margaret Street, 'a service to make me happy', Margaret wrote. This is a rather startling statement, both to readers of her memoirs and to those who knew her in later life, when she habitually referred to a church where ritualistic practices were combined with appeals for funds as The Beggar's Opera. Standing in a redbrick close, designed, with the church, by Butterfield in 1856, All Saints has been called the Anglo-Catholic Cathedral, but, as has been said, happiness at its services did not stop Margaret's retreat to the Evangelicanism of her upbringing.

Friendship and religious sympathy made it natural for Lady Galloway to be godmother to Margaret's second surviving daughter, born not long after the friends had met. In consequence this baby was called Mary, but Lady Galloway herself had another name of historical significance. She had been christened Arthur after the Duke of Wellington, almost as devoted to Lady Galloway's mother as he had been to Lord Salisbury's first wife. In all four sons of Lord Salisbury were named after the Duke, whose godchildren, including among them a son of Queen Victoria, must have been as the sands of the sea.

Lady Galloway's sponsorship did not stop with Mary, for the second son and youngest child of the Jerseys, born in 1883, was christened Arthur on her account. This little boy became the pet of his three sisters, a devotion which lasted into their married lives. Each sister gave their firstborn son the name of Arthur, a tribute to the Great Duke having become, by descent, a gesture of affection.

One of the last incidents in Margaret's diary concerned a Warwickshire election, in which her brother Gilly was standing as a Liberal against Lord Yarmouth. Family feeling overcame Margaret's Toryism. She drove down to the telegraph office at Heyford Station where, against regulations, she coaxed or bullied the clerk into sending a message up the line to Leamington. Gilly, she learnt, was elected, though the order of the poll came back facetiously as 'Leigh . . . Yarmouth Bloater . . .' In her delight Margaret was not to know how short a time Gilly had before him. Her own life was also full of a new excitement for, when she abandoned her journal, Osterley, the palace of palaces, was just about to become her most beloved home.

7

'The joy of my life'

THE DEATH OF the ninety-one-year-old Duchess of Cleveland, the tenant of Osterley Park, took place in November 1883, three weeks before the birth of Arthur Villiers, which perhaps prevented Margaret from immediately realizing the change that this death might make in her life. As the Duchess, a careful and generous tenant, was clearly doing her best to live for ever, the Jerseys, when she failed to do so, found themselves with no idea for the house's future beyond finding a new tenant. Although they had once spent a night there as guests of the Duchess, the magic of the treasure house, lapped by pink walls and roofed by blue domes, had not made itself manifest to its owners.

Margaret's delay in grasping the opportunity before her may have been due to nervous exhaustion after the birth of Arthur. This weakness, most unusual for her, was due, she believed, to overdoing the Christmas shopping. The following year, she mentioned in her diary, Jersey had an idea of keeping a house on the Osterley estate as a surburban home, but she doubted, rightly, if this plan would come to anything. Then they decided to give one garden party before seeking a new tenant. More guests than they had expected arrived to enjoy a perfect afternoon in a perfect setting.

Suddenly it became obvious that Osterley itself was an ideal surburban home. At least that is how Margaret described the decision to make it so. With the willingness to declare her enjoyment which was one of her most attractive traits, she added that '[Osterley] became the joy of my life and a great pleasure to my husband'. In reality, Margaret had fallen in love, and the object of her affections gave her a return as generous as the love she poured out upon it.

Unlike Middleton Park, demolished and rebuilt forty years ago, Osterley Park still presides over its cedar dotted lawn, now open for all to visit. Some pictures and furniture have been dispersed, but enough of Adam's inspiration remains for imagination to understand Margaret's feelings when she entered into her new kingdom. She was never daunted by its splendours into treating the rooms as too sacred for everyday use. Her children did their lessons in the Etruscan room, and, it must be admitted, whiled away the tedium secretly by peeling the paint off the chairs designed to match the wall decorations. If the house was full of visitors, the hostess would herself sleep in the state bedroom next door, in the four-poster bed whose valance was embroidered with the marigold flower, the emblem of Child's Bank. The marigold turning towards the sun's rays and the motto 'Ainsi mon âme', was a sentiment more high-minded than botanically accurate, the flower that reputedly turned to the sun being the girasole.

Both the Etruscan room and the State Bed came in for disapprobation from Horace Walpole on the visit in which he called Osterley 'the Palace of palaces'. He thought the decoration of the Etruscan room unworthy of the house. As for the great dome of the state bed, he asked what Vitruvius would have thought of a dome decorated by a milliner. Finding no gothic majesty in the Park, 'the ugliest spot of ground in the universe', Walpole drove back, comforted, to the elegance of Strawberry Hill four miles away. A century later trees had grown up to soften the flat landscape of orchards and market gardens, whose produce poured into the great maw of London. Now secluded in its groves, the Park seemed a spot far from ugly to generations of courting couples.

In the autumn of 1884, when the prospect of making a home at Osterley was opening before her, Margaret's own family was blasted by a tragedy, as a result of which two generations were to pass before direct descent was re-established. It has been mentioned that Lord and Lady Leigh had seven children who survived infancy, Margaret, Gilbert, Agnes, Dudley, Rupert, Rowland and Cordelia. These names had family, literary or historical asssociations, though to a later generation their familiar abbreviation to Markie, Gilly, Aggie, Duddy (or Duds) Rupy, Rowly and Cordie (or Cords) has an echo of Walt Disney's Seven Dwarfs. None had married, but Gilly, now an M.P., was expected to take on more responsibilities in due course, including a wife, and the begetting of an heir to succeed him at Stoneleigh.

Accustomed to going on shooting expeditions in the Rocky Mountains, Gilly rode off from his camp during one of these, never to be seen alive again. His companion William Grenfell, later Lord Desborough and a famous athlete, searched for days before finding Gilly's body at the bottom of a precipice, down which he had fallen to instant death. Years before Lady Leigh had written a lament for the ewes of Kingairloch, when their lambs were taken away. Now it was for herself that she wrote a lament, touching in its unselfconscious striving for comfort at the loss of her eldest son. The poem ended,

> But to him come not again
> Cold or heat or grief or pain.

After an agonizingly long wait the body reached Stoneleigh for burial. Margaret did not comment on the particular loss to herself of the brother who had been her closest companion in her growing-up years. She only wrote that her mother placed a bunch of white rosebuds in the coffin, because Gilly, as a little boy, had once said that his idea of love was a bunch of roses.

Even before Osterley opened a wider field of hospitality, Margaret had made many friends among distinguished men. She was prepared to welcome guests from both political parties, inviting Joseph Chamberlain to her house at a time when he had not yet split with Gladstone. She was not, herself, on familiar terms with Gladstone, but enjoyed Lady Galloway's letter on that formidable thinker's theory concerning the immortality of the soul. Gladstone had conveyed this theory to Lady Galloway during a house party at Knowsley, but the latter, excusably, found it hard to grasp. Based on the idea that every soul was not 'of necessity immortal', Gladstone suggested that immortality was lost through sin and gained through Christ. Lady Galloway was glad to assure her friend that Mr Gladstone was not speaking *ex cathedra*.

Margaret found speculation on the hereafter perfectly compatible with adherence to the Church of England by law established. Consequently she took pleasure in comparing Gladstone's idea of the soul's future with that of Robert Browning, with whom she was well acquainted. Having watched more than one person die, Browning told her that, observing the last movement to be a flicker between the eyebrows, he believed it was there that the soul last lingered in the body. Margaret was sceptical, both on this point and on the poet's remark that he had expressed what he felt about immortality in *Old Pictures in Florence*. The lines ending 'I have had troubles enough for one' seemed to Margaret in contradiction to the strong faith, expressed in *Prospice*, that he would find Elizabeth Barrett again.

Talking of his late wife, Browning told Margaret that he was in the habit of sending autographs to those who wrote requesting them, a practice, he added, that Tennyson did not follow. He had come to see that there was something in Tennyson's attitude, when, having received Browning's autograph, a correspondent wrote again asking for Mrs Browning's: if there happened to be no separate signature available, surely the widower could cut one off any letter he happened to have preserved.

In recollecting the opinions of great men on immortality, Margaret mentioned that she had 'perpetrated' an article on Buddhism for the *National Review*, to which she was an intermittent contributor. The article brought her a kind letter from Edwin Arnold, author of the immensely popular poem *The Light of Asia*, a disquisition on the Gautama's idea of Buddhism. He also begged her not to consider Nirvana to be annihilation, but rather as an escape from the embodied life onto a higher metaphysical level.

The correspondence, begun on a high metaphysical level, developed into a friendship, in which Margaret, on one occasion played a rather witch-like role. A friend, renowned for her powers of reading both palms and thoughts, came to call. Hearing that Margaret had met Edwin Arnold, the caller expressed such admiration for *The Light of Asia*, that she was asked to dinner that same night, the poet being already engaged to dine with the Jerseys. According to Margaret, she put this admirer, Augusta Webb, on the other side of the guest of honour in order to please her, but it seems likely that she wished to display Miss Webb's psychic powers. In any case Miss Webb was called upon to tell Edwin Arnold what was his favourite flower, which she did by looking at his hand, although the flower's name was unknown to her and she could only describe it as 'white, strong-smelling and something like a tuber-rose'.

A different approach was, naturally, correct when Margaret found herself seated next to the newly made Cardinal, John Henry Newman, at a dinner given in his honour at Norfolk House. The evening had begun rather farcically when the host, that Duke of Norfolk who had been so loved by Margaret's nurse Mrs Gailey, led the Cardinal into the room where the guests were assembled in a circle. The ballroom had been decorated in what has been called 'a florid and rather free Louis XV manner' about forty years before. Against this background of ornate gilding reflected in mirrors, an elderly lady, a convert to Roman Catholicism, broke ranks and fell on her knees, grovelling before His Eminence as she effusively kissed his hand. The Cardinal was embarrassed, but even more appalled was Margaret's aunt, the Duchess of Westminster, who was handsome but portly. 'Margaret,' she whispered in anguish to the niece beside her, 'shall we have to do that? Because I shall never be able to get up again.'

Luckily no such drastic obeisance was required, as Margaret herself must have been pregnant at the time. At dinner she found the Cardinal most attractive, though he responded with a denial to her inquiry as to whether the Gerontius of his poem was a real person. Bane of authors though this particulat query often is, it did not take away from the Cardinal's enjoyment in finding that this charming Countess had read his poem. Two years later he sent her a book on the Russian Church which he had edited. With the book came a letter to say that, at his age, this might well be the only opportunity of showing his appreciation of her kindness when they had met at Norfolk House.

As it happens, Margaret's account of this reception at Norfolk House can be checked against that of Matthew Arnold, who described the evening in a letter to his sister dated May 15th 1880, the party having taken place three days earlier. He thought Norfolk House less fine than he expected, and perhaps the Cardinal in his costume also less fine. Arnold wrote that Newman was 'not in full Cardinal's costume, but in a sort of vest with gold about it and the red cap'. The poet had come in after dinner when the Cardinal was in state receiving the devotees. Like Margaret, Arnold thought some of their zeal excessive. 'That old mountebank Lord—— dropped on his knees and mumbled the Cardinal's hand like a piece of cake.' Meeting a cousin of the host, who piloted him through the crowd to the Cardinal's chaplain, Arnold was able to jump the queue and make a deferential bow to Newman. The Cardinal took the poet's hand in both of his and charmingly said he had suggested to the Duchess that Arnold should be invited. To quote Newman's best-known hymn, it is like 'a kindly light in the encircling gloom' to know that after a life of struggles and doubts he could still take pleasure in meeting a woman of charm and a poet of genius.

Although Matthew Arnold and Browning were acquaintances of Margaret's, the poet with whom she had the closest friendship was James Russell Lowell, brought into her life by Thomas Hughes. So determined was Hughes that Lady Jersey should learn to like and admire the American Minister to the Court of St James's that he gave her a letter from Lowell written on his appointment. This not only dealt with the delicate health that kept Mrs Lowell inactive, but discussed the comments by the British Press on the new Minister. Resentment was still felt for Lowell's harsh words on those British actions which had favoured the Confederates during the American Civil War. There was speculation that he might arrive in a spirit of bitterness. For his part Lowell complained that the English were ever unsatisfied unless the outsider liked England better than his own country.

Thomas Hughes may have been unworldly to a fault when he planned an Utopia in the New World, but he was shrewd when he saw that the Jerseys would be ideal people to soften any bitterness in Lowell's spirit. With them there was no umbrage, or insistence on unconditional surrender to the superiority of England to impede a new friendship. Between Lowell and Margaret, thirty years his junior, there developed a literary flirtation to the obvious enjoyment of both parties. Unlike many of Margaret's correspondents, all the letters from Lowell which she preserved are dated with official competence, day, month, year. Only too many of the letters she thought worth keeping are headed, for example 'Tuesday', leaving readers in later years to guess on which Tuesday pen had been put to paper.

If Lowell teased Margaret as an irreclaimable Tory, which indeed she was, he also made play in prose and verse that she had been named for a pearl. Two of the poems that appeared in his collection, *Heartsease and Rue*, were originally written for Lady Jersey, and were perhaps not improved when the poet had worked over them. The first celebrated the green peace of Middleton Park after 'London's noise and smoke' and ended,

> Sun sink no deeper down the sky,
> Nature, ne'er leave this summer mood,
> Breeze loiter thus for ever by,
> Stir the dead leaf or let it lie,
> Since I am happy, all is good!

Concerning Margaret, the pearl, he wrote a letter of infinite courtesy, when a sudden decision as to the date of the Queen's official birthday forced him to postpone a dinner party. If the alteration meant that his table would lose its pearl, the Minister insisted that he would give a dinner specially for Lady Jersey. He continued the word play on her name in a second poem, after he had given her a copy of Omar Khayyám. From aboard ship he sent her verses on the subject of his gift; his pen, he wrote, dancing to the dancing of the ship.

When published the poem's inspirer was not identified, but the verses spoke of 'Omar's pearls of thought', strung on Fitzgerald's 'English thread', 'fit rosary for a queen',

> 'Fit for a queen? Why, surely then for you!'

Nearing the centenary of her birth and driven from her London home by war, Margaret kept a few books beside her, indeed her sight had failed. She did, however, still cherish the volume of Lowell's poems that Thomas Hughes had given her, and in which the poet had written of the repose to be found at Middleton. The lines on the gift of Omar Khayyám, she had, as Lowell suggested, pasted into the book, and this book was also with her to the end. These were reminders of the evenings when Lowell had delighted to sit with her in the garden at Osterley, watching the blue haze that softens the landscape of the Thames valley. Although never one to make claims for herself as an influence on public affairs, Margaret might well have been justified if she felt that this friendship had been an element in building a better understanding between the country of the American Minister and her own.

Lowell's poems mingled serious thought with compliments to his hostess, but Osterley and its owners frequently received more frivolous tributes from a widower in his forties called Lionel Ashley. He celebrated the doings of the two countesses, Jersey and Galloway, so constantly that they called him 'the Bard'. They enjoyed his effusions, though to judge from the one which Margaret quoted in *Fifty-One Years of Victorian Life* these were more remarkable for punning dexterity than poetical feeling. Having made play with the idea of 'Villiers' and 'suburban villas', (as the name is pronounced) and ingeniously rhymed 'Grandison' with 'stand his own', the Bard may still have felt that he was outpointed artistically by the American Minister. In any case Ashley took what might be called a swipe at Lowell's attitude on the Irish question, in lines which have still a harrowing relevance, although ninety years have passed since they were written.

> The Irish question, in masterly way,
> Mr Lowell made easy and clear.
> We must make them content without further delay,
> But the method was not his affair.

Lady Galloway's appearance as she handled the ribbons of a Shetland pony four-in-hand, is illustrated by a photograph taken at Cumloden, her husband's Scottish home, in 1889. She was remembered by her step-great-niece, Lady Harlech, as being smartly dressed, with the kind of smartness that chose to have country clothes subtly different for England or for Scotland. She is certainly more coherently fitted out than the niece of her husband who sits beside her in the pony carriage.

There is a more spectacular representation of Lady Jersey to be found in the National Portrait Gallery, a fact which gave her great pleasure whenever she happened to see it, as it contravened the rule that no portrait should appear in the Gallery until ten years after the sitter's death. As the artist, H. J. Brooks, had placed Margaret in the middle of a large group, standing very much detached, she had some reason to feel pleased. The occasion was the Private View of an Exhibition of Old Masters, held at the Royal Academy in 1888. It was a loan exhibition and the prominence of Lord and Lady Jersey may have been due to their having lent what must have been one of the largest pictures on show, Rubens' Apotheosis of George Villiers, 1st Duke of Buckingham. Removed for a season of public display from the Gallery at Osterley where he dominated one end, Buckingham can be seen cavorting in the background.

Margaret is flanked by Lord Leighton, the President of the Royal Academy and King of this occasion, and by Sir Richard Wallace, illegitimate son of Lord Hertford and heir to what is known as the Wallace Collection. Lord Jersey stands to the right of the group, leaning on a stick, bans on sticks and umbrellas not then prevailing. Margaret herself is holding an umbrella, and gazing into space, but the artist has painted more than a formal likeness, and her vivid face makes the rest of the crowd appear to be waxworks. The photograph of Lady Galloway and the portrait of Lady Jersey give an idea of how they must have appeared when they made two continental journeys together, journeys of intense enjoyment which took them from Berlin to Athens.

8

From Prussia to the Peloponnese

SINCE HER MARRIAGE there had been more than one winter in
which Margaret had been bustled off to the Mediterranean to
favour her weak chest by avoiding the latter end of that season
in the north. Paradoxically this consideration seems to have been
ignored when she set off to join Lady Galloway in Berlin, in 1887.
Her friend was returning from a visit to Russia, and, though the
month was February, no one seems to have attempted to stop Margaret from this reunion in the notoriously harsh Prussian climate.
Mary Galloway and Margaret Jersey were guests of the British
Ambassadress, Lady Ermyntrude Malet, who steered them
through the social obstacle race dictated by the iron rules of Prussian Court etiquette. After leaving cards on the entire Corps
Diplomatique, the last obstacle was presentation to the Empress's
Obermeisterin, an appointment only next to royalty in rank and
filled by a Gräfin Perponcher, irreverently described by Margaret
as a funny old soul in a wig.

World War I was still a raw wound in the minds of many, including her own war-widowed daughter, in 1922 when Margaret
wrote her reminiscences. Consequently she was obliged to handle
her experiences in Imperial Berlin with caution, but she was not
able to conceal that she had had a wildly enjoyable visit. As half-
sister of Lord Salisbury, British Prime Minister, Lady Galloway was welcomed with a respect that seemed to the English
ladies, accustomed to the tidal rise and fall of Ministers in England,
slightly comic. Margaret was made welcome for more personal
reasons, her grandmother, Lady Westminster, having been on
terms to exchange birthday presents with the Emperor William I.

French was still the language spoken in court circles in Berlin.
The Empress Augusta, dressed like an idol and with eyes glittering

as if from belladonna, made a neat speech in French to each of the ladies seated before her on a Stonehenge of chairs. She had been trained as a child to address a polite speech to a circle of empty seats. The Emperor, on the other hand, although aged and ailing, had a more active enjoyment of social life. The upsurge of Prussian military pride in their victories had boosted the Emperor's popularity, but was destined to have a sinister effect on the future of Europe. In the meantime, the Emperor was amused at Margaret's curiosity in going to see him when he looked out, as he did every morning, to watch the parade of his soldiers. Previously, he told her, no one had troubled to come and look at him, but now he was 'devenu la mode'.

The Crown Princess, eldest daughter of Queen Victoria, kept up her habit, already mentioned, of tactless speech in her meeting with Margaret. Replying to a conventional compliment on the splendour of the scene in the Weisser Saal at the Carnival Court Ball, the Crown Princess said that at Buckingham Palace not only was the spectacle finer but the faces prettier.

A call on Princess Bismarck resulted in the Iron Chancellor joining the circle of ladies in his wife's drawing-room. Here the conversation, in French, reached its most significant when Bismarck misunderstood Margaret, thinking that her remark that he wished to change 'les caractères allemandes' referred to the character of the German people rather than to the script in which they wrote. Bismarck said he would hardly be capable of such a transformation. However he added, 'On m'accuse d'avoir changé une nation de poètes en nation de politiques militaires, mais c'est parce que nous avons été si longtemps l'enclume il fallait le faire. Il faut toujours être l'enclume ou le marteau, maintenant nous sommes le marteau. Nous étions l'enclume jusqu'à Leipzig et Waterloo.' Margaret, with commendable firmness, suggested that at Waterloo 'nous étions deux marteaux'. Bowing, Bismarck replied, 'J'espère que nous les serons encore ensemble.'

Bismarck's ambition to drink ten thousand bottles of champagne in his lifetime seems to have been an excellent preservative, for Margaret was struck by his eagerness for social life. However, only three years after the discussion about hammers and anvils, when William II had succeeded Frederick, his doomed father, Tenniel had cause to draw for *Punch* the immortal cartoon that showed the Dropping of Bismarck, the Pilot. Sitting next to the future Emperor William II himself at a concert, Margaret found herself cross-examined on the subject of the Primrose League, in which she had a position. She was left with the impression that the Prince, who as Kaiser was to become the bogeyman of the next generation, thought the Primrose League dangerously promoted women in public affairs. Margaret, on her side thought it symptomatic of Teutonic rigidity that in a morning's walk in Dresden she was checked three times for walking in places *verboten*. In fairness to the police of Saxony, it should be mentioned that Margaret congenitally lacked a sense of direction, an embarrassment to her descendants when they found themselves following her against tides of one-way foot traffic.

A year later, the two friends set off for Greece, but only after some family protest, owing to possible dangers from brigands. Seventeen years earlier Lord Muncaster, his wife, and a party of friends had been captured by brigands near Marathon, the traditional twenty-two miles from Athens of the legendary runner. The women of the party were allowed to go, Lady Muncaster having cleverly hidden her rings in her mouth. One man was to go with them to arrange a ransom, and the lot fell on Mr Vyner, a bachelor. He insisted that Lord Muncaster should go in his place, but the Greek Government sent troops instead of money. The brigands were wiped out, but not before they had murdered the prisoners. In her youth Margaret thought that Lord Muncaster's habit of carrying his head to one side came from his grief over this tragedy. He was a brother-in-law of Margaret's Aunt Jane, born Grosvenor, so cries of alarm now went up from Lady Leigh and her family.

Apprehension was also felt by the Bard, Lionel Ashley, who insisted on giving each lady a revolver and ammunition. Unable to refuse, but convinced she would miss and only enrage the brigands, Margaret hid the revolver on her person and the ammunition in her luggage, neutralizing her weapon of defence. Having had sixteen years of matrimonial experience, Galloway and Jersey took the view that their wives were a match for any number of brigands. Lord Jersey calmly assured them, 'If you are captured Galloway and I will come with an army to rescue you.'

It was only when the friends found berths available on a Messageries boat from Marseilles to Athens that they finally decided to explore Hellas, or rather to spend three days in Athens, imagining that even Marathon, where Mr Vyner and his companions had been massacred, would be out of bounds. However, from the moment that they were met at Piraeus by William Haggard, the British Chargé d'Affaires, who took them off their ship in a boat from the Harbour Master's Office, their visit became a triumphal progress, the three days visit planned being extended to a four weeks' tour. The Haggard family were of good omen to Margaret. William Haggard was the eldest of a septet of brothers, of whom Rider Haggard, creator of *She*, was the fifth. Four years later the second brother, Bazett Michael, was to be Margaret's host and guide in Samoa, where he introduced her to Robert Louis Stevenson. It will be seen that this meeting, and the consequent expedition, remained for Margaret the most excitingly delightful of all her adventures of travel.

Against a background of olive groves, sight-seeing was taken over at the highest level of government. If Lord Salisbury's half-sister was treated with respect in Berlin, in Athens the Ministers treated her almost with awe. As it happened Lady Galloway had another connection with Greece, her mother's second husband, Lord Derby, had been offered the throne of Greece, when, as Lord Stanley, he had been a young politician. There is a legend that he had refused with the inquiry, 'Don't they know I am going to be Earl of Derby?', certainly a more solid prospect. At the time of Margaret's visit the King was a prince imported from Denmark, George, brother of Alexandra, Princess of Wales. Lady Jersey thought that he kept his balance admirably, calling him an astute monarch. In practice the country was under the control of M. Tricoupi, Prime Minister and Minister of War.

In Margaret's bedroom at Middleton there hung a watercolour of one of the rooms in the Royal Palace of Athens. This pink wedding cake of a palace had been built by the Bavarian occupant of the newly-made Greek throne, King Otho, who, turning out to be unsatisfactory, had been returned to stock. During his reign, however, King Otho had sent M. Tricoupi and his devoted sister on a visit to England, their luggage including a picture of the Royal Palace to be presented to Sarah, Lady Jersey. This shared memory made it easy for Margaret to make friends with M. Tricoupi and his sister, who had devoted her life to her brother's political career. While Parliament was in session, this lady sat on a sofa in her drawing-room, at home to all classes among her brother's supporters. Although embittered by the Allied Powers treatment of Greece during the First World War, she continued to correspond with Margaret, until death came to fetch her from the sofa on which she still sat. Coming of a long-lived family, Margaret regarded fulness of years as a natural phenomenon, but even she remarked that Mademoiselle Tricoupi must have been very old.

M. Tricoupi himself was determined that the English ladies should see every glory of Greece in high style. When a sea landing was necessary, gunboats were supplied by M. Theodoki, Minister of Marine, mentioned by Margaret as the most amusing of the ministers and 'not averse to a little innocent flirtation'. This theory was supported by a glance from M. Theodoki in Margaret's direction when the bachelor Prime Minister, judging from the behaviour in public life of his sister, declared that he favoured women rising to Cabinet rank. Any question of the distracting effect on their male colleagues was brushed aside with the assertion that it might be arranged that only married men should hold office. From the look on the face of the Minister of Marine, Margaret concluded that he did not share his Chief's belief in the powers of matrimony to regulate the impulses of the heart.

In theory, a German courier was responsible for the safety and comfort of Lady Jersey and Lady Galloway, but he became a background figure in the court that grew up around them. Even the name of The Courier was taken from him and applied in joke to M. Bakhméteff, a Russian diplomat. M. Bakhméteff came on their expeditions, interpreting when the gap between Greek and English ideas of comfort became too wide. If he was under orders from his government to keep an eye on the half-sister of the British Prime Minister, he must have done so unobtrusively, for such a suspicious thought does not seem to have occurred to Margaret.

At a party the night before an expedition into the Pelopennese, the Greek Prime Minister himself dictated extra telegrams to improve the tour's organization, sending the Foreign Minister, 'a white-haired statesman', to dispatch them. The telegrams decreed that the hotel at Nauplia (still ill-reputed when one of Margaret's grandchildren was on a Greek honeymoon half a century later) should be thoroughly cleansed. Its charming façade was well-known to conceal insanitary horrors. When the visitors arrived they found that the hotel had been scrubbed and kept sacrosanct for the previous four days. Groans and coughs came from the back room in which the landlord had been sequestered, his place being taken by what Margaret called 'a very smart individual, a Parisian doctor of law'.

Known to be travelling under the protection of the Prime

Minister, the party was the object of anxious efforts to provide
domestic comforts. Margaret was grateful, though amused when
the provision of only one small jug and basin obliged her friend
and herself to borrow earthenware pans from the kitchen in which
to wash. She omitted from her memoirs the story she told her
grandchildren, concerning the closet in which two commodes had
been placed side by side, thoughtfully chosen to be of different
heights, in consideration that some legs might be shorter than
others.

At Nauplia they awoke to find that snow had fallen, and that
their coachman was refusing to drive to Epidaurus. M. Bakhméteff proved worthy to be called The Courier by summoning the
Prefect of Police, who over-ruled such cowardly behaviour.
Drawn by four horses, with a spare trotting behind, they drove
for four hours through mountain country, breath-takingly lovely
at any time, but particularly so when the hills had been touched
by snowy fingers. At Epidaurus the theatre had only recently been
excavated. Its perfect acoustics were tested for the visitors by an
Ephor of Antiquities ordered up from Athens. They sat in the top
row of an auditorium built to hold twenty-five thousand Epi-
daurians, while he spoke from below, his words rising like a lark's
song. This Ephor, and indeed all the Nauplians, thought that the
madness of going to Epidaurus in the snow was only surpassed
by doing so in an open carriage, a fact carefully recorded by the
local newspaper.

In Athens also the newspapers that supported the Government
found the expeditions of the English ladies, and the parties given
in their honour, to be excellent copy, occasionally pausing to sneer
at the opposition papers for ignoring the presence of the half-sister
of Lord Salisbury. The Greek royal family were continually
hospitable, but its isolated domesticity was less lively than the din-
ners and balls of the *corps diplomatique*. For a fancy-dress ball at
the Austrian Legation, Lady Galloway dressed as 'Dresden China'
or a 'bouquetière', though Margaret did not say if her friend travelled prepared for a fancy-dress occasion. Margaret herself bor-
rowed a Japanese costume from her Russian friend M. Bakhméteff, which must have suited her pale skin and almond eyes.

Concerning one of the balls, a reporter became almost lyrical
at the gaiety which had overtaken the Prime Minister, in consequence of the visit of the English ladies. 'He [M. Tricoupi] frequently accompanied the two English ladies to the Buffet, and

with very juvenile agility he hastens to find for them their *sorties de bal* with which the noble English ladies are to protect their delicate bodies from the indiscretion of that cold night.' Both the English ladies had reputations unblemished by indiscretions of nights cold or warm, but had it been otherwise it seems it would have been from Greek Ministers, rather than from Greek brigands, that their husbands might have had to recapture them.

9

The Golden Jubilee

IT WAS IN the summer that followed the visit to Berlin that the
Osterley house-party took place about which Lionel Ashley had
written verses. Besides the punning lines already quoted, the Bard
wrote,

> In a nice little church a grave sermon we heard,
> Which reproved Christianity flabby,
> And urged that in heaven a place be preferred
> To a Jubilee seat in the Abbey.

The Thanksgiving service, to which only a heavenly seat would
be preferred was to celebrate the Golden Jubilee of Queen Victoria, and the sun shone on the rejoicings throughout the summer
of 1887. As it rose on the royal train that was bringing the Queen
down from Balmoral, a lady-in-waiting looked out to see, in the
dawn, groups of the Queen's subjects, who had come down to
the railway line simply to watch the train go by. Outside Buckingham Palace, Margaret heard a policeman remark, 'Mother's
come home', and felt that he expressed the general sentiment. To
express similarly affectionate feelings, Lady Leigh took up her pen,
and produced twelve stanzas, comparing the bloody fights that
attended the Triumphs of ancient Rome with the kisses that the
Queen, at her triumph, gave to her children and her children's
children.

Although, as will be seen, Margaret's verses in connection with
the Jubilee were of a facetious and narrative order, she appears
to have made a certain reputation for herself in the debatable
ground between amateur and professional journalism. The
publishing house of Cassell, in that summer of 1887, had offered
Oscar Wilde the editorship of the *Ladies World*. On accepting, he

insisted that the name should be changed to *Woman's World*, as having a more serious sound that would be likely to attract intelligent readers, and contributors, of both sexes. In the third person, Wilde wrote to Lady Jersey, suggesting that 'a contribution from her on any political or social subject would add a charm and interest to the magazine'. There is no way of knowing how Margaret replied, but she must have been complimented to preserve the letter in the first place, and to keep it throughout the period when Wilde's name could not be mentioned in mixed society.

Margaret's own verses were to commemorate a particularly enjoyable party of pleasure, the Jubilee Naval Review at Spithead. Lord Jersey went as the guest of the P. & O, in one of their ships, but Lady Jersey, Lady Galloway and the latter's stepfather, Lord Derby, were invited to stay on board the *Mirror*, described as 'one of Sir John Pender's electric cable ships'. Although the Jerseys lived most amiably together, having many interests and sympathies in common, it is undeniable that, on a junket with Lady Galloway, without their respective husbands, a particular jolliness becomes apparent in Margaret's recollections. As for Lady Galloway her childless marriage ended in a separation, Lord Galloway having a predilection for girls below the age of consent. There was a tradition in the Villiers family that, in writing to his wife on the subject of their separation, his letters continued to begin, 'My own darling'.

At the Spithead Review, as the Queen sailed in the *RSY Victoria and Albert* between the lines of warships, she was followed by the *Euphrates*, a ship that had been allotted to the House of Lords. Those on board saw a wonderful spectacle, and the company included Lady Jersey and Lady G., as Margaret's children called her. They had persuaded the Captain of the cable ship *Mirror* into sending them off in a boat, leaving the rest of the guests to damn women for keeping their dinner waiting. On Sunday morning farce took over completely, when Sir John Pender, Chairman of the Cable company, but a Nonconformist, decided that it was his privilege to read the lessons at the Church of England Matins. Sir John, a little man, stood up to read the first lesson, beginning 'And Satan stood up', only to be pulled down by the Captain as the passage, although appropriate, was not that appointed to be read.

It was after this religious scrimmage that Margaret broke into verse to describe an afternoon's expedition in 'that splendid tug *Undaunted*'. Besides herself, Lady G. and Lord Derby, the rest of the party consisted of General Lord Wolseley and Sir William des Voeux, a former Governor of Fiji. The General claimed, like other great captains, that he could fall asleep and wake at will, a gift that came in handy when the tug began to roll. Having acquired no resistance to sea-sickness in the Pacific, the unhappy ex-Governor of Fiji was reduced to lying prostrate at the bottom of the boat. After going ashore the company found that the splendid tug *Undaunted* had left them marooned,

'Dauntless perhaps but useless quite,
She's stranded on the bar.'

Lord Derby was the hero of Margaret's verses, and she took pleasure in describing this statesman, known for his solemnity, happily playing ducks and drakes with stones from the shore until rescue arrived.

If Lord Derby represented the still unimpaired power of the House of Lords, Margaret had also for a friend Joseph Chamberlain, representative of the industrial expansion of nineteenth-century England. In London society there were still Conservatives who were unwilling to meet such a dangerous Radical, but after meeting the Jerseys at luncheon he was immediately asked to dinner. His hostess had been Lady Jeune, a woman about ten years older than Margaret, who, as a young girl had learnt the art of holding a political salon from Lady Palmerston.

It was in 1886, when Joseph Chamberlain had split with Gladstone over the agonizing question of Home Rule, that Lady Jeune gave the luncheon party after which Chamberlain, and the Jeunes themselves, were invited to dine at the Jerseys' house in Great Stanhope Street. Margaret recorded that Lady Jeune had forgotten who had met who in her house. Arriving, Lady Jeune anxiously asked her hostess if she would object to meeting Mr Chamberlain at dinner in the near future. ' "He [Chamberlain] is in the house," was my reply, whereat she gasped and nearly fell backwards.' This is the only mention of Lady Jeune (whose husband became Lord St Helier) in Margaret's memoirs, although it seems that they frequently entertained each other. Lady Jeune called her own memoirs *Memories of Fifty Years*, and she makes something of a point that there had been no successors to such hostesses of the past as Lady Palmerston. There is no mention of the hostess who had swept Mr Chamberlain into her fold at Osterley Park.

Freeman, Lord Jersey's butler, felt differently from his employers on the subject of Joseph Chamberlain. When a dinner party, at which the Radical from Birmingham had been a guest, was followed by one of what Freeman regarded as more worthy friends, he made a point of telling Lady Jersey that they had had a very nice dinner the night before. When she had agreed, the butler added, with emphasis, 'All very nice people.' Margaret recognized that she had been rebuked, but continued to invite Mr Chamberlain. Indeed she believed that some of her Conservative friends had their first sight of him at the oars of a boat on the lake at Osterley. He must have looked rather as if he had escaped from a picture by Daumier, for he wore a top hat and had a pipe in his mouth.

The occasion was a garden party in the summer of 1888, when most of the company wore mourning for the Emperor Frederick. Margaret had found him charming to meet in Berlin only the year before, but additionally his death was a tragedy that cleared the way for his son the paranoiac Emperor William II. The blackness was nearly uniform, and it was remarked that the party had the air of a funeral wake tempered by strawberries. The guests included the ambitious political beginner George Curzon, and by way of contrast Prince Louis Esterhazy, Jersey's cousin from feudal Hungary. Standing out, like a pigeon among crows, was Miss Beatrice Chamberlain, Joseph's daughter, in a dress of coloured plaid. She was at pains to explain that her nonconformity was not due to Radical principles, but to absence abroad which had prevented her from knowing that London Society was wearing black for Queen Victoria's son-in-law.

Margaret learnt, incidentally, that Beatrice Chamberlain belonged to a society in Birmingham whose members were pledged to wear mourning for none but the closest kin. With a strong dislike of mourning, Margaret thought this a most sensible idea. On her side Miss Chamberlain always remembered the Jerseys' kindness as an emollient factor in her entry into the life of political London. Although they had political differences Margaret's friendship with Joseph Chamberlain continued until his life was ended by a long sad illness. He was even prepared to take part in some after-dinner game at Osterley, which obliged him to trot down the gallery holding a poker at arm's length to keep it clear of his nose. Neither this unkind game, nor his adoption of Protection while his hostess remained a Free Trader, spoilt Chamberlain's pleasure in sitting, as Lowell had done earlier, at the top of the steps overlooking the garden.

Emollience was, perhaps, Margaret's most useful contribution to the political life of her time, and in this the background of Osterley was an essential part. Taking possession, she found not only the joy of her life but an outlet for her energies. Hospitality meant a continuous attention to the details of house-keeping. Even though absorbed in their games or their gardens, her children could remember how rare it was on summer mornings that their mother had time to step out, even for a moment, from the Gallery onto the landing of the wide springing double staircase. Careful planning had its reward. When her guests joined her she had leisure to enjoy with them what Henry James called 'a rich English voice of the early part of the eighteenth century'.

10

Through the Eyes of the Master

IT IS Henry James who has left the clearest picture of Osterley, and the guests who wandered through its gardens, in his novella, *The Lesson of the Master*. Margaret had an idea that James had been introduced to her by Lowell, but as he was also a friend of Mrs Kemble and her daughters, Mrs Wister and Mrs James Leigh, he must have been already well-known to her by reputation. James regarded Mrs Kemble with respect that was sometimes touched by uneasiness, an attitude different from Margaret's cheerful pity for Mrs Kemble's melancholy spirit. His admiration for Mrs Wister, mother of Owen, had been warm enough for him to write reassuring letters on the subject to his own family, when he, in Rome, was Mrs Wister's escort on rides on the Campagna. In Mrs James Leigh, Henry James found a sympathetic friend with whom he was happy to spend an English family Christmas. When Alice, Lady Butler, daughter of the James Leighs, died at the age of ninety-two, she must have been the last person who could boast that Henry James had helped to decorate the Christmas tree in her childhood's nursery.

In his great life of Henry James, Professor Leon Edel has much to say of the author's friendship with the James Leighs, and the use of Osterley as a background for *The Lesson of the Master* seems to have given considerable pleasure to their niece. James himself admitted the picture in one of three letters to Lady Jersey which she preserved. The first is only an acceptance of a dinner invitation, dated May 9th. No year is given, but the address is 13 De Vere Gardens, to which James had moved in 1886. The second is obviously in reply to one from Margaret, written from New South Wales, where she had gone with her husband on his appointment as Governor-General. The subjects dealt with in her letter may be largely deduced from James' reply, which may be quoted in full. Slightly disingenuous over details, there is a characteristic flavour of the Master's style in approaching an English hostess.

> Hotel de Sienne
> Sienne
> Italy.
>   June 11th [The recipient added '1892']

Dear Lady Jersey,

Your kind letter finds me in a foreign land – the land in the world, I suppose, least like New South Wales – and gives me very great pleasure. It is charming to hear your voice so distinctly round so many corners of the globe. Yes, 'Summersoft' *did* venture in a timorous and hesitating manner to be an affectionate and yet respectful reminiscence of Osterley the exquisite – of whose folded and deserted charms I can't bear to think. But I beg you to believe and as indeed you will have perceived if you were so good as to look at the little story, that the attempted resemblance was only a matter of their dear old cubic sofa cushions and objects of the same delightful order, and not of the human furniture of the house. I take the liberty of being, in your absence, so homesick for Osterley that I can scarcely conceive of the pangs by which you and your children and Lord Jersey – with your much greater right to indulge in them – must sometimes be visited. I am delighted, however, to gather from your letter that you have occupations and interests which drop a kindly veil over that dreamland. It must indeed. I can imagine, be a satisfaction to be really lending a hand in such a great and growing young country – doing something in it and with it and for it. May the sense of all this make the years roll smoothly – till they roll you back into our ken. – I am also an absentee, but (I confess I thank my fortune,) in a blissfully irresponsible way – When Osterley is closed there seems to me so little to stay in London for that I came to Italy without a scruple. I am not fond – without that compensation – of the rush and crush of the Season; and I am finding for this month a happy refuge in this admirable old Siena, which, I think, is as romantically mediaeval a thing as Europe still holds. It is high and cool (more or less all summer) and at this moment the tangle of the luxuriant green country – the corn and olives and orchards – breaks in wonderful waves directly at the foot of the old golden-red ramparts of the city, which has no suburbs, nothing outside of its gates. My old friend Paul Bourget, the French writer, is here – and one enjoys doubly when one enjoys also through another's eyes. London, after being atrociously cold all spring, is now atrociously political – that is electoral – but I fear I can send you no prophecies. Besides, you receive them from greater oracles. I saw Mrs Jimmy Leigh just before coming away – pretty happy in the first social steps of that handsome and natural Alice. Please give my very friendliest rememberance to Lord Jersey – to whom I wish – as to all of you – and indeed to myself that you may serve your term with an appearance of rapidity. And please believe, dear Lady Jersey, that when it is over no one will more heartily rejoice than

Yours faithfully,

Henry James.

With its assurance that Siena still stood where it did, and that Aunt Fanny's Alice, for whom James had decorated a Christmas tree, was a satisfactory débutante, this letter must have been a pleasure to receive in the Antipodes. On the subject of the compensations of Margaret's position, working for a 'great and growing young country', James probably wrote from a wish to be agreeable rather than from conviction. His attitude to his own 'great and growing young country' was frequently less than enthusiastic. It should perhaps be mentioned that though both Henry James and the formidable Edith Wharton took pleasure in the company of Paul Bourget, the former objected to the whorish heroines of Bourget's novels and the latter to the coarseness of his dinner-table conversation. To Lady Jersey he was, understandably, presented as nothing worse than an intelligent sightseer.

This enjoyable letter was written on black-edged paper, James being still in mourning for his sister Alice. After a life of neurotic illness, Alice had, as sometimes seems to be the case with neurasthenics, developed a mortal complaint from which she had died the previous March. Settled in England, she had lived periodically in Leamington Spa, which was in the orbit of Stoneleigh Abbey. From her couch Alice James had noted in her diary many things about the English class structure of which she disapproved. There was, however, one anecdote which would have pleased Lord Leigh's eldest daughter. Alice wrote of an American woman who was amazed by the flutter caused when an excitable Miss Kingsley, forgetting the respect due to rank, called out to Lord Leigh, 'Come here.' 'Why not,' asked the American lady, 'you know he is a very handsome man.' To this transatlantic tribute to her father Lady Jersey would certainly have agreed.

Margaret thought the portrait of Osterley in *The Lesson of the Master* a delightful compliment, accepting without hesitation the author's assurance that the human furniture was not portrayed. She noted James' admission of the debt to Osterley, and his mention of the cubic sofa cushions, in her presentation copy. She does not seem to have had any objection to a remark put into the mouth of one of the elder guests, 'It's a nice little place ... but there's nothing much to do,' an irreverence shocking to the young man through whose eyes the drama is seen.

The description of Osterley, comparing the lack of creepers on the rosy brickwork to a woman with the confidence not to wear a veil, opens *The Lesson of the Master* with a flourish. The reader is put into a receptive frame of mind, but the background is not particularly relevant to the story, which quickly moves back to London. In spite of the author's disclaimer, Lady Watermouth, the hostess, the 'human furniture', has touches which those who knew Lady Jersey in her more acid moments might recognize. She had an intolerance for any physical weakness which might cause ladies not to join the party that took the mile-long walk to Heston Church on a Sunday morning. Whether James had encountered this impatience in Lady Jersey, or whether he had received one of those telepathic signals, the use of which often causes writers to be unfairly censured, he reproduced the trait in the hostess of 'Summersoft'.

The second chapter of *The Lesson of the Master* ends with the aspiring young writer, both pupil and observer of the Master, facing an awkward encounter with Lady Watermouth. He is obliged to explain that Mrs St. George, wife of the famous novelist and already a truant from church, has been obliged, from bodily frailty, to abandon a walk round the park.

' "She oughtn't to have come out at all," her ladyship rather grumpily remarked.

"Is she so very much of an invalid?"

"Very bad indeed," and his hostess added with still greater austerity:

"She oughtn't really to come to one!" '

There is no record that any wife of a distinguished frequenter of Osterley died from living a social life beyond her strength, as eventually happened to Mrs St. George in James' story. But had such a disaster happened Margaret's likeliest reaction might well have been that such folly could only be expected to bring its own penalty.

The third letter to be preserved from Henry James belongs to the summer of 1895, and concerns the visit of Alphonse Daudet to London. This visit has supplied Professor Edel with the material for one of his most splendid passages in *Henry James: The Treacherous Years*, the occasion itself being a shot-silk of tragedy and comedy. It appears that Margaret had sent a note to James suggesting that the author of *Lettres de Mon Moulin* and *Tartarin de Tarascon* might, with his family, be brought down to Osterley.

Alphonse Daudet, Madame Daudet, their sons Léon and Lucien, their daughter Edmée, together with a grandson of Victor Hugo's and his wife, had arrived in London on May 6th, Daudet having appointed James as literary and social tour-director. The French writer was struggling with stoic heroism against increasing paralysis, the penalty of a recklessly amorous career. Bath-chairs had to be provided for occasions when the support of his legs failed. However, from his base at Brown's hotel, he had gallantly followed James' hospitable programme, including a visit to George Meredith, another dying lion, and a dinner at the Reform Club for French-speaking admirers.

James had also to advise Madame Daudet as to the hour when London society might best be observed in Hyde Park, so she was probably disappointed when a visit to Osterley proved impracticable. He found her well-dressed, worldly and amusing. She must have mellowed since her days as a young married woman, when, as the Goncourt Journal describes, she had made the mistake of returning home unexpectedly, to surprise Daudet and his mistress both naked. The subsequent scene, with its threat of suicide, was delayed by Madame Daudet for six months, but did not thereby lose anything of its violence.

It is not possible to say how many of this somewhat unwieldy party were included in the invitation to Osterley. By that time they had been in London for three weeks, and there is a hint of relief at their departure in James' reply.

Saturday 34, De Vere Gardens S.W.

Dear Lady Jersey,

All thanks for your most kind notes and your so liberal hospitality. Your offer is so really dazzling that I deeply regret the

Daudets have come to the end of their stay. They depart on Monday next, definitely, so they necessarily lose the great pleasure of accepting your invitation. Had they been able to, it would have given them, I am very sure, not only their pleasantest view of la campagne de Londres, but the happiest experience they would have had in England. All I can do is to embitter them with regrets and make them feel very badly. Please be sure they will highly appreciate your offer and Lord Jersey's part in it.

Yours, dear Lady Jersey, most truly

Henry James.

This was a relatively formal letter, handsome in its expression. To a closer friend, Professor Edel tells us, James wrote of the Daudets' London visit, 'They clung to me like a litter of pups to an experienced mamma.' He then had an attack of gout which swelled his foot 'like the Dome of St. Paul's'.

11

The Indian Experience

DRIVING THROUGH LONDON in her carriage, Margaret was hailed one day by a friend in a hansom. The friend was Robert Bourke, a former Under Secretary for Foreign Affairs under Lord Salisbury. It is a scene that might have been handled by Balzac – noble lady entreated by passionate politician for an assignation – but in fact Mr Bourke wished to consult both the Jerseys about his political future. Like the figures of Rain and Fine in a weather house, Mr Gladstone had recently retreated into opposition, while Lord Salisbury had emerged as Prime Minister. He had, however, conveyed to Mr Bourke that no further promotion might be expected in England by offering him the Governorship of 'the benighted Presidency', Madras.

Mr Bourke came down to Osterley in a disgruntled state. Doubting if he was material for the Cabinet, the Jerseys talked him into feeling more warmly towards what Margaret called 'gubernatorial glories'. Encouraged by their attitude, Mr Bourke asked if, should he accept the appointment, his friends would come and stay with him. Possession of Osterley had left Margaret's wish to travel unabated. She was at once charmed with the idea of India. Two years later, in the autumn of 1888, she and her husband sailed from Marseilles in the P & O liner *Arcadia*.

Lord and Lady Leigh agreed to undertake the supervision of the younger children, with an additional promise of a visit to Stoneleigh. At Middleton, in spite of Miss Mason for education and Mrs Bourne to care for health in the nursery, a long absence of their parents was apt to lead to the growth of hair-raising legends to be passed on to the next generation. A demented man-servant was said to have had to be disarmed of the carving knife, with which he was setting off to the nursery. It was also insisted that, when Mary became ominously ill, no doctor was summoned, the local medical practitioner having come under the cloud of Lady Jersey's disapproval. Fear of her displeasure was, apparently, greater than any anxiety that the last two lines of Thomas Carew's Epitaph on a 17th century Lady Villiers might again be apposite. Addressed to absentee parents, the lines run,

> 'For thou perhaps on thy return
>   May'st find thy Darling in an Urn.'

Villiers, of a more convenient age for travel and always privileged, was allowed a half's leave from Eton for what was thought to be an educational experience. His parents sailed with the expectation of meeting him in Calcutta, when they had zigzagged across the Indian Sub-continent. As a queasy sailor, Margaret took an eager interest in the improvements that modern science was bringing to steamships, recording that the S.S. *Arcadia* was fitted with electric light. She was also something of a Jonah when afloat, and not only in such vessels as the tug *Undaunted*. As will be seen, marine furies frequently pursued the ships in which she sailed.

The tedium of the voyage was beguiled by Sir Samuel Baker, discoverer of Lake Albert Nyanza and the Murchison Falls. His stories of his adventures among the sources of the Nile, and of big game hunting, paid tribute to the devotion and endurance of his wife Florence, in the face of perils from man and beast. Baker's first book had been called *The Rifle and the Hound in Ceylon*, a title that any satirist of British tastes would have been proud to invent, and which, incidentally, was still being reprinted forty years after publication. Adventures in Ceylon were mild compared to what occurred when he travelled in Africa with the gallant Florence. Incongruously, when the Bakers met Grant and Speke, the explorers refused to enter the Bakers' camp, considering themselves too ragged to meet a lady. Later, living among slave-traders, sun-struck, and with a local king demanding her surrender to him as the price for helping her husband's expedition, Florence Baker must have recalled the *pudeur* of Grant and Speke, and the pleasure of mending their clothes, as something in a lost civilization.

Travelling in the second class of S.S. *Arcadia* was Colonel Olcutt, the antithesis of Sir Samuel Baker. No dangers seem to have been too great for Baker not to have overcome by resourceful heroism. Few sensations were too weird for Colonel

Lady Jersey, 1880s

Lord Jersey, 1880s

Private view of the Exhibition of Old Masters, Burlington House, 1888; detail from a painting by H. J. Brooks, 1889. Lord Leighton, PRA, is in the centre with Lady Jersey on his right, and Lord Jersey on the right of the picture in a top hat

Arthur, Beatrice, Margaret and Mary Villiers, Osterley Park, 1890

Olcutt, President of the Theosophical Society, not to have claimed to have experienced, or indeed precipitated by the cosmic force of his personality.

Margaret was among those anxious to invite Colonel Olcutt to expound Theosophy to the first-class passengers. She had an appreciation of the occurrence of the inexplicable, though on at least one occasion her phenomenally retentive memory aided scepticism rather than credulity. Talking, at dinner, of ghosts to Lord Cairns, the Lord Chancellor, he told her that he had been impressed by a story related to him by the wife of the Prussian Minister. This concerned a man in Berlin who had thrice dreamt that a friend had been murdered, the body being smuggled out of the city hidden in straw. Alerting the police, he found the dream to be true. Margaret remembered to have read the story in the poems of Dryden, when she studied them as a girl of thirteen beside the Mediterranean. She also remembered that Dryden had taken the story from Chaucer, and, on looking up the subject, found that Chaucer had taken the story from Cicero. The Lord Chancellor accepted the provenance with the aplomb of a lawyer accustomed to the emergence of awkward facts. Colonel Olcutt was to find himself more actively embarrassed by Lady Jersey's quick wits.

When taxed with his association with, and the charlatanism of, the raffish Madame Blavatsky, Olcutt looked down through his blue spectacles and remarked that all religions must be manured. This fertilization presumably included a ring that he wore, which, he assured Margaret, had been conjured by Madame Blavatsky out of the heart of a rose. On the voyage he tried to induce Lady Jersey to sign a document declaring her interest in Theosophy. This was to be locked away as a private matter, but Margaret was firm in her refusal, pointing out that if privacy was maintained the document would be of no use to the Theosophist.

As a girl Margaret had arrived in the dark at Glengariff, and awoken in the morning to what she called 'glorious scenery quivering in sunshine and colour'. She had the same pleasure at Mahableshwar, reached in the dark after a five hour drive from Bombay. The glittering light which the precipitation of dust seems to cast over the Sub-Continent at once put its spell upon Margaret.

Her host, Lord Reay, Governor of the Bombay Presidency, pro-duced for her another variety of religious experience in the person of the Aga Khan, a boy of fourteen, but already venerated as a god. Recording the strange story in which the followers of the Hindu Vishnu had accepted a Mohammedan Persian prince as an incarnation of their god, Margaret also mentioned that, being allegedly descended from the Tribe of the Assassins, it was by assassination that the succession was said to pass.

Margaret, after thirty years of acquaintance, could write that the Aga Khan, first seen at Mahableshwar, was certainly still unassassinated. Indeed his greatest triumph on the British Turf, winning the Triple Crown, was yet to come. The Aga Khan also remained undaunted by the life-long tendency to corpulence, apparent even in his boyhood. It was his habit, when in London, to eat a solitary tea at Gunter's cake shop in Berkeley Square, where among a clientèle of creamy young English girls he gave himself up to the enjoyment of equally creamy English cakes.

Although she suffered much at sea, Margaret was, on land, an uncomplaining traveller. Chugging by train through the Deccan for two days and nights only increased her interest in the Indian scene. Naturally, at that date, there was no air-conditioning, and even in the cold weather season the dust and heat would be trying to weaker spirits. Margaret rarely mentioned any discomfort in her Indian travels, dwelling instead on the marvellous scarlet of the dawn, and the startling end to the day, with its rapid transition from rose pink to black velvet night. At a race-meeting the day after she arrived in Hyderabad she became particularly conscious of the sudden dying of the light, fading on a scene of richest colour, on riders in white muslim with black and gold turbans, the tails of their prancing horses dyed pink, and on the Nizam's syces in liveries of yellow and blue.

With unusually sharp criticism for the ruler of a country she was visiting, Margaret described the reigning Nizam as an effete individual. He only relaxed from poker-faced apathy during a display of his jewels, when he smiled faintly in responding to an inquiry from Lord Jersey about black pearls, producing two for inspection from a calico bag. Margaret slightly relented in her disapproval of the Nizam, when she learnt that he was responsible for four thousand women, some of them inherited from his father's zenana. Some time before the Jerseys' arrival the women were said to have lured the Nizam into their quarters and given him a flogging, but whether from sexual frustration or to get their pensions raised was not, it seems, known.

Fortunately for the State of Hyderabad, the Chief Minister, Sir
Salar Jang, was an able and intelligent administrator. He was also
a collector, and his palace is now a splendid museum of Eastern
and Western objects. Some of the latter are more beautiful than
others, a copy of a Reisener desk, unhappily overburdened with
additional bronze nymphs and a clock inset into a sunburst, being
balanced by a exquisite group in white Dresden china of Frederick
the Great with a pair of whippets. It was more on the human furniture that Margaret concentrated at a banquet at the Salar Jang
Palace. Stuff for the men's coats had been imported from Paris,
while their fezzes came from Lincoln and Bennett of London. The
ladies wore brocade dresses with divided skirts, specially designed
by Howell and James, rather surprisingly, as this firm had been
pilloried as the antithesis of aesthetic sensibility by W. S. Gilbert
in *Patience*.

In spite of her respect for well-educated women, Margaret was
forced to admit that the problems of education for women in purdah were complex. Not only would girls educated, but still in purdah, be apt to become discontented with their seclusion, but their
attempts to emerge would mean rejection by possible husbands.
On the other hand some husbands, willing that their wives should
come out into the world, met resistance from the wives themselves, reluctant to abandon the strength given them by the soli-
darity of the zenana. Finally Margaret had breakfast with two
sisters of Sir Salar Jang, who she described as the most empty-
headed of all the Indian ladies she ever encountered. In parrot-
bright clothes, yellow, crimson, green, with stockings of pink,
they squatted before a low table covered with dishes of assorted
curries and rice. As they ate they chattered of food, clothes and
jewels, their only interests. Empty headed they may have been,
but their guest admitted that their contentment seemed complete,
and their happiness superior to that of their more educated contemporaries.

To fulfil their promise to visit Mr Bourke, who had taken their
advice and become Governor of Madras, the Jerseys travelled on
to the Bay of Bengal and the capital of the benighted Presidency.
If Margaret took a dutiful interest in the education of women in
purdah, it was a relief to turn to religious discussion which she
approached with the zest of a theological explorer. In Madras she
happily settled down to compare the words of a Munshi of the
Advaita sect with those of an ascetic who expounded a form of

the Sankhya philosophy, 'which presupposes eternal matter with which the eternal mind unites itself'.

There was also a family connection that Margaret wished to explore. The elegant spire of St Mary's Church, Fort St George, rises from a circle of some of the oldest British tombstones to be found in India, and in the church register it is recorded that John Floyd, a distinguished soldier, married Julia Rebecca Darke in 1791, the witnesses being the bride's parents, Charles and Rebecca Darke. As has been mentioned, the Floyds' daughter Julia was born in Fort St George, returning to England with her parents. John Floyd became a General and a Baronet, while his daughter became the much loved wife of Sir Robert Peel and the mother, as has been seen, of Julia, Lady Jersey. It was, however the surname of Darke which had started the romantic idea that Julia Floyd was of Indian ancestry. In fact Charles Darke had come out to India from Herefordshire as a young man, his wife having been born Rebecca Gyles.

For some reason, Margaret was unwilling to accept the obvious Englishness of the Darkes. She shook her head over the reluctance of her husband's cousin William Peel, subsequently Earl Peel and head of an Indian Commission, to dive further into his grand-mother's origins. William Peel, she maintained, had definitely an Indian cast of countenance. She does not seem to have reflected that there was no genetic reason why her husband should not have shared these characteristics, Julia Rebecca Darke being equally the ancestress of the 7th Earl of Jersey and the 1st Earl Peel. Re-search has shown that it may have been his forefather's financial misfortunes, rather than the question of mixed blood, that made Lord Peel unanxious to explore the Darke pedigree. Darke's ruin had occurred in the service of the Nawab of Arcot. Matters were complicated by bribes given 'at the time of the arrest of Lord Pigot', a Governor of Fort St George who, according to *Burke's Peerage*, died 'in illegal confinement, supposedly by violence'.

The area ruled by the British around Fort St. George was now the far-flung Madras Presidency, but scandals and dramas still abounded. The Governor, Mr Bourke, instigator of the Jer-seys' Indian journey, had become Lord Connemara, but this had done nothing to ameliorate an uneasy relationship with his wife. Usually firmly disapproving of frivolity on the subject of divorce, Margaret found the farcical elements of the Connemaras' domestic upheaval too much for her seriousness. Lady Connemara hovered between Government House and a local hotel, where she stayed in company with a doctor attached to the Governor's staff, choosing to decamp when a large dinner party was due to arrive at the official residence.

Possibly the Jerseys felt that they had some responsibility for Lord Connemara's situation, for they agreed to extend their visit, to give cover to the myth that Lady Connemara was indisposed in her own apartments. They played their part with such conviction that fellow guests were completely deceived. Margaret quoted, in this connection, the cabman who said he would not say the policeman was lying, but that he handled the truth rather carelessly. Divorce followed eventually, then remarriages. 'All dead now, faults on both sides,' was the pithy summing-up of Lady Jersey.

A prolonged visit to Madras gave the Jerseys time to travel to Tanjore and Madura, Margaret being ever more impressed by the power of the Hindu faith, which had raised such towering Gopurams to guard the treasures of its temples. They had also the opportunity to visit an Ashram, at Adyar, where their fellow traveller from the *Arcadia*, Colonel Olcutt, presided over devotees of mixed nationalities.

Even as they arrived the comic element which dogged Colonel Olcutt became evident. Driving towards the Ashram they saw a number of people sitting on a verandah, who obviously saw the carriage, but did not suppose themselves to be visible. Scattering in haste, the company left Colonel Olcutt to arrange himself in abstracted meditation, from which he emerged to welcome the guests. The other followers were then discovered, as if accidentally and introduced – 'a Russian Countess – the Countess of Jersey', 'a Japanese nobleman – the Earl of Jersey'. Two portraits of Mahatmas, Colonel Olcutt explained, had been painted by an artist called Schmiechen, implying that inspiration was involved, for the painter had never seen his subjects. With Olcutt's usual luck some of the Jersey children had been painted by Schmiechen, so, on reaching home, Margaret was able to ask if he had not set eyes on the Mahatmas before painting them. Certainly he had not, said the artist, but he had been supplied with excellent photographs.

Still seeking to assure Lady Jersey that Theosophy was not an anti-Christian cult, Colonel Olcutt lent her copies of a magazine which would prove his point. Margaret found the publication to be innocuous, not to say colourless, but reduced Olcutt to red-faced embarrassment by showing him that the advertisements, which he had overlooked, offered literature that was strongly anti-Christian in tone. However, when Colonel Olcutt visited Sydney during Lord Jersey's period as Governor-General of New South Wales, he had not given up all hope of winning a declaration of interest in his work from Lady Jersey. But even a poem addressed 'To Our Lady of Leigh' and containing the appealing lines,

> 'Sign; I entreat you,
> Bishops will greet you,
> Clergy entreat you,
> Lady, to join
> This league confraternal ...'

failed to melt the hard heart of Our Lady of Leigh.

A sequence of accidents, both ludicrous and dangerous, disrupted the Jerseys' plans to reach Calcutta in time for Christmas. Their ship, the *Pundua*, had trouble with her loading gear. Then, after the Governor had taken his guests on board, through the impracticable harbour that then served Madras, there was an explosion. The unlucky ship had blown the top off one of her three cylinders. Slinking back to Government House, the travellers had the humiliation of their re-appearance emphasized by having to attend the Governor's 'Dignity Ball'.

When the *Pundua*, her speed reduced to nine knots, finally limped out to sea, it became apparent that cylinders were not alone in blowing their tops. Margaret was given the ladies' cabin and its bathroom to herself, being assured that the only other lady on board was not in the habit of bathing. In fact this heroine was more or less a prisoner in a second class cabin, the captain having disarmed her of a revolver. She, unlike Miss Darke, was of mixed blood, married to an English husband. He had been prostrated with sea-sickness early in the voyage from England. Meanwhile, Margaret was enthralled to learn, his wife, besides swearing and drinking, had carried on a flirtation with another passenger. On her husband's recovery, she had insisted that he should shoot her admirer, and, when he refused, tried to shoot her husband.

On Christmas Day, only, was this termagant allowed out by the captain to dine with the first class passengers. Always keen on a good plot, Margaret thought it regrettable that the fiery lady could not be united with another passenger, an orchid-hunter. Outraged to discover that a rival was known to be heading for a place where a previously unknown plant was said to grow, this botanist was avowedly setting off to hunt a human quarry. Margaret felt that such a pair, armed with a revolver, would be well suited to any hunt.

Although the bewitched *Pundua* stuck on a sand-bank at the mouth of the Hoogli, the Jerseys finally reached Calcutta, then the seat of the Government of India. Here they received a welcome telegram to say that their son Villiers had reached Bombay. In contrast to her attitude towards Villiers, there is a hint of exasperation in a letter Margaret wrote to her sister Cordelia concerning her younger son, left behind at Stoneleigh. Arthur, aged six, had apparently suffered from some illness or accident, and if Margaret wrote as an equal to Lady Leigh to Cordelia, now in her twenty-third year, her letter was marked by elder sisterly condescension. Arthur's mother wrote that she was sorry if he had been a nuisance, but if the local doctor had been pleased at being called in it was, at least, an ill wind.

As Christmas Day was spent on board the *Pundua*, and Villiers was met at Benares on New Year's Day, there can have been little time at Calcutta. In the light of Margaret's determined study of comparative religions, it is not surprising to learn that she managed to receive a call from the head of the Brahmo Somaj, a religious body that accepted much from the Holy Books of all nations. Although this seemed to Margaret to offer a prospect of Hinduised Christianity, its all-embracing aspects had been no protection against schism, when the founder arranged a grand marriage for his daughter under the age he had, himself, laid down as the lower limit for a bride.

The family reunion at Benares was a happy beginning to the year 1889, but following her practice of omitting reports of sight-seeing, Margaret did not dwell on the teeming city. She gave more space to the party's guide and interpreter, a Jain, who escorted the family when they visited the Maharajah. Here they were entertained in feudal dignity, by music, dancing and an inspection of the Maharajah's tigers. The Jain was a teller of tales, of his own early life, and of his campaign as an adherent of the Raj. An acute judge of human attitudes, Margaret suspected that their guide's professed contempt for Hindus in general was exaggerated for her benefit. Herself prepared to accept the customs of any country with interest rather than disapprobation, she appreciated the setting down that the Jain's wife had given a philanthropic English lady, who was protesting at the practice of child marriage. She herself, said the Jain's wife, had lived happily ever after from being married at seven years old to a husband of nine.

At Lucknow there were sights to be seen that recalled terrible episodes of the Mutiny only thirty years before. Here they made friends with Sir Frederick Roberts, later Earl Roberts and a Field-Marshal. As a young subaltern he had been present on the historic day when the breach was made that linked the besieged with their relievers. Sir Frederick Roberts' kindness included lending a pony to Villiers, who promptly gave his parents a fright. Overdaringly, he rode the pony down a steep nullah, and, though the inevitable fall only gave him a green-stick fracture of the wrist, he was handicapped for the rest of the Indian tour.

Except for memories of the Mutiny and the accident to Villiers, the Jerseys had, it seems, met little to remind them of disease and death, the dark side of the glittering Sub-Continent. From Delhi, however, they went to Meerut for a Saturday to Monday visit, where George Wombwell, eldest son of Jersey's sister Julia and the Balaclava survivor Sir George Wombwell, was stationed. This boy, in his twenties, a lieutenant in the 60th Rifles, was found to be laid up with typhoid in the house of his Colonel. As he seemed to be recovering, and was being well looked after, the Jersey's hurried their own convalescent son away from the infected cantonments. There was a relapse, and Lord Jersey was called back from Agra to his nephew's deathbed. Two years before, almost to the day, Kipling's poem *Christmas in India* had appeared. Its most melancholy line, 'Youth was cheap / Wherefore we sold it', might be quoted as an epitaph for young George Wombwell, buried, like many others, far from his home.

Among the introductions by which Sir Edwin Arnold repaid the Jerseys' hospitality was one to the young Maharajah of Bhownugger, a state that lies to the north west of Ahmadebad. The invitation to visit the Palace (Bhownugger) has survived. Written in a flawless copper-plate hand, it expresses the fear that 'Sir Edwin Arnold's description of me and my state exceeds reality.' The Maharajah's welcome was, in fact, of the most splendid order, host, in green velvet, wearing the Star of India, high officials in attendance and a guard of honour. It was offered to three guests who were deeply stained by travel. Usually ignoring the heat, Margaret did record that the thermometer had been close on 100°Fahrenheit in the railway carriage.

Arnold's introduction had probably not dwelt on the lurid perils, worthy of the Italian Renaissance, that surrounded the Maharajah. His marriages had included a love match with a wife of too low a caste to please the Brahmins. Knowing that there was a plot to murder him if he did not dispose of this favourite, he consulted the Political Officer, the British appointed adviser to states administered by native princes, choosing a moment on the tennis court, where spies could not eavesdrop. The immediate solution was that the favourite Rani's position should be regularized by a call from the Political Officer's wife, and that the Maharajah himself should stick closer than a brother to the Political Officer.

Essentially without shyness, and the melancholy it induces, Margaret was probably the member of her party who made friends most easily. At Bhownugger, however, although both Jerseys liked their host, it was to Lord Jersey that the Maharajah became devoted, telling the English landowner of the difficulties facing an Indian prince in carrying out his duties towards his people. ' "We must do the best we can and leave the rest to God", [he said] – then looking up at the chandelier ... "God is like that light, and the different religions are the different colours through which He shines." ' This idea of the prismatic nature of God remained with Margaret, and returned to her in her nineties. When the people around her had become clouded, like photographs out of focus, she still spoke of the light of God shining through different lustres of a chandelier, as the young Maharajah had suggested half a century before.

Some years earlier Sir Richard Burton had praised the liner *Bengal* as a ship that had taken all the terror from ocean voyages. When the Jerseys boarded the *Bengal* at Bombay they could only be thankful that the sea was calm, for to them she appeared almost dangerously antiquated. Between Bombay and Suez Margaret gathered her thoughts together, and settled down to write the article on her Indian experiences that was to appear in *The Nineteenth Century*. She must have felt the line from Lowell's poem in her copy of Omar Khayyám, 'Groping, you may at least bring back a pearl' to be applicable many times over.

As she sorted her handful of pearls, she came to a conclusion which Sir Edwin Arnold told her was original to herself. The Taj Mahal, that monument to love stronger than death, was, Margaret wrote, too perfect, lacking the mystery of 'unfulfilled aspiration'.

Unlike Aldous Huxley in the nineteen-twenties, who complained that the Taj Mahal was both anti-classical and only admired by tourists on account of the expense of building it, Margaret's criticism might be called an objection to the absolute. She did not, apparently, consider that the sight of the pearly dome swimming mistily under a full moon, its arched gateway being both a frame for a picture and a case for a jewel, conveyed a message to 'the soul with her god-given wings'. If Governors and Maharajahs had been her hosts during her Indian experience, it was conversations with assorted sages that moved her to write verses which she called *Meditations of a Western Wanderer*, from which the phrase quoted above is taken.

After three and a half months in India, the Jerseys found their response to Cairo and its neighbourhood less lively than it should have been, even though the arrival of Lady Galloway injected fresh life into the party. They also met the Sirdar, Sir Francis Grenfell, and his adjutant, Colonel Kitchener, who was to become to Margaret a much-valued friend and correspondent. The party then boarded a ship belonging to an Egyptian line, sailing to Athens, where these insatiable travellers were pausing on their way home.

Egyptians were not highly prized as sailors at that date, so the crew were chiefly Turkish, while the Captain was Maltese. Proud of his British nationality, he insisted that a plum pudding, boiled for twenty-four hours as his mother had taught him, should be served to his English passengers. Before the twenty-four hours had passed the sea had risen, but Margaret felt that she could not risk shaking the loyalty of a British subject by rejecting a so intensely British pudding. Performing, she wrote, the single heroic act of her life, she sat through the meal until she had tasted and praised the pudding, before seeking her berth to await, in squeamish stoicism, the arrival at Piraeus.

Since the visit of Lady Galloway and Lady Jersey the year before, the teeming nursery of the Greek Royal family had received a seventh baby. With the knowledge that Lady Leigh would consider such behaviour as extravagant as she did herself, Margaret wrote to her mother that competition for the baby's favour was so strong that the Queen caused her guests to sit on the floor so that he might be worshipped at his own level. The Queen was a Russian Grand Duchess by birth, and her eldest daughter, a particularly merry girl of eighteen, was soon going to Russia to marry a brother of the Czar. At the time Margaret speculated that the little princess would find life grimly different at the Russian court, but commented later that the poor girl, dying at the birth of her second child, was at least spared from the fate that engulfed her husband and so many of his family.

Margaret also wrote about the tragedy at Mayerling, where, in January 1889, the Crown Prince Rudolf, only son of the Emperor Franz Joseph, was found shot dead in his shooting lodge, beside the body of the beautiful young Baroness Mary Vetsera. Mysterious even to this day, at the time the scandal somewhat obscured the political consequences of the death of the direct heir to the Dual Monarchy of Austria-Hungary. It was, in reality, the first rumble of a storm which was not to break until twenty-five years later, when the next Austrian heir's murder at Sarajevo submerged Europe in war, and washed away three imperial dynasties.

Having met those who knew her, Margaret wrote, all were agreed on the loveliness of Mary Vetsera. These acquaintances included the Sirdar, Sir Francis Grenfell. Baroness Vetsera and her beautiful doomed daughter had spent the winter in Egypt, Mary falling in love with an English officer. They had also had an introduction to the Sirdar, who was persuaded to take mother and daughter to a fortune-teller renowned for prescience. On some excuse the seer refused to look into Mary's future, confiding to the Sirdar that over the radiant girl there hung a cloud of a blackness indicating a speedy death.

Athens was the last stop from which Margaret wrote a traveller's letter to her mother, but her spiritual reactions appeared publicly. *The Nineteenth Century* not only published the article written on board the *Bengal*, but also the nine verses of *Meditations of a Western Wanderer*. Written after the author had read Alfred Lyall's *Meditations of a Hindu Prince*, this consideration of the different images of religion also owed, in its last lines, something to Whittier's 'still small voice of calm'.

'It is not the voice of the whirlwind, nor the bolt from the storm-kindled dome;
'Tis stillness that bringeth the tidings—the child knows the accents of home.'

As it happened, within two years, the accents of home were to be drastically changed for the Jerseys themselves and their own children.

12

The Empress at Home:
Two Countesses Abroad

TRAVELLING THROUGH INDIA, the Jerseys had been constantly
struck by the interest taken in the Empress, not only as a ruler
but as a personality. Among princes and politicians, Lord Jersey
found, knowledge of leading English public figures was of a
vagueness that might have been salutary had those concerned been
aware of it, but all was liveliness and interest at the mention of
the Empress. This interest was reciprocated by its object. Sir Henry
Ponsonby, meeting Margaret by chance, asked her to send her
article on India to the Queen, to whom he was then Private Secretary. This she obediently did, and the result was an invitation to
dine and sleep at Windsor.

Although Jersey had stayed at Windsor before, it was, for Margaret, a first visit, remembered with the zest with which she
greeted any new experience. Their rooms in Windsor Castle overlooked the Broad Walk, which allowed them to watch the Queen,
then aged seventy, returning from her afternoon drive. When
some of the Household came in for a chat, the atmosphere was
made increasingly friendly by the revelation that no one had
remembered to send to Windsor Station to meet Arthur Peel,
Speaker of the House of Commons and Jersey's uncle.

Margaret was nearly ready for dinner, when her husband
appealed to her for help in a strange sartorial crisis. At that date
the breeches worn for dining with the Queen were known as 'the
funny trousers'. These garments, an uneasy blend of trouser and
knee breeches, buttoned into a band round the calf, leaving the
socks visible well above the ankle. The clocks in Jersey's socks happened to be marked in white, and he demanded that Margaret
should at once pick out the stitching. Even allowing for his wife's
lack of skill in sewing, or rather unsewing, the light was dim and

time was short. Margaret's maid saved the situation by the brilliant suggestion that the white stitching should be obliterated with ink.

Curiously there is another recorded case of Queen Victoria's dinner guests having to resort to ink. The wife of Sir Howard Elphinstone, Prince Arthur's governor and a great favourite of the Queen's, once found that she had brought no black chemise to wear under her black gown, a white one being visible through the laces which criss-crossed her spine. Fortunately Sir Howard, a talented artist, had some Indian ink at hand, and deftly blacked-in the eyelet holes.

Presumably unaware of inky improvisations, the Queen's welcome for the Jerseys was particularly warm. By chance they gave her an opportunity to talk of one of her favourites who was far from popular with her own Household. Among her Golden Jubilee presentations in 1887 there had arrived two Indian servants, with the idea that daily contact with some of its inhabitants would increase her knowledge of her Indian Empire. One of these arrivals, Abdul Kerim, became almost as much of a support to the Queen as John Brown had been, and in the process almost more of a plague to her entourage.

Usually known as the Munshi, Abdul Kerim began to raise his status by giving the Queen lessons in Hindustani, supplying the mixture of coaxing and bullying which seems to have been a need of her temperament. Soon the Queen was giving orders that any photographer showing the Munshi in an earlier, menial, rôle should be suppressed. His father, she claimed, was a distinguished doctor of medicine, whose son, by his industry and his invaluable help to her in her daily business, was worthy of a position of consideration. As Elizabeth Longford has written in *Victoria R.I.*, it is difficult not to feel some sympathy for the Queen's determination to lean on the help available, but the opposition from her advisers on Indian affairs, and from her Household, is understandable. Not unnaturally, her other Indian servants were racked by jealousy, but the Queen remained unshaken in her favouritism. She ignored the report from Frederick Ponsonby, son of Sir Henry, who visited Agra whence the Munshi had originally come, and returned with the deflating news that Kerim's father had been the apothecary at the jail.

As it happened the Munshi had been on leave at Agra during the Jerseys' visit. In fact their host, Sir John Tyler, Superintendent of the Jail, had, Margaret believed, been responsible for the almost too successful selection of the Munshi for the Empress's service. Besides arranging for the prisoners to weave some splendid carpets for Osterley, Sir John took his guests to a Nautch, given for the Bismillah of a nephew at the house of the Munshi's father. This must have strengthened the Queen's hand in her claim that the Munshi's background was distinguished, and whenever the Jerseys went to Windsor she made a point that the acquaintanceship should be renewed.

Margaret wrote guardedly that she understood that later the Munshi became swollen-headed. By the Government he was also suspected of being the tool of Muslim agents of the Czar, but not an actively dangerous spy in his own person. On the other hand, the Household almost reached the point of taking industrial action, when it was suggested that the Munshi might join them at meals during one of the Queen's visits to the South of France. Their mistress, however, continued to regard the Munshi as valuable, giving a photograph of him, inscribed by herself, to a little granddaughter of Lord Salisbury the Prime Minister. The child would have been more honoured had the inscription read 'Mary' rather than 'Mabel Cecil', which the Queen misapprehended was her name. To Margaret, the Queen explained that it was only her age and propensity to sea-sickness which held her back from visiting India herself. Had she been able to do so the question of the Munshi's antecedents would, presumably, have been settled to the Empress's satisfaction.

Obviously accepting Lady Jersey as someone of considerable intellectual and moral qualities, the Queen urged her guest always to keep a journal and never to forget England. Margaret's journal keeping was intermittent, but her remembrance of England, and what she considered to be her country's civilizing mission, was steadfast. Perhaps on account of the Jerseys' Indian journey and Margaret's writings on the subject, shortly after the visit to Windsor, Lord Jersey was offered the Governorship of Bombay. His wife wrote that he liked the idea, but refused it on grounds of delicate health, having not long recovered from an attack of typhoid fever. She gave no more details of the illness, which seems strange after her experience of its dangers when Jersey's nephew had died at Meerut. From Osborne, the Munshi wrote in a fair hand and good English, regretting that Lord Jersey 'was not strong enough to take up an appointment in Bombay'. If not an active intriguer, the Munshi obviously kept an eye on what was going into the curry.

Instead of this governorship Lord Jersey accepted the post of Paymaster-General, a department in which everyone was paid except the Paymaster. Something of the Child banking blood seems to have risen in his veins, for he engaged in a persevering campaign against the Treasury. In the end he was able to have the triumph of proving that his department was in the right over the misplaced sum of two shillings in an expenditure of thirty-five millions.

Once again, to avoid the worst of the winter, Margaret went abroad with Lady Galloway in February 1890. Jersey had some idea of following them, but, as on a previous occasion he was a non-starter. With thirst for sight-seeing unslaked by other civilizations, the ladies returned to Egypt. Colonel Kitchener, as he then was, had stayed at Osterley after their earlier visit, and under his increasing friendship their way was made smooth. An attempt by Cook's Office to fob the ladies off with two berths on a Nile boat, instead of the cabins ordered, was dealt with arbitrarily. Kitchener declared that the ladies represented two, slightly mythical, aunts whom he was expecting.

Shortly before, Kitchener had escorted Joseph Chamberlain up the Nile, the tour being the foundation of a speech made in Birmingham on the subject of the British presence in Egypt. With pleasure, Margaret wrote that Chamberlain's readiness to learn from facts had been demonstrated by his conversion from his Radical point of view to the conviction that Egypt was then in no state to be abandoned by England. Whatever others may have thought, she retained a belief in Chamberlain's political integrity. When she differed with him over Protection and Free Trade, and he asked her to believe in the honesty of an old friend, she was able to say that she did so from her heart.

On the Nile boat from Luxor, Sir Francis Grenfell, the Sirdar, was travelling on a tour of inspection, so the boat was picturesquely escorted by the camels of the native guerilla police, galloping along the bank behind their Sheikh. The High Dam at Assouan had not yet been built, and the boatmen taking tourists through the cataracts made the passage appear as perilous as possible. Margaret considered that there was no real danger, but a fellow passenger, an Austrian Prince, looked distinctly uneasy, as the boats sheered off from the rocks at the last moment, amid yells from the boatmen.

The Austrian Prince got a rather bad time retrospectively when Margaret came to write about him. Mourning a young wife, he was in a mood of deeply religious melancholy, though he did become more cheerful during the voyage, possibly helped by Lady Jersey's distinctly bracing attitude. The Prince had been impressed by the spontaneous politeness which left a portion of the deck free for the Sirdar's party, without any official order. Austrians, anyway of the middle-class, he said, would not have done so voluntarily. On the other hand, he expressed astonishment that it was the practice of English boys, such as Margaret's sons, to play games with the boys of the village. Her tone in describing the prince's surprise at English good manners, and English democracy in sport, verged on the complacent. She does not seem to have reflected that cricket, the great village leveller in England, was not a game likely to have been familiar to Austrian magnates.

There had been a row between French and German passengers on board the *Arcadia*, when one of the former played the 'Boulanger' hymn amid French cheers and German hisses. In the interval General Boulanger had met a great fall, but sympathy for him still seems to have lingered in unexpected places. The 'Boulanger' hymn was played, rather bizarrely, by a nun in an Italian Franciscan convent, whither a local Pasha had conducted Margaret's party. Although raising no objection to the 'Boulanger' hymn, the Prince's sense of religious decorum was outraged that supposedly cloistered sisters should entertain three men, himself, a British official and the Pasha, even calling the last 'un bon papa'. The 'bon papa' also took the ladies to visit his wife and daughter, more closely secluded than the nuns. When the Egyptian women had retired the European male guests were invited to rejoin the party by a Nubian servant, with the simple phrase, 'Pasha, ladies, harem', suggesting that *Entführung aus dem Serail* might be necessary. However, though they found the Pasha on his knees, it was not in supplication but to unpack his portmanteau, wishing to display some antiquities he had packed in his socks. The visit, which it is to be hoped cheered the melancholy Prince, ended with an evening meal at which sweet pastry was followed by a large turkey.

Before they left Cairo, Margaret sat next to Stanley, the explorer, at a dinner party of Kitchener's. On her way to India she had heard much about him from the Bakers, and, after a sticky start, he expanded, talking of his famous book *In Darkest Africa*, on which he was working. There were to be three pages, he said, given up to a beautiful white lady, met under the Equator and 'fragrant with the odours of Araby'. Margaret, on her side, told Stanley of the loss of Mr Powell, who, with her brother-in-law Mr Jenkins, had made the expedition of vengeance to Abyssinia. Subsequently Mr Powell had gone up in a balloon, and never been heard of again. Like a hound picking up a scent, Stanley quickened at the idea of a search for such a human needle in a hay stack.

On a Russian boat the two friends now sailed to Jaffa, driving to Jerusalem, amid hordes of Russian pilgrims bound for the Easter celebrations. As well as their Egyptian dragoman, they were escorted by a Sheikh, bribed to keep off thieves, and a Turkish soldier, provided in compliment to Lord Salisbury's half-sister. Railways had not yet come to the Holy Land, and when they paused at the inn between Jerusalem and Jericho to rest their horses, it was, they realized, the obvious spot for the good Samaritan to have deposited the man who fell among thieves. Although they had paid to be protected from thieves themselves, the Bible stories were made even more real by the arrival of a family, a husband leading a donkey on which was seated a woman with a baby in her arms, as though they might be setting out for the flight into Egypt.

Nicholas, the dragoman imported from Egypt, had naturally little knowledge of the Bible, so his employers could not resist ragging him. On the shores of the Dead Sea, Margaret flummoxed him by asking if Lot's wife was to be seen. Told by Lady Galloway that Lot's Wife had been turned into a pillar of salt, Nicholas hastily pointed to the nearest salt-caked hillock. Subsequent visitors to Sodom would, they felt, benefit from this identification.

At Jerusalem, ever a centre of international intrigue, the Russians, builders of barracks ostensibly for pilgrims were regarded with much suspicion, though the Sultan Abdul the Damned had just encouraged the German Emperor by giving him control of the Church of the Knights of St. John. The two friends came under hostile suspicions themselves from an eccentric female traveller. This woman was said to be travelling with her husband's ashes, about which she had a dispute with his trustees. Incensed by an escort granted to Lady Galloway, when she herself had none, she went so far as to threaten to shoot Lady G. as a reprisal. The enraged woman was shaken off between Jaffa and Damascus, but caught up with them at the latter city, which they had entered in state under an escort sent out by the Governor. This must have exacerbated their enemy even further. She certainly displayed a disregard for good manners by entering the restaurant smoking a big cigar, and she was, additionally, rumoured to be an alcoholic.

There were also hints that the captain of the Austrian boat, which carried the two friends from Beirut to Constantinople, was too fond of the bottle, although, Margaret kindly mentioned, 'A mild lover of little birds'. The ship touched at Smyrna in time for Easter to be celebrated in the Consular church by a canon travelling to Constantinople. The Consul himself was so apprehensive of brigands that he would not allow the ladies out of his sight, until he had seen them re-embark. In spite of his reputed alcoholism, the Captain brought his ship through the Dardanelles, in a storm of mist and rain, safely to anchor at the Golden Horn.

Arranged by their host Sir Edgar Vincent, Governor of the Imperial Ottoman Bank and afterwards Lord D'Abernon, their programme was comprehensive. Like many before and since, Margaret complained that the nobly soaring roof inside St Sophia was marred by the garish grass-green shields painted with the names of the companions of the Prophet. In passing it may be mentioned that the continual complaints eventually had an effect on the directors of the museum that St Sophia became. Latterly, the shields were toned down from the true green of the Prophet, and, darkened almost to black, became comparatively inoffensive.

The British Ambassadress, Lady White, invited Margaret and Lady G. to a picnic party at Scutari, on the Asiatic side of the Bosphorus, described by Margaret, with reason, as 'a quaint expedition'. It was a diplomatic gathering, the French launch setting out first, to be followed by a launch from the British Embassy. On board the latter, besides the Ambassadress and her two English guests, there were the Ministers of Norway and Persia, and a pair of Belgian ladies. The French launch started first in a sea that got up rapidly, but national honour required that the British launch should follow without hesitation. Margaret and her friend managed to sit in silence as the waves rose almost dangerously, to the accompaniment of screams from the Belgian ladies. The Norwegian Minister encouraged the company from the prow, but the Persian Minister 'wept hot tears', which Lady White tried to staunch with a lace-trimmed handkerchief and a bottle of eau-de-cologne.

Although the Asiatic shore of the Bosphorus was dominated,

as it still is, by the grim barracks with its four towers, where Florence Nightingale wrestled with dirt and corruption, the object of the 'quaint expedition' was to see a performance by howling dervishes. Margaret found the atmosphere so stifling that she left the building, to be at once surrounded by a crowd of dishevelled Turks, in a situation from which the Consul at Smyrna had taken such pains to protect her. However she always, she wrote, made a point of learning the words for 'hot water' and 'go away' in each new country she visited. Private hospitality had made the Turkish words for 'hot water', superfluous, but she pronounced the word for 'go away' as 'Haiti' in a loud indignant voice, which dispersed the crowd with a competence the Consul at Smyrna could not have failed to admire.

Invited to dinner by the Sultan, Margaret refused the invitation, as she was setting her face for home. Additionally, she had been warned that, if an invitation was accepted by distinguished tourists, Abdul the Damned invariably postponed the event, in order to add a touch of style to his ramshackle dominions by retaining them as long as possible. In the archives of the present Lord Jersey, there was recently discovered the medal and ribbon of the Order of Chefakat, the Order of Chastity presented to ladies, about which jokes have not been few. Margaret's only sight of the Sultan had been when he drove to the ceremony of the Selamlik. It is unlikely that the Chefakat was presented to her at such long range, so its recipient remains mysterious. No one would have been more suitable to wear such an order than Margaret, and no one would have been more appreciative of jokes on the subject.

If the expedition to Scutari had been a quaint drama, the journey home on the Orient Express was a roaring Balkan comedy. The habitual shortage of sleeping berths was increased by the presence of a Queen's Messenger and Sir Edgar Vincent, each bound, statutorily, to have a separate compartment. Margaret and Lady G. had a compartment reserved, only to find that their enemy with the cigar and revolver had installed herself with such determination that Sir Edgar Vincent had to be invoked to get her ejected.

At Sofia, Prince Ferdinand, Tsar of Bulgaria, joined the train, escorted by an imposing, subsequently assassinated, Prime Minister. These were only briefly fellow-travellers, as it was Ferdinand's habit to take his *déjeuner* on the train, get off at the frontier, and take the next train back to his capital, an innocent diversion considering his reputation for foxiness and sinister habits. (His son, the last Tsar of Bulgaria, carried matters further by actually driving the engine.)

Ferdinand complained, unreasonably, that the English travellers had not been presented to him, but they blamed him for making no advance. In any case there had been a disappointment over the menu. As Margaret wrote, 'some apricot omelettes were seen walking about', but were said to be reserved for a *déjeuner commandé*. Additionally, an American fellow-traveller had inquired if Sir Edgar and his friends had been allowed the asparagus he had seen going by. When assured that they had not, the American said he was prepared to overlook a general deprivation, but had those sitting next to the princely party been specially favoured he would have made a cataclysmic row.

It was just as well that another row had not been added to those already raging, which included a determination by a Greek to fight a German with whom he shared a compartment. The Greek was, in his turn evicted, and shut up in the saloon, reducing the accommodation still further. At midnight, at Buda-Pest, the sister of the Queen of Serbia joined the train, to be welcomed with a bouquet of flowers. Her welcome ended there, for, faced with sharing the compartment of the cigar-smoking woman, who terrified her by barking like a dog, or going into the saloon with the enraged Greek, she chose to spend the night in the corridor. This grand finale on the Orient Express brought the two countesses to Vienna, where their ways divided. Margaret returned to her family, having shown exemplary, indeed perhaps excessive, attention to her husband's wish that she should avoid the treacherous English spring weather.

13

Queen and Exile

THE ELDER CHILDREN of the family to which Margaret had returned were now leaving childhood with the speed that is always surprising to parents. A photograph taken at Middleton in January 1890, before their mother left for Cairo, showed the elder girls as still very much children, dressed in the same dresses and hats as their younger sister, hats and dresses that managed to be both over-trimmed and frumpish. Their mother looked distinctly older than her age, for she wore a bonnet and her shoulders were wrapped in a shawl. The group included one of Lord Jersey's brothers, probably Reggie the favourite, and Rupert Leigh who was to share his sister's most enjoyable travels. In the background there stood some young men, but they clearly belonged to the grown-up world, remote from the cluster of little girls at their feet.

Six months later a series of photographs were taken at Osterley and suddenly Markie and Mary seemed to have made a bound forward in their development. Markie, in particular, had grown to nearly her full height and developed the sparkle which never left her. Mary, later to be the tallest of the sisters, had lost the cuddlesome air of her babyhood, but had still a chubby charm. A waif-like element was contributed by Beatrice and Arthur, both solemn-eyed. It might not be too fanciful to suggest that something of the secondary position of these children in their parents' eyes, compared with their eldest brother, appeared in their demeanour when they faced the camera.

The family scene that summer at Osterley was, as it happened, crystallized by Augustus Hare in *The Story of My Life*. This autobiography began as a horror story, for the brutality of the kins-folk of Hare's aunt and adoptive mother was only surpassed by ill-treatment at school. In middle age he had settled down to a life divided between art and society, leading sketching parties of ladies through picturesque parts of London. Violet Leigh, Margaret's cousin was among his younger pupils. Although she drew reasonably well, she was bored at trailing after the older ladies, except on the occasion when Hare led his party, by accident, into Billingsgate and, a weirdly inappropriate figure in top hat and morning coat, had to appeal to a policeman for rescue from mocking fishwives. Violet herself was responsible for disrupting a morning's drawing at the Tower of London, when an admirer in the Brigade of Guards relieved her boredom by turning out his men for a fire practice with hoses spouting at full strength.

After such scenes the peaceful ritual of a house party at Osterley must have been infinitely soothing to Mr Hare's nerves, and his praise was unrestrained. In her own memoirs, though she quoted Hare's description, Margaret wrote that she had omitted what she called 'the over-kindly portraits of ourselves'. These occurred after a mention that the Osterley gardens 'would now bloom unseen for five years, as Lord Jersey has accepted the Governorship of New South Wales . . . an immense self-sacrifice, though he and Lady Jersey can never fail anywhere to be the centre of all that is most interesting and useful. To English society her absence will be a terrible loss, as, with the utmost simplicity, she is the one person left in England capable of holding a salon and keeping it filled to the advantage of all who enter it. Nothing can be more charming than the relationship of Lord and Lady Jersey to their children, and the fact that the latter were always of the party, yet never in its way, was the greatest testimony to their upbringing.'

After this tremendous bouquet to his hostess, Hare went on to name some of the guests, 'M. de Stael, the Russian Ambassador; Lady Crawford, still lovely as daylight . . . Lady Galloway brimming with cleverness, . . . Mr and Mrs Frank Parker, most amusing and cheery.' (The Parkers belonged to the vast family of Margaret's aunt, Lady Macclesfield, and it is sad that Hare gave no example of their cheery wit.) It was an August Bank Holiday party, and on Monday three carriages took the guests to Doughty House at Richmond to see Sir Francis Cook's collection. Hare praised the Jerseys' arrangements for their guests as 'most unostentatiously sumptuous', but was rather unjustly doubtful of the attributions of the Cook pictures.

The party was treated to a 'luxurious luncheon' at the Star and

Garter Hotel, just below Doughty House, and later used by Gals-worthy for a powerful scene in *The Man of Property*. Then they drove to Ham House where the collective ghost of the Cabal still seems to walk. Hare described the display of ancient dresses taken from a chest in the gallery. It is to be hoped no souvenirs were carried away involuntarily, for it had been found necessary some years before to burn every bed in Ham House to exterminate the bugs. The day ended with Hare telling the children a long story in a glade of the Osterley garden. He found them a splendid audience, and thought the scene might have recalled the Deca-meron.

To Augustus Hare, with only the blackest memories of child-hood, the Villiers children must have seemed to lead a paradisaical life, and indeed some aspects of it were delightful. Summer days at Osterley were recollected by Mary, who shared her mother's propensity for sea-sickness, as an anodyne on the long, rough pass-age to New South Wales, which was the adventure that now faced the family.

'You are a Queen and an Exile,' wrote Lord Derby to the wife of the new Governor-General. 'Are you to be congratulated or condoled?' Her children had no doubts on the matter. Five years on the other side of the world appeared to them as exile unrelieved. Torn though they all were from familiar homes, gardens and pets, Markie had, in addition, the prospect of making a colonial début, coming-out as a princess being, in her eyes, no compensation for a season in London.

To accept a colonial governorship that did not threaten his health, appeared as a duty to Lord Jersey, even if it was 'the im-mense self-sacrifice' that Augustus Hare considered it to be. Peers, or their eldest sons, were considered suitable for such posts, and in 1890 Victoria, South Australia and New Zealand, all had titled governors who had been, like Jersey, Lords-in Waiting to Queen Victoria. The Queen brought up this fact when the new Governor and his wife had been summoned to Balmoral for a farewell visit. Whenever she had a nice Lord-in-Waiting, the Queen com-plained, Lord Salisbury sent him off to govern a colony, though she smiled graciously when Lord Jersey pointed out that this was a tribute to how well she brought them up.

The summons to Balmoral had come hastily, the Queen having forgotten how soon the Jerseys were to sail for the Antipodes. The visit had a special interest for Margaret as it was the only time that she saw the Duke of Clarence, eldest son of the Prince of Wales, a young man who was to die less than two years later. Margaret was apt to take a generous view of the good qualities of royalty, but in this case she was obviously sincere in her surprise at the lack of self-importance of the Duke of Clarence. He had been left a gold chain, a relic of Marie Antionette, in whom his grandmother had a fascinated interest. When he showed it to the Queen he seemed genuinely surprised that any such gift should have been left to him. The emotional instability, which led him to conduct two or three simultaneous courtships, and caused acute anxiety to anyone who contemplated the future under such a king, seems, at Balmoral, to have been in abeyance.

Preparations were made for the migration, the London house was let, and the family were waiting at Claridges, then a relatively simple hotel, for what might be called 'the off', when Margaret was smitten with typhoid fever. No one was more distressed than the Queen. Typhoid had killed the Prince Consort and she thought of it with horror, blaming herself for having summoned the Jerseys to Balmoral when they were in the turmoil of packing-up. Margaret wrote firmly that Balmoral had not been a factor in her illness. It would, indeed, be hard to blame the drains of that recently modernised castle for playing the sinister part that the drains of Windsor Castle had done in the mortal illness of the Prince Consort. Frequent telegrams came from the Queen, and, when the Court returned to Windsor, she sent daily to inquire, Margaret having been moved from Claridges to Lady Galloway's house in Upper Grosvenor Street.

Lady Galloway showed all the devotion of a real twin, nursing Margaret until she was convalescent. At this time occurs Margaret's first mention of another friend who became almost equally dear to her, Alice, wife of Sir Stafford Northcote. She was the niece and adopted daughter of Lord Mountstephen who had made a vast fortune from the Canadian Pacific Railway. Her husband, subsequently made a peer, was a political figure, who, unlike Jersey felt strong enough to accept the governorship of Bombay, and in his turn, that of New South Wales. The Northcotes and the Jerseys made a congenial foursome, a matter of some bitterness to Lady Galloway, who now had no companion to offer Lord Jersey.

Lady Northcote even showed her friendship by offering her house as a fever hospital, with Lady Galloway as the matron. In the end Margaret remained with Lady G., while Lord Jersey sailed with only his official 'family', or staff. Actually his staff had a family flavour consisting of his wife's brother Rupert Leigh, her cousin Harry Cholmondeley, Lord Ancram, the son of Lord Lothian and, as private secretary, George Goschen. This last was the son of the first Viscount Goschen, who became Chancellor of the Exchequer when Lord Randolph Churchill, supposing himself to be indispensable, resigned and had to admit, 'I forgot Goschen'.

Although still recovering, Margaret must have found that the opportunity of a Christmas at Stoneleigh a compensation for her illness. This unexpected treat not only took in the Twelve Days of Christmas, but a celebration of the marriage of the eldest son and heir. Dudley had proudly arrived home with an American wife, Hélène, of great prettiness, but of an age somewhat mysterious. As a girl Hélène Beckwith had been a beauty at the Court of Napoleon III, and she had remained a friend of the Empress Eugénie. She had also retained her good looks and her dark curls, but simple calculation showed her new family that to have been a beauty at a court that had disintegrated in 1870 she was unlikely to be less than forty in 1890, which made the question of an heir somewhat speculative.

Hélène, however, made no concessions to what her age might be presumed to be. She followed her husband, a dynamo of energy through many a long round of social engagements and strenuous sight-seeing, with a devotion that was said to have shortened her life. At home she rose early to bicycle round Battersea Park, a fashionable scene for that new exercise. Abroad, she would bid farewell to any sluggard niece with a resigned, 'Good-bye, dear, I won't be back till dinner-time.'

This arduous life was in the future. At Stoneleigh there was rejoicing and health drinking, Duddy causing protest by invariably returning thanks with, 'I and my wife'. On Twelfth Night a little judicious rigging cast the lots of Queen and King of the Revels to Markie, the eldest granddaughter, and to Arthur, aged seven, the youngest grandson. He brought the house down by firmly returning thanks for the health-drinking with, 'My wife and I.'

The happy interlude came to an end, and there was the farewell to Villiers to be faced, as he had to be left to finish his Eton career. The children were also taken to say good-bye to their father's mother, Julia Lady Jersey, called by them Grandmama Lily, after a dog she owned. Age seems to have softened her notoriously hard heart, for she wept at the idea that she might not live to see these children again. The sight was surprising to her grandchildren, who had never before seen an Olympian grown-up in tears.

Still devoted, Lady Galloway travelled through bitter weather with the family caravan, struggling to keep them all warm and fed on the long haul through France and Italy to Brindisi. There, with a promise of a visit to New South Wales, she said good-bye to a party which, besides the mother and children, included Miss Mason, the English governess, Fräulein Witzell, the German governess, and Mrs Bourne, the nurse, brought because the children had cried so terribly at the idea of leaving her behind. They sailed in the *Arcadia* which had already carried the Jerseys to India. Unaware that the claim was made for each newly-built ship of increased displacement, the children believed the assurance that no one could be sick in a liner of five thousand tons, and awoke in their bunks on the first morning to find the *Arcadia* remarkably steady. Disillusionment set in when they discovered that she was still alongside.

In a journey punctuated by anxious telegrams from the Queen, Margaret spent most of her time resting in her cabin, while her children, sitting on trunks in theirs, struggled rather mutinously with their lessons. Their English governess did not waste her free time on board. She collected an admirer, a professor, who she married in Sydney, where he rose to academic eminence. Comic drama, which dogged Margaret's travels, did not fail. One young man always appeared in purest white, with a sash that matched the ribbons of his lady love. At Colombo an outbreak of smallpox prevented washing from being sent ashore, and he was mocked by fellow passengers for his despair at falling away from his standards of spotlessness. Enraged by this rudeness, the unhappy young man ran up and down outside his cabin with a drawn sword in his hand.

The *Arcadia* was still commanded by the Captain who, on the voyage to India, had made short work of the intransigent Frenchman, player of the 'Boulanger' hymn, by sending a steward to tell 'the man to stop that noise'. On the nine days sailing between Colombo and Australia all the Captain's firmness was needed, for he had to steer his ship round what was said to have been the worst typhoon of a generation. Those who could face food found that the fiddles were on the tables in the saloon for days at a time. When the Governor's rather battered family were finally landed at Sydney they were, understandably, sent to Hill View, the Governor's country residence, for recuperation.

If Lord Derby hesitated as to whether his friend should be congratulated or condoled with over her husband's new position, Hilaire Belloc, at a slightly later date, had no doubts on the matter. One of Belloc's gallery of peers, Lord Lundy, has disappointed his backers ('It was arranged that you should be/The next Prime Minister but three') Lord Lundy is cast out from all hopes of a splendid future with the cruel words, 'And as it is my language fails / Go out and govern New South Wales'.

Although cosseted herself as a girl, Margaret's care of her own daughters varied from the fussy to the Spartan. When in the comparative freedom of Hill View they were still forbidden to leave the house without the protection of gloves and veils, the latter being a handicap when on official occasions bouquets were presented, and the veils had to be raised before the presenter, a small child, could be kissed. On the other hand, when Lady Jersey discovered that Miss Mason had asked for soup to be sent to the schoolroom instead of cups of milk and slices of bread, which was all the children had after their evening ride, she countermanded it as unnecessary. Miss Mason's own marriage delivered her from a certain amount of ragging from her pupils, who found her plumpness tempting. At Baglan, absence of parents had encouraged an upsurge of mischief. Mary had given her governess a sly push at the top of the steep Welsh garden, and it was said that only the garden gate had halted her from running down into the town of Briton Ferry. Together Markie and Mary had behaved even worse, creeping up to a lavatory door known to have an uncertain lock, and suddenly flinging it open when Miss Mason was seated inside.

Fräulein Witzell, called affectionately 'Frl', was not given such rough treatment, and her flirtations at balls at Sydney were followed raptly by her pupils. Mrs Bourne was still an anchor in the nursery, steering the girls through the onset of puberty with the philosophical assurance that menstruation was the curse that lay on every woman 'from the Queen downward'. Mrs Bourne also gave Arthur encouragement when one of the ADC's dressed to kill, wished to add a buttonhole to his outfit. Stooping to gather some flowers from a bed regarded as belonging to the nursery he found himself dowsed with water from a jug poured by the Governor's youngest child.

This assertion of the nursery's rights became a family legend, but Mary met with less sympathy when, afflicted by the curse, her plea to her mother to be let off a game of tennis with her father was swept aside. The apparent callousness may have arisen from a wish not to disturb the Governor's temper, always an incalculable element in dealing with his children. Joking among themselves at Sunday luncheon about the game of cards among the choirboys in the Cathedral, which they had observed from the Governor's pew, during the sermon they were struck by a thunderbolt. Their father's rebuke for his children's irreverent inattention during the service reduced them to silently quivering jellies, though it might, with more justice, have been directed at either the choirboys or the choirmaster.

14

Buried and Dug Up

LETTERS OF SENSIBLE advice continued to arrive from Lord
Derby. Warnings against trusting to information that was not up-
to-date, because of the rapid changes in a developing country,
were added to counsel on the non-interfering attitude that a Governor should maintain towards his Ministers. Hospitality on a scale
beyond the Governor's salary was inevitable, wrote Lord Derby,
but that alone would not induce good will. Fortunately his recom-
mendation of mixing in the local amusements was one that
appealed to Lord Jersey, and he was remembered with approval
in New South Wales for his sociable habits. It is possible, with his
knowledge of her character, that Lord Derby wrote his letters of
advice as directives by which the Governor's wife would coach
His Excellency. Margaret herself made the point that on her arrival
in Australia the terms 'colony' and 'colonist' were still used un-
selfconsciously by all, pejorative implication only growing up
after Federation was established.

Escorted by her cousin Harry Cholmondeley, gorgeous in his
ADC's uniform, Margaret made her first appearance as the Governor's lady at the initial banquet for the Federation Convention,
attended by delegates from all the States of Australia. Being accustomed to acting with the Cholmondeley family, she had an impression of private theatricals, when the company rose to their feet
as she entered the gallery of the Town Hall. She had a link with
Sir Henry Parkes, then Premier of New South Wales and the chief
promoter of Federation, for he had been born on her grandmother's property at Stoneleigh. Besides attending the village
school, Henry Parkes had had his first pair of breeches made by
Job Jeacock, the village tailor and parish clerk. Job Jeacock's
reliance on Margaret in her girlhood had been so complete, that

baffled by the new-fangled service of Harvest Festival, he had left his desk in the three-decker pulpit, and marched across to ask Miss Leigh to find the special psalms for him.

On the other side of the world, these children of Warwickshire met. Parkes made a speech, and so did the new Governor, the latter making an apt reference to the Saxon Heptarchy as a precursor of the Federation of Australian States. A Sydney newspaper treated this historical parallel with frivolity, declaring that some of the audience believed that 'Heptarchy' was a Jersey ancestor who had fought at Crecy, while others fancied it to have been a kind of cake. Cake might indeed have come in useful, for when Margaret increased her popularity by attending the debates of the New South Wales Parliament she observed that at six o'clock, whatever the topic, whoever the orator, a cry of 'Tea, tea, tea,' emptied the house.

Republican tendencies were already to be found in Australia in the eighteen-nineties. Sir George Dibbs, a huge man, chief political opponent of Sir Henry Parkes, was thought to have such sympathies, but demonstrably they were not deeply rooted. During the Jersey's term of office Dibbs visited England, where he was fêted at the highest level, not least by the families and friends of the Jerseys. In Sydney his progress was reported by splash headlines–'Dibbs meets one King–several Princes,' 'Dibbs visits the Queen,' Then a family note, 'Lady Leigh asks Dibbs to bring out Lord Jersey's son'. Dibbs returned to Australia with not one but two cigars given him by the Prince of Wales, He was also full of new-found Imperial ardour, while a Sydney paper published a caricature of Parkes' chagrin of his rival's social success in England. Margaret, who had had her finger in the pie and enjoyed making a sly thrust, said to Dibbs that she supposed the talk of Republicanism had been 'only his fun.' ' "Only my fun," was [Dibbs'] hasty reply.'

In any case, it appears that Dibbs' republican outlook had been modified before he left for England, judging from his exertions on the Governor's behalf at a vast picnic to celebrate the inauguration of the Yarrangobilly caves. The caves lay in an administrative no-man's-land between two districts, each refusing to accept responsibility for feeding the Governor's party. The gathering for this Governor's Picnic was five thousand strong, but, in the reverse of the biblical situation, everyone except the Governor's party had brought their food with them. Seizing a sword from an attendant trooper, the immensely large Dibbs descended on a party of picnickers who had sat down to eat their meal. He demanded how they dared to eat cold mutton when the Queen's representative was facing starvation. He returned in triumph with the joint.

In the meantime a packet, said to be Brand's Essence, was produced, and Lady Galloway, who had arrived on a visit, declared she knew how to make soup. Only when she had emptied the packet into a soup plate full of water were its contents discovered to be tea. A meal was scratched together, but on the following day matters went to the opposite extreme. On their way to a municipal banquet the party was halted by a district magistrate, determined to forestall his neighbours by giving the Governor a champagne reception at nine o'clock in the morning.

Brought up in old houses, and travelling much among ancient civilizations, Margaret felt at times that she had been buried in her previous life, and had now been dug up in a world where nothing was old. As her first sight of the delegates at the Federation banquet was of a body of men averaging over six feet in height, she may also have felt that she had been dug up in a new world peopled by giant politicians. Among the giants was the Chief Justice, Sir Frederick Darley, another link with home as his resemblance to the father of Margaret and her brother Rupert was remarked on by all who knew them both. Sir Frederick was kin to the poet Darley, but his wife had closer literary associations, being the sister of Rolf Boldrewood (Thomas Browne) author of the Australian classic *Robbery under Arms*.

The Darleys had built a house in the Blue Mountains beyond the waterfalls of Katoomba, where the Jersey family and Lady G. were welcomed into a sympathetic circle. This beauty spot was reached by a railway of extravagant loops, constructed, it was said, by an engineer anxious to keep within visiting distance of an innkeeper's daughter who lived along the way. Lilianfels, the Darley's house, looked down on wooded valleys, secret and inaccessible, in one of which Boldrewood had placed the headquarters of Captain Starlight, chief of the bushrangers in *Robbery under Arms*. Starlight was a vastly idealized projection of the real bushranger, Ned Kelly. Margaret learnt that Kelly had been, in reality, 'a common sort of villain', in spite of his personal magnetism. She found it repulsive that Kelly's brother and sister had cashed in on his myth by appearing for a fee on the stage in Sydney on the night of their brother Ned's execution.

An early Governor of New South Wales had been Captain Bligh of the Bounty, whose characteristically harsh standards of discipline had led to something approaching a mutiny on land. Between Bligh's term and Jersey's the harrowing days of transportation had run their course and ceased, but some idea of past horrors could be imagined when a visit was paid to the French Colony of New Caledonia, where there was still a penal settlement. Convicts at times escaped from thence to Australia, where they were resented both as an increase of a criminal element, and a reminder of the unhappy origins of the forcibly settled Australians.

Margaret's account of New Caledonia, sent to her mother, to whom her travelogues were always vivid, is a Firbankian narrative with lapses into Grand Guignol. To reach Noumea they sailed for three days in the *Armand Béhic* of the Messageries line, run at a loss by the French for prestige. By now something of a seasick expert in shipping lines, Margaret wrote that this ship was no exception to the Messageries fleet's practice of ordering ships of an elegant appearance but of frame so slim that they rolled in the smoothest seas.

A tremendous salute of guns greeted the *Armand Béhic* as she sailed into Noumea, the effect being spoilt by everyone being put into a twenty-four hours quarantine for small-pox. It was thought that this futile precaution (three weeks being the incubation period for small-pox) was due to the lack of a cable-link between Sydney and Noumea, so that the date of *la visite* had been unannounced. Panic was caused by the sight of the ship flying the White Ensign, which meant that the Governor-General of New South Wales was on board. Small-pox was virtually unknown in Australia, but a few cases, at once contained, were known to have arrived at Sydney, an excuse for a twenty-four hours hold-up at Noumea while preparations were hurried forward. The Jerseys, left on board, were only inconvenienced by the delay, but the rest of the passengers, penned in a tiny quarantine station, had their dirty linen ruined by a soaking in disinfectant.

When it came, the delayed welcome was imposing, headed by the Mayor girt with his tricolour sash. At Government House the visitors' apartments were lavishly prepared, flags, flowers, scent bottles, toothbrushes, and 'splendidly bound copies of Byron and Milton to make us feel at home'. Heavy rain began to fall and, as these preparations seemed to have exhausted the domestic

Government House, Sydney, New South Wales, circa 1890

Back row; Lord Ancram, ADC, George Goschen, Private Secretary, Lord Jersey,
Governor-General, Captain the Honble Rupert Leigh, ADC. *Front row*; Harry
Cholmondeley, ADC, Margaret Villiers, Mary Villiers, Beatrice Villiers, Lady
Jersey, Arthur Villiers

Lady Jersey and Robert Louis
Stevenson, riding to visit the
rebel King Mata'afa. Drawing by Belle Strong

Robert Louis Stevenson in
Samoa

impetus, the floors of the Governor's residence grew ever deeper in unswept mud. The only attempt at cleaning came from a party of Kanakas, who sometimes ran in with feather brushes, stirred up some ritual dust and ran out again. George Goschen, the Private Secretary, had to point out to Henry the footman, a boy from Middleton village, trained in the English discipline of departmentalized domestic service, that either he or Henry would have to make His Excellency's bed.

If Henry was taken aback by the inadequacy of the Kanakas, which obliged him to undertake housemaid's work, Goschen was equally shocked by the lackadaisical habits of the staff of M. Laffon, the Governor of New Caledonia. Their habit of remaining unseen, until *déjeuner* was ready, fitted the Firbankian aspect of Government House, but M. Laffon's own position had a more Balzacian background. As the chaos of his household indicated, he was a bachelor, but a clever and charming young man. He had been appointed through the influence of a Paris Rothschild, a friend of his father's and a main shareholder in the profitable nickel mines of New Caledonia. As a civilian, the Governor had had no word in the choice of his own staff. Goschen continued to be scandalized by their contempt for their chief, while he, tortured by rheumatism, struggled after Lord Jersey through storms of tropical rain.

M. Laffon was a devoted host, rising early to escort his guests, while his staff neglected even elementary duties, such as putting round place-cards on the dinner table. (The Minister of the Interior was, rather appropriately, obliged to undertake this job.) To Goschen, the Staff explained that they pleaded headache as an excuse to absent themselves from any activity that promised boredom, wondering if the Governor felt any surprise at the frequency of this indisposition. Goschen, examined as to the corresponding behaviour of British ADCs, took pleasure in assuring the Frenchmen that Lord Jersey's ADCs never had a headache, never allowed their feelings to interfere with their duties and, above all, never permitted that more than one of the four should be ill at the same time.

During the *Fêtes de Juillet*, co-incident with the Jerseys' visit, the grimmer side of New Caledonia became apparent. At the three balls which had been arranged the company danced to the music of the Convict Band, dressed, Margaret wrote, in their penal garb, but playing very well. Such an accompaniment must have seemed inappropriate for a celebration of the Fall of the Bastille, but a tour of the Convict Settlement brought an even more acute reminder of the Revolution. The first point of interest to be shown to the visitors was the site of the guillotine, which to at least one prisoner represented an escape from the miseries of solitary confinement.

Although the visitors were not shown the prison which held the worst criminals–'Ils out des temps durs ceux-la,' one of the French ladies told Margaret – they were shown one cell which held a large man who had assaulted a waiter. He had been condemned to seven years in his tiny cell, and, standing up when the visitors came in, implored the Governor to put him out of his misery by execution. Margaret supported his plea for more liberty, hoping that M. Laffon's promise to look into the matter would result in improved conditions, and feeling profoundly thankful that such days had passed in the Colony that her husband governed.

Hopes that her appeal for the unhappy assaulter of the waiter might have been effective were increased by the success of another appeal, which she had cause to make to the authorities in New Caledonia. Just before sailing for Sydney, she had received a letter written in 'flowery English' from a French *poilu*. He had married, or so he wrote, a girl who now lived in the State of Victoria with their child. However, 'France had called him to serve'. Now that his service was over, and he wished to rejoin his wife, France proposed to ship him back to Marseilles.

On reaching Sydney, Margaret got in touch with the office of the Charity Organization in Melbourne, asking if the heroine of the story could be traced. By a flagrant coincidence, she turned out to be employed in the office of the Charity Organization itself, and was said to be of a respectability barely flawed by some informality about her marriage lines. The Colonel at Noumea, described by Margaret as 'very amiable', was pleased to arrange that the love-sick *poilu* should be demobilized in Australia. For her part, Margaret requested that the Charity Organization should see that an impeccable marriage ceremony was now performed. A letter of thanks then arrived from 'two grateful young hearts for ever made happy'. She had never seen this romantic pair and could only hope that no disaster followed her god-like interference.

15

An Island Night's Enchantment

A FORMAL GROUP shows how the establishment at Government House faced the camera when on official photographic duty. Photographs at Hill View might be more relaxed with the children feeding a pony, nursing a kangaroo or a puppy, though even on what was obviously a halt in a game of tennis the Governor did not dispense with a high-crowned bowler hat. In Sydney everyone was on their best behaviour, and in their best clothes, Margaret Villiers' advance in age being shown by a dress and hat that marked a difference between her and her sisters, if only by an unhappy number of buttons and bows. As Private Secretary the devoted George Goschen had no hat and only an undress uniform, a sober contrast with the other ADCs. Lord Ancram had aquiline good looks which made him look delicate compared with the robust figures of Rupert Leigh and Harry Cholmondeley. Arthur Villiers also had an undress white uniform with a cap, presumably as a junior hereditary ADC.

Prepared to deflate a ghost story, when her memory supplied its ancient source, Margaret took an interest in the occult when it came to her firsthand. She watched with fascination when Lady Darley displayed her power of drawing shadow profiles, which grew under her fingers, sometimes recognized by others though never seen by the psychically inspired artist. It may have been this exhibition that incited Margaret to experiment with automatic writing during her time in Sydney. She was almost too successful, for she found herself obliged to tear up the words that came from her pencil. They concerned two people present, indicating that it was 'the hope of money' that actuated the girl at that time courted by the impecunious ADC, Harry Cholmondeley.

On another ADC the occult laid a tragic shadow in the form of a premonitory dream. Lord Ancram told Margaret that in his sleep he had returned to his home to find his brother in his place, and he himself ignored by everybody. This was far from the case in Sydney where he was immensely popular. His delicate appearance did indeed indicate a fragile constitution, so when he came to say good-bye to Her Excellency, before leaving on a shooting expedition with Rupert Leigh, her last words were to be sure to put bedding below him as well as above, should the party sleep out. It was the Australian custom to shoot from the saddle, and one of the party remounted with a gun thought, wrongly, to have been discharged. The gun went off and Ancram, shot through the head, died instantly.

Only six months before, the Staff had been almost overwhelmed by answering and forwarding condoling messages at the death of the Duke of Clarence, of whom Margaret had a kindlier opinion than most of those who knew him. Ancram's death was a more acute and personal grief, to all who had known him in New South Wales, and particularly to George Goschen, who was nearly prostrated. A telegram of anxious inquiry came from the Queen, the agonizing business of breaking the news to Ancram's parents being taken on by his uncle, who happened to be the Admiral commanding the station. This accident took place in June 1892, just before the Jersey's visit to New Caledonia. Soon after their return, Margaret set off again on a journey which she was ever to remember as the summit of enjoyment in all her experience of travel and literature.

Whether or not the choice of Rupert Leigh as ADC had been made partly because he would be an impeccable chaperon, when Margaret wished to travel without her husband, it was an ideal appointment for that purpose. When his sister and Lady Galloway went to visit Lord and Lady Onslow in New Zealand, Rupert went with them, on one occasion carrying the picnic luncheon basket on his head to the two countesses, adrift on the waters of Lake Rotorua in a boat that had lost its rudder. Lady Onslow had crowned her husband's service as Governor-General by the handsome gesture of giving birth to a son called Huia, after the bird whose feathers decorated the Maori chieftains. Margaret did not go to such extremes, as a Governor's lady, limiting herself to studying the history, myths and legends of every place she visited. Nowhere did she find this interest more fascinating than when she sailed through the South Seas to Samoa, in the company of her daughter Markie and her brother Rupy.

Although the group of Samoan Islands had, at that date, a population of under a hundred thousand souls, its politics were a bub-
bling pot. More suitable, Margaret suggested, to the arena
of the League of Nations were the three Land Commissioners and
the three Consuls, English, American and German. There were
also rival kings, with an additional pretender, whose father had
once been given a uniform by the Germans to support his claim.
The Prime Minister was a German, for his countrymen had set
up coconut plantations. This attempt at industrialization had met
with little response locally, and had had to rely on imported
labour. Sensibly, the Samoans preferred to exist on a two-day
week, which sufficed to keep them in the fish of the sea and the
fruits of the earth.

A Swedish Chief Justice legislated over questions of land in dispute between the three Great Powers, though this neutral umpire
had known no English on his appointment, and had had to go
to Fiji to learn it. Religious representation was triangular, London
Missionaries opposed to Wesleyan Missionaries, Roman Catholics
at odds with both. In spite of rival nations and faiths clashing about
their ears, the Samoans had an easy-going air of contentment. It
was here that Robert Louis Stevenson had settled. It was the end
of the long trail in search of health, which had already begun at
Mentone, where he had watched the fireworks organized by Margaret's father to celebrate the marriage of the Prince of Wales.

The invitation to visit Samoa had come from Bazett Haggard,
the British Land Commissioner. He was the brother of Rider Haggard, the author, and of William Haggard, who had guided the
two countesses on their first visit to Greece. Loudness of voice distinguished the many Haggard brothers; it had once caused
them to win a contested election in their native Norfolk by shouting in unison. Bazett Haggard, it would be said to-day, was
obsessed with Samoa, and, with an endearing naiveté, took his
position there with deadly seriousness. The possession of a Foreign
Office uniform and a red box transformed him in his own eyes
from a lawyer into a diplomatist. On requesting Margaret to dance
with him as the first representative of the Foreign Office in Sydney, he explained solemnly, that it was etiquette for him to wear
his sword, only laying it aside when the State Dance was over.

It was after this splendid, if encumbered, appearance on the ballroom floor that Haggard invited Her Excellency, Lady Margaret
Villiers and Captain the Honble Rupert Leigh ADC to visit him

in Samoa, offering them the hospitality of Ruge's Buildings, his residence. Always full of interest and enjoyment in new, remote places, to Margaret the days spent in Samoa were of a pleasure unsurpassed in a lifetime of travelling. Her daughter was equally enthralled, and Rupert rode at their heels, in his eye an eyeglass that was to be immortalized by Stevenson.

The party sailed from Sydney in the *Lübeck* of the Norddeutscher Lloyd, yet another ship of a line subsidized for reasons of prestige. In spite of the current distaste for all things German, Margaret, in retrospect, felt obliged to mention the kindness of the Captain when the almost inevitable storm got up. Not only did he move mother and daughter out of their swamped cabin into his own, but struggled to find food which their stomachs would not reject. The immediate reward for this rough passage was a visit to Tonga, where the King was called George after George III. His wife, Queen Charlotte, had, however, died. In King George's comfortable villa of a palace, Margaret found the portrait, full-length in oils, of an old acquaintance of her days in Berlin, Emperor William I of Germany, a gift to the King in return for Tonga's declared neutrality at the time of the Franco-Prussian War. Unfortunately, an effort of counter-propaganda by the British High Commissioner in Fiji had only resulted in the arrival of a much less imposing head and shoulders engraving of Queen Victoria.

The most beautiful moment of this visit was the sunrise as the *Lübeck* sailed from Tonga. Margaret and Rupy both remembered a little picture in their copy of Ballantyne's *Coral Island*, from schoolroom days when she had been Head Girl and he the wildest of her little brothers. Now they felt themselves to be in a realized dream, 'as if a rainbow or the tail of an angelic peacock had fallen into the ocean'. Margaret thought that St John's Revelation might compare with the glory, but that nothing on earth could surpass the splendour of crimson, green and purple.

At Apia, capital of Samoa, Haggard was awaiting the party with the British Commission's boat, smartly rowed by Samoans whose bodies were tattooed from waist to knee under their red lava-lavas. On the first floor of Ruge's Buildings, in bedrooms off the fine reception-room, Margaret, her daughter and her maid were established. Haggard carefully locked the three women in at night, though they never knew against what peril. Fascinated by what appeared to her to be Utopia, for the next three weeks Margaret was held in the spell woven by the Enchanter of the Islands. He had not been slow to manifest himself, for the Stevensons had arrived for dinner the day after Margaret and her party had landed.

Bringing with her the current number of the *Illustrated London News* in which Stevenson's story *The Beach of Falesa* was running as a serial, Margaret had some familiarity with the background against which she was meeting the author of that magnificent tale. Appearing with his wife in the doorway of the panelled room in Ruge Buildings, Stevenson made an impression never forgotten by Margaret and her daughter. Tusitala, 'the Teller of Tales', was indeed a figure of romance, dark, bright-eyed, with a black velvet jacket worn over a white shirt and trousers, his waist wrapped in a scarlet sash. 'By his side [stood] the short dark woman with cropped, curly hair and the strange piercing glance which had won for her the name, in native tongue, of "the Witch Woman of the Mountain".'

The sympathy that immediately arose during dinner was helped by a discussion, ever enthralling to authors, on the subject of royalties. The number of thousands said to have been received by Margaret's friend, Mrs Humphry Ward, for her last book was declared to be incredible, by Bazett Haggard on his brother's account, and by Stevenson on his own. It was then decided that an Apia Publishing Company should be formed, its initial production to be a story in which each chapter should be written by a different hand. While their host was absent it was agreed that he should be the hero, unbeknownst to himself. Stevenson, in Margaret's recollection, invented the title, *An Object of Pity, or the Man Haggard,* and also arranged an adventure to keep the plot moving. To Margaret it must have been a glorified return to the days of her girlhood, when stories, plays and poems had been turned out like hot buns, but now there was the genius of the Teller of Tales to increase enjoyment.

After hardships to which he had nearly succumbed, literary success had provided the money for Stevenson to settle in Samoa and build Vailima. This was about two years before Margaret's visit, at which time his household included his wife Fanny's son and daughter by her first and disastrous marriage. The son, Lloyd Osbourne, had grown up to be his step-father's collaborator. The daughter, Belle Strong, had just divorced a husband who added excessive drinking to the unfaithful habits with which her own father had made her only too well acquainted. The ladies of

Vailima had taken to wearing the loose native clothing, and they
had also, Stevenson wrote, accepted the local custom of communal
repose. As he expressed it, 'sleeping to them has long been a public
function'. In these circumstances it must also have been essential
to have customs which dictated where and when copulation
should take place, a matter on which Stevenson's published letters
are silent.

Aged only seventeen and full of enthusiasm, Margaret Villiers,
as she openly declared to the next generation, fell in love with
Stevenson, gazing bewitched as he recited verses by the light of
a glowing bonfire. Her mother, at a more cautious age, had feelings that were only implicit when she compared Stevenson to
Matthew Arnold's *Empedocles on Etna*. She made the reservation
that while Stevenson would have rejoiced to have 'Advanced true
friends and beat down baffling foes', unlike Empedocles he would
never cast himself into Etna's crater.

Stevenson, who had once referred to Scottish history as 'one
long brawl', found a sympathetic resemblance in Samoan politics.
He supported Mata'afa, the rival to the official king, raising his
glass and drinking to him as 'Charlie over the water'. It was Stevenson's friendship for Mata'afa that led to Margaret making an
expedition which she always remembered with pleasure unabated,
firmly ignoring any politically compromising aspects.

According to Margaret, it was Stevenson and Haggard between
them who decided that she must pay a visit to the rebel king,
Mata'afa, a visit that could only be made incognito. Lady Jersey
was to be disguised under the name of Amelia Balfour, and to
pose as a cousin of Stevenson's. This was an easy choice of name
as Stevenson had forty cousins called Balfour, one of whom, Graham Balfour, was staying at Vailima and joined the expedition.
Even with this extra cover, to conceal the fact that the wife of
a Colonial Governor was committing the indiscretion of visiting
a rebel chief, the attempt at secrecy proved to be futile. Nobody,
however, enjoyed the conspiracy more than the principals, even
when its pretences collapsed into farce.

Stevenson celebrated the adventure in an unfinished poem
called the 'Samoid', which began with an exaggeratedly dramatic
account of his party, himself, Lloyd Osbourne, Belle Strong, Graham Balfour and an interpreter, awaiting the arrival of Lady Jersey
and Rupert Leigh, who were to go with them. Haggard and Margaret Villiers came as far as the rendezvous, and then returned to

Ruge's Buildings, where Haggard presumably locked her in with
her mother's maid.

In the poem, Haggard was described as 'the Judge of the Titles
of Land / He of the lion's hair, bearded boisterous bland'. The
young lady was complimented as 'the maid that was named for
the pearl, a maid of another isle / Light as a daisy rode and gave
us the light of her smile', which must have been a tribute to delight
the heart of the maid that was named for a pearl.

Stevenson continued the narrative:

'But two to pursue the adventure: one that was called the
     Queen
Light as the maid, her daughter, rode with us veiled in green,
And deep in the cloud of the veil, like a deer's in a woodland
     place,
The fire of the two dark eyes, in the field of the unflushed
     face.
And one her brother that bore the name of a knight of old,
Rode at her heels unmoved; and the glass in his eye was cold.
Bright is the sun in the brook; bright are the winter stars,
Brighter the glass in the eye of that captain of hussars.'

There could hardly have been a more elegant way of saying
that Lady Jersey had a sallow complexion. As far as her riding
was concerned, Haggard had found her an animal so tall and
skinny that it was called both 'Pedigree' and 'Starvation'. Stevenson rode beside her on a fat little pony, and Belle Strong did a
drawing of the pair, Stevenson looking up rather as Sancho Panza
might have gazed up at Don Quixote. There was a personal element in Belle's emphasis on Lady Jersey's tiny waist, indicating
the tightness of her stays. By Margaret's account, Fanny Stevenson
and her daughter regarded any fitting garment as 'an absurd super-
fluity'. Belle had indeed put on a pair of stays for their support
on the long ride, but, when twilight came and the end of the ride
was near, she slipped them off, bidding a servant be a good boy
and carry them.

When the paths through the tangled vines and the little stiles,
to keep pigs in, not, as some had thought, to keep out Mata'afa's
enemies, had been negotiated, the party was greeted by the whole
population, a man beating a drum at their head. From references
overheard to the Tamaiti Sili, or Great Lady, it was clear that
Markie's cover as 'Amelia Balfour' had been blown. This was

confirmed at the kava cermony. Correctly, Mata'afa should have first offered the half-coconut shell, with its liquid distilled from the roots of the pepper tree, to the most important guest present, Stevenson, a man and the head of a family. 'With an indescribable expression of suppressed amusement,' however, Mata'afa handed the cup first of all to the Tamaiti Sili. 'Oh, Amelia, [said Stevenson] you're a very bad conspirator!' As the conventions of the day would have prevented any ordinary exchange of Christian names, both Stevenson and Lady Jersey obviously enjoyed the fiction by which he could address her, without impropriety, as 'Amelia' in a letter planning the expedition, while she could begin her reply 'My dear cousin'.

At the end of the evening Stevenson and the captain of hussars retired to one hut, while in another, the main hut of King Mata'afa, a pile of mats under mosquito nets was prepared for Margaret and Belle Strong. The hut's boat-shaped roof was thatched with palm leaves, and the mats were beautiful to honour a king. With a nonchalance worthy of the Stevenson family, Margaret explained that, as a rule, sleeping arrangements were communal, but on this night a big tappa curtain was let down to separate the ladies from the king and his warriors.

Sleep, as has been mentioned, always came easily to Margaret, but in the interval before it arrived, Belle Strong entertained her companion with stories of her life in America. As this life had included a runaway marriage, and perpetual financial troubles with a husband of abysmal irresponsibility, there was plenty of material on which to draw, though Belle may have edited some of her more outrageous experiences. It is probable that she also suppressed her present, unrequited, passion for Stevenson's real cousin, Graham Balfour.

On her side, Belle was entertained by the tooth brush which was Margaret's sole piece of luggage. Actually teeth cleaning had a special significance in the Leigh family, for Mr Gould, the chemist in North Audley Street, had made up an individual prescription for Margaret's mother, which he had been given permission to market as *Lady Leigh's Tooth Powder*. Ever faithful to this product to the end of her days, it was presumably with this in her hand that Margaret stepped outside the hut to clean her teeth. Although constantly bathing in the sea and in the streams, all washing by Samoans was done outside the huts to avoid damage to the handsome mats. The tooth brushing was watched,

enthralled, by the guards clustered round the visitor in the dark-
ness, Stevenson taking pleasure in assuring her that her teeth would
certainly become historic.

The visit ended with a formal kava, at which Margaret, ever
on the lookout for religious comparisons, was struck by the ritual
of a chief who refused the cup five times, in memory of an ancestor
who had refused water when his king had none. This recalled to
her the Bible story of King David, pouring out, undrunk, the
water for which his captains had risked their lives. At the formal
kava Mata'afa behaved with perfect courtesy, accepting the fiction
of Margaret as 'Amelia Balfour' by first offering the cup to Stevenson.

There was yet another, rival, royal family to visit, that of Tame-
sese, son of the king who had been promoted by the Germans.
His wife, Viti, a handsome, polite lady, wore, on top of her lava-
lava a kind of double bib of cotton pocket handkerchiefs, not yet
cut apart for sale, and printed with the portraits of prize-fighters.
It was during this visit that Rupert Leigh was seen by his sister
to be sitting in the centre of a ring of admiring ladies, including
Viti, and the Taupau, or Maid of the Village, a girl customarily
chosen for her beauty to represent her community in local revels.
The bright glass in the eye of the captain of hussars was shining
out from under the wreath of flowers that had been placed on
his head.

Mostly visiting in Samoa was done by boat, which Margaret
found delightful, but once rough weather prohibited landing at
a certain islet. Haggard sent a message of apology and a promise
that a photograph of the 'Tamaiti Sili' would be sent. This had
been particularly asked for by the London Missionaries there
established, as a precaution against any backsliding into Wesleyan-
ism. Margaret had experienced the intensity of religious rivalry
when on an evening visit to these same London Missionaries. A
servant interrupted with the news that the Roman Catholic priest
was giving a magic-lantern show, in which Margaret's host was
represented as resident in hell. Anxious to support her friends,
Margaret arranged for a photograph of herself, in an elaborate
frame, to be sent from Sydney. Something of a failure as a fetish,
this picture was reported to have been hung upside down in the
guest house, before being carried into the hills, when its owners
had been defeated in a fight.

When Tamasese came to pay a farewell visit, Haggard put on

his uniform to add splendour to the occasion, on which he made a speech that was a masterpiece of grandiloquence. Having dwelt on the importance of these visitors to Samoa, he went on to expatiate on the sadness of the imminent parting, but he ended on a note of encouragement. 'Partings must always occur on earth; there is but one place where there will be no more partings, and that is the Kingdom of Heaven, where Lady Jersey will be very pleased to see all those present.' Delighted at the idea that Lady Jersey was in a position to issue a blanket invitation to Heaven, Stevenson told Margaret how much he would regret the end of her visit. The prospect of the departure of Haggard he also found depressing. The loss of such a splendidly idiosyncratic friend would, he knew, increase his sense of isolation.

Before the farewell – a final one for Stevenson – *An Object of Pity or The Man Haggard*, composed by six separate hands, was read aloud by Stevenson to its subject. A festive luncheon at Vailima had been arranged, and the garlanded hero accepted the production as a tribute of friendship. Stevenson had written the dedication to Ouida, whose style the book attempted to imitate. Unluckily the photograph taken to celebrate the occasion though posed with an attempt of Ouidaesque extravagance, was nearly a failure. Only Belle Strong, lying at Haggard's feet with an apple held provocatively, came out visibly as a temptress. Taking with her a cable to be sent from Auckland to his publishers forbidding alterations to the text in book form of *The Beach at Falesa*, Margaret sailed from Samoa on September 2nd 1892. She was glad to be of help to Stevenson in a matter of literary business, for she had just spent what she called, 'three of the happiest weeks of my life'.

If the Samoans had seemed to Margaret to lead a life of perpetual celebration, singing as they rowed from lagoon to lagoon, the Stevensons had found life hard in their early days at Vailima. By the time of her visit Margaret found an Enchanted Palace that had been carved out of the wilderness. Less happily in November 1889, the American historian Henry Adams had arrived at Apia with an introduction from Henry James. A devoted and sympathetic friend to the Stevensons, James' introduction came at a grotesquely inopportune moment, for the writer and his wife had only a ramshackle hut in which to entertain their new acquaintance.

Adams was almost comically revolted by the Stevensons' clothes, which he described as 'pajamas and nightdresses and dirty ones at that'. He considered Stevenson's love of squalor to be a result of a poor education, and continued association with the second rate. (Professor Edel has pertinently inquired why Adams ignored Henry James as an indubitably first-rate associate of Stevenson's.) Adams thought that Fanny Stevenson was mortally broken in health by her husband's restless travelling, though in fact 'the Apache Squaw', as he called her, was to live at full pitch for another twenty years. Adams felt, unjustly, that Stevenson disapproved of his 'Bostonianism', with perhaps a defensive feeling that he, Adams, was showing little appreciation for American ideals of pioneering and democracy when he met them in the raw. Finally Adams thought that the Stevensons should have bought less land and more soap.

Margaret, on the other hand, sympathized with the hardships of Stevenson's early struggles, particularly when, as she discreetly put it, he had just undertaken a wife and her children. She had faith in the writer's buoyant nature, being convinced that the pleasures of success had been greater than the temporary depression of failure. This was surely a reflection of her own buoyant nature, while Adams' distaste was a reflection of his sceptical melancholy.

If there was a variance between the views of the Boston historian and the English vicereine on the subject of Vailima, the Stevensons had equally divergent opinions on the personality of M.E.J. To the Teller of Tales, Lady Jersey was 'in all ways admirable, so unfussy, so plucky, so very kind and gracious', an opinion of value if the rigours of the expedition with 'Amelia Balfour' are remembered. Fanny, on the contrary, instantly took against Lady Jersey and her brother, though she thought Margaret Villiers a charming girl. To her Fanny confided that she had, herself, seen the personal devil. This information startled Markie at the time, but, had she known of the description that her hostess was cooking up in her diary, Markie might well have thought that Mrs Stevenson's idea of the personal devil had some of the traits of Lady Jersey.

Stevenson had described his wife as 'a violent friend and a brimstone enemy'. Years of watching his perilously fluctuating health, while wrestling first with poverty and then with the problems of success, had upset the balance of Fanny's temperament to a degree that made life a misery for her family. In the months before Lady Jersey's visit she had taken her daughter's divorce more hardly than Belle herself, for whom Joe Strong's final dismissal was a welcome end to years of sponging and cheating. Fanny was more outraged than her daughter to discover that Joe Strong's visits to the dentist in Apia had been an alibi for seeing his native mistress, and that duplicate keys had allowed him to rob the stores at Vailima.

Already showing symptoms of the psychotic illness which, at intervals, made her unmanageable during the last years of Stevenson's life, Fanny's jealousy of his attentions to Lady Jersey made the visit what he called a 'wretched period' at Vailima. In fact it was Fanny who was the real Object of Pity, while Margaret was enjoying three of the happiest weeks of her life. It must have been additionally galling that Lady Jersey had the dark colouring, which Stevenson found so physically attractive, that he had written an undisguisedly erotic poem on the appeal of a Dark Woman, blooming like a 'tiger lily, / In the snowdrift of the bed'. Although Fanny could certainly appropriate this particular poem to herself, Stevenson's lines on Lady Jersey, 'The fire of the two dark eyes, in the field of the unflushed face,' can have done little to improve her temper.

Fanny's comments in her diary were unrestrainedly vitriolic, Lady Jersey being only allowed the quality of courage. To those who knew Margaret as a kindly grandmother it was a mental shock to read that Fanny had thought her to be 'too much like [Kipling's] Mrs Hawksbee ... They were a selfish "Champagne Charlie set", with the exception of the daughter, a tall awkward young girl, of the best English sort; gracious and gentle and simple with the pretty simplicity of youth . . . Lady Jersey tall and leggy and awkward, with bold black eyes and a sensual mouth; very selfish and greedy of admiration, a touch of vulgarity, courageous as a man and reckless as a woman.'

Having herself married at seventeen, and at once become the mother of the ebullient Belle, Fanny may have been attracted by a phase of girlish simplicity of which she had had little personal experience. Her comparison of Lady Jersey with Mrs Hauksbee (the correct spelling) had a certain shrewdness, but was more of a compliment than Fanny intended. Had Margaret been a grass widow in Simla no one could doubt that she would have made her personality felt, but she definitely lacked the mischief-making propensity which, Kipling wrote, was the main fault in Mrs Hauksbee's character. The idea of the 'Champagne Charlie set' was probably suggested to the disgruntled Mrs Stevenson by the forethought of the Jerseys. Warned that the supply of imported goods was difficult in Samoa, they had not only brought with them a consignment of tinned meats but additionally a stock of champagne.

Fanny's strictures on her unloved guest's appearance are comprehensible when it is remembered that Fanny was stocky, not to say square, in build, which would account for accusations of legginess and lankiness in women of average size. Lady Jersey was only a year older than Stevenson, so the 'bold black eyes' and 'the sensual mouth' belonged to a woman ten years younger than Fanny. It is not clear in what way Margaret fell below Fanny's standard of non-vulgarity, but 'courageous as a man and reckless as a woman' could equally have applied to Fanny herself.

As a result of this visit, Stevenson wrote an exposition of the crisis that was boiling up in Samoa, between the rival kings which he sent to Lord Jersey. He had hopes of travelling to Sydney to discuss the matter in person with the Governor-General, but, fortunately for his domestic peace, he did not make the journey until after the Jerseys themselves had left. If Fanny had been exasperated by Lady Jersey incognito, to be obliged to contemplate her as 'the Queen of Sydney' would have certainly caused a major eruption of brimstone.

Only too soon the merrymakers of the islands showed the dark side of their nature in a hideous outbreak of warfare. Mata'afa, defeated, escaped to exile, but his nephew and heir was decapitated, together with his wife, 'a maid of the village', who had refused to leave him. Two more women's heads were brought in to the Government, grisly examples of the primitive horror that had been let loose. Only a precarious peace returned to Vailima, where Fanny's neurosis had added to the perils of Stevenson's involvement in the 'long brawl' of Samoan politics.

Then, on December 3rd 1894, Stevenson, whose terrifying haemorrhages had for years been an anxiety to his family, had an apoplectic stroke and died in two hours. From England Margaret wrote her condolences and Fanny replied at length and amiably. No difficulties were made by the widow when Margaret wrote a preface to *The Object of Pity*, nor to the reproduction of Stevenson's verses on the visit to Mata'afa. Margaret cherished her bright memories, and when Fanny wrote to her she spoke fondly of 'my Lou'. Jealousy may be as cruel as the grave, but in a grave it can also be buried.

16

Return to the Old World

IF THERE WERE any repercussions from the indiscretion of the
Governor's wife hob-nobbing with a rebel king in Samoa, Margaret chose to leave them unrecorded. Instead, she wrote of how
much her regret at leaving the enchantments of the islands had
been mitigated by the pleasure of the arrival of her eldest son.
Villiers was a clever boy, who, on returning after a half's absence
in India, had gratified his parents by winning the Junior Oppidan
Exhibition. They learnt of this success from a report in *The Times*,
the boy having kept his own counsel. His tutor at Eton wrote that
Villiers had taken the examination in his stride, vindicating the
tutor's good opinion of the pupil's abilities, though later he came
to lament that the boy chose to rely on ability rather than industry.

Villiers had travelled out across the United States and the Pacific
under the supervision of the Prime Minister of New South Wales,
Sir George Dibbs, who, when he reached Sydney, was to be teased
by Villiers' mother as a recanted Republican. In the States a
reporter, evidently confused between the Governor-General and
the Prime Minister of New South Wales and ascribing Villiers'
paternity to the latter, expressed surprise at the young man's
English aspect considering his Australian origin. Villiers was now
a formidable young man, over six feet in height. It is possible to
speculate that his separation from his immediate family, at an age
when character often crystallises, increased his natural reserve, for
in later years he was known for a reticence that at times approached
the enigmatic.

His sisters were still at an age when they were alternately taken
about by their parents, or put back into cold storage in the schoolroom as convenience dictated. Spartan daily life was varied by
spells of being treated like princesses. At the Races, in the Gov-

Villiers, as an undergraduate, 1892

Margaret Villiers, dressed as Henrietta, Duchess of Orleans, for a Fancy Dress Ball at Devonshire House, circa 1895

Golden Wedding Party at Stoneleigh Abbey, August 22nd, 1898. Lord Leigh in centre, on his right Hélène, wife of the Honble Dudley Leigh, on his left Lady Jersey

Lady Northcote and Lady Jersey Bombay 1900

ernor's box, they were given leather-bound race cards and hints on the form by the Staff. After this privileged treatment Mary Villiers could never reconcile herself to the hurly-burly of the Royal Enclosure at Ascot. She had another splendid moment when she was asked to launch a ferry-boat, christening it with her own name. Against her judgement, she followed the advice that all she needed to do was to let the bottle of champagne swing against the bows. No breakage, well-known as a sign of bad-luck for a ship, resulted, and Mary's second attempt was made with all the force of her hockey player's arm. The smash that resulted did not avert the bad luck, for the last her namesake heard of the *Lady Mary Villiers* was that she had gone aground on a sand bank.

The girls made friends, whom they entertained, but one of these children appears to have been suborned by a gossip writer. This ungrateful little guest reported, with a sneer, that Lady Beatrice had only the low count of twelve buttons on her boots, instead of the fashionable sixteen. As it happened, Beatrice herself had asked to be excused the tedium of buttoning thirty-two buttons every time she left the house. In spite of her unfashionable boots, Beatrice, aged twelve, had a young admirer, who felt so strongly at her departure that his parents did not dare tell him the date on which she was to sail for England.

It was not only in Samoa that Beatrice's mother was apostrophised, if with less elegance than in the *Samoid*. The failure of the ubiquitous Colonel Olcutt's verses to win her theological support, when he visited Sydney, has already been mentioned. A more public effusion, a cutting from a Sydney newspaper, has also been preserved. Entitled 'A Paean to the Countess of Jersey', it began 'O, Queen of Song, our soul's delight', an inappropriate address if the subject's lack of musical sense is remembered. By her own account, in her dealings with Colonel Olcutt, Margaret was a reader of newspaper advertisements, so she presumably looked at the reverse side of the poem. It advertised an Indian Medical herbalist, 'admitted to be the most successful Medical Expert and Specialist in all Private diseases'. She did not, however, consider this sinister medical puff as a reason for not preserving the paean.

Lord Jersey's appointment had been for five years, but early in 1893 he felt himself obliged to resign. His health was affected by the climate, as it seems to have been by most climates. Additionally, the agent of his Welsh property had died, so there was a need to turn his attention to his own affairs, and those of his rapidly growing-up family. Among his children's grievances at being taken to the other side of the world had been his eldest daughter's complaint that she would be obliged to 'come out' in Australia. Now that her début was imminent her parents may have come to appreciate her point of view. In any case Villiers was due to return and start his Oxford career, and Lord Jersey can hardly have forgotten what a mess a young man with no father at hand could get into. The Jerseys' term of service had been a success, largely due to the sympathy with which they had regarded the advance towards a Federated Commonwealth. Writing a letter to entertain and inform Queen Victoria, Margaret had reported that one female guest, dazzled by the fairy lights at a Governor's Ball, had expressed her belief that she had arrived in Heaven. With all respect to Government House, Sydney, Margaret wrote that the lady's celestial expectations must have been distinctly modest.

On leaving Government House, the Jersey family split, and sailed for home in opposite directions. Margaret Villiers travelled with her parents, who planned to complete the circuit of the globe by way of the Pacific Ocean and the United States. The rest of the household boarded the *Ophir* in February 1893, with the addition of Villiers to make up the numbers, the English governess being left behind as the wife of the professor who had courted her on the voyage out.

According to their parents' plan, Stoneleigh should have been ready to receive Margaret's children, and keep them in loving care until the Jerseys reached England. This scheme was accidentally sabotaged by Mary Villiers, who, enjoying the opportunity of taking a decision on her own, arranged that the party should not disembark at Marseilles, but continue on board in order to visit Gibraltar. Unhappily, some other child passengers came down with German measles, and had to be segregated in company with a traveller whose son had just committed suicide, and a party of animals on their way to an English Zoo. Worse still, the *Ophir* flew the yellow flag, and the quarantined Villiers family could only gaze at the Rock from the deck.

Landing in England, they found their grandmother to be equally unaccommodating. Her daughter Cordelia, Lady Leigh declared, had already had measles twice, if not three times, and the risk of another attack was too great. It seems to have struck no one that Stoneleigh was big enough for the children to observe a separate quarantine. Still in command, Mary directed the party to Claridges, which she remembered as a hotel frequented by her family, and where, only two years before, her mother had been smitten by typhoid fever. No one could blame a girl of fifteen for failing to foresee that two years would have turned a family hotel into something infinitely more fashionable. Claridges did not close its doors, but its welcome for the quarantined party was frigid. Oddly enough, Lady Leigh's attitude did not suggest to her granddaughters that quarantine should be viewed sensibly, to be modified according to the inconvenience its strict observance might cause. On the contrary, they grew up to regard the period of the incubation of a disease as requiring more attention than the disease itself.

Ostensibly the Jerseys took their eldest daughter with them on the homeward journey for the pleasure of her company, but having seen much of the emotional excitements endemic to a long voyage, Margaret may have thought it wiser to keep 'the maid that was called for a pearl' under her own eye. They said goodbye to Australia at Port Darwin, where there was an increasing problem of immigrant Asiatics anxious to open up the empty continent, while the Aboriginal Australians were losing their own culture before waves of multi-coloured invaders.

By a fortunate chance the Corroboree, a battle dance of Aboriginal warriors, almost extinct as a custom, could still be seen in the neighbourhood of Port Darwin. By the light of bonfires, the men danced, wool stuck in patterns on their bodies, their own blood being the fixative. On their heads were mitres of bamboo, in their hands spears for their mimic warfare. The rhythmic accompaniment came from the women, the 'gins', who lurked in the gloom, only visible by the stripes of white paint on their bodies, while they smote their thighs with their hands. To Margaret it was like a Walpurgis Nacht, made all the more like a dream next day, when the wild dancers, tidily dressed, came to be rewarded by Jersey with tea and tobacco, money being banned as certain to be spent on drink.

If the Corroboree was an eerie sight with which to say goodbye to Australia, a visit to the prison at Port Darwin was positively macabre. The procedure by which death sentences were confirmed from Adelaide, the State capital, had not been overhauled since the invention of the telegraph. Consequently the visitors were faced with a row of seven or eight Malays, condemned to death for such crimes as piracy, and awaiting confirmation of their fate to arrive by slow mail. Margaret made a protest at such a parade of those so close to death, only to be assured that it would be a cheerful interlude, which seemed to be corroborated by the smiling faces of the condemned.

At Timor, the Portuguese colony, the *Catherthun*, carrying the party from Port Darwin to Hong Kong was slowed down by being obliged to take in tow a Portuguese gunboat, in whose boiler inefficient management had caused forty-nine holes to appear. Owing to this brake on progress, a storm overtook the ship, but only after Margaret had done her best to keep a Portuguese Archbishop up to his duties. With his priests, the Archbishop had come on board at Timor. He was thought to be in some sort of ecclesiastical hot water, and to be on his way to Macao for an inquiry. In a fine spirit of religious toleration, Margaret suggested to the first officer that, as the Captain was to conduct a Church of England service, and a Chinese Wesleyan missionary the appropriate service for the Chinese crew, it would be proper that the Portuguese should be invited to celebrate the rites of their persuasion. On the Sunday the offer was accepted with gratitude, but when the former theological *enfant terrible* suggested that March 25th, the Annunciation, should also be honoured by a service, the Archbishop refused to accept that heretics could have any knowledge of such a Feast.

Dragging the Portuguese gunboat behind them, the Jerseys reached Hong Kong, where Markie was carried in a chair to her first ball as a come-out young lady. The ball was at Government House, such occasions, according to Lady Jersey being a paradise for the young, meaning young girls. In a colony abounding with sailors, soldiers and young men from offices only nine girls were of an age to be invited. Markie's 'first social steps', to use Henry James' phrase, were such enjoyably dancing ones that it seems that her father took fright at his daughter's attractiveness. She always remembered the bitter moment on board ship between Yokohoma and Vancouver when, having filled her card for the evening's ball, her mother broke it to her that her father wished her not to dance that night. Lord Jersey's fussiness about his daughter's partners was labour in vain. Like the magnet in W. S. Gilbert's *Patience* she was always to be surrounded by a loving crop.

A readiness to disregard rules, which had led to the visit of King Mata'afa, came into play when the Jerseys visited Kowloon, across the harbour from Hong Kong. Here the Commodore of the

Station took the party to a Chinese gambling hall, an illicit proceeding which inhibited Lady Jersey, even after thirty years, from
mentioning his name. Galleries ran round the high hall, with small
rooms behind in which opium smokers lurked. The visitors were
given baskets to let down from the gallery, so that their bets could
be registered on a game that two or three Chinese were playing
below. Ignorant of the game, only small coins were lowered, but
either from Chinese courtesy, or from recognition of the Commodore, the sums had increased when the baskets were hauled up
again, a rare example of anyone making a profit in an opium den
and gambling hell.

Sailing up the Pearl River to Canton, it seemed to Margaret
that the Chinese wallpaper in her nursery at Stoneleigh had come
to life. This feeling was increased in the garden of a rich merchant
when his wife was introduced. She tottered in, supported by her
maids, but her face was so rigid with paint that speech was as
difficult as walking on her tiny, bound, feet. With the loan of the
consulate guard to create an air of importance, Lord Jersey paid a
ceremonial call on the Viceroy of Hong Kong, and, through the
interpreter, managed to hint that his wife and daughter would be
gratified to meet the Viceroy when the call was returned.

Amid general satisfaction, this meeting took place. Never having seen a European woman before, the Viceroy examined Margaret's get-up with close attention, wishing to know why she wore
no ear-rings and what would be done with her jewellery when
she died. The seven grand-daughters eventually to benefit were,
of course, still out of sight below the horizon of the future. The
conversation, with inquiries for the Queen, was closely monitored
by the Consul and Vice-Consul, so that no remark derogatory to
the British might slip by in Chinese. Once a term, its nature unrecorded by Margaret, was used in reference to the Queen's sons
and was not of the highest propriety if applied to princes. However
the extreme good temper of the Viceroy, and the success of his
interview with the exotic English ladies, decided the monitors that
this one lapse might be overlooked.

If Canton brought memories of the nursery wallpaper at Stoneleigh, Japan evoked visions of the Middle Ages. Expecting 'toy
houses and toy people', as Margaret wrote to her mother, she
found herself contemplating feudal castles, formidable in size, and
haunted with legends of knights, witches and enchantments. The
Viceroy of Canton might have never before seen a white woman,

but the Westernization of Japan had moved to a point when the wife of the Vice-Chamberlain of the Court was, herself, English. Complications of ancient etiquette still remained, however, dictating what might or might not be worn, as in the days of Lady Murasaki.

For an audience with the Empress at ten in the morning, the ladies were told to appear without bonnets, but in high-necked dresses with trains. This posed a problem, for, as Margaret had to explain, her 'latest Paris morning frock' had only a short train, and her daughter's dress had none at all. Although she wrote that it was fortunate that she had even a token train in which to appear before the Empress, Margaret does not explain by what means Paris gowns arrived in the Antipodes, or if Mrs James Leigh, knowledgeable about *haute couture*, picked them out. The Empress, herself, wore a gown of purple silk, its train of the length required for presentation at Queen Victoria's drawing-rooms. There was an exchange of bows, curtseys and a few stilted sentences, but the Empress was said to have been very pleased with the interview. 'She must have been easily gratified, poor dear,' Markie wrote, contemplating the life of stifling etiquette lived by a childless consort, whose adopted children were those of the Emperor's secondary wives.

With a hundred first cousins to draw on, Margaret found, as she wrote herself, that wherever she travelled a first cousin was almost certain to appear. In Japan the cousin was the Revd. Lionel Cholmondeley, brother of Harry, the ADC. He was Chaplain to the British Embassy, and a missionary of much experience. The mass crucifixion of Jesuit missionaries in the seventeenth century, which preceded the closing of Japan to foreigners, had practically eradicated Christianity. When the country was re-opened a German was employed to teach Court etiquette, with the suggestion that this might include the full ceremonial for a Court Christening. The idea that this might be superfluous in a non-Christian country was waved aside in the interest of getting the full package of ceremonial arrangements which might come in useful in due course. It seemed to Margaret that this foresight had been unfruitful, the Japanese appearing to take their ideas of Christianity from the materialistic activities among foreigners, rather than from the work of her clergyman cousin.

The Pacific Ocean and the North American continent still lay before the Jerseys. An outbreak of small-pox among the Chinese crew was the only hazard of this particular voyage, but the threat of quarantine at Vancouver was averted by some brisk perjury on the part of the ship's doctor, supported by the Captain. A private car, supplied by the Canadian Pacific Railway, took the travellers through the Rockies, where Gilbert Leigh had met his death, and on to St Paul, Minnesota. Snow and ice, not seen for two years, added to Margaret's pleasure in the grandeur of the scenery, which she passed through on the way to Chicago. Here they paused to visit the Exposition, a production celebrating the fourth centenary of Columbus's landing in America.

Normally, as Stevenson remarked, a plucky and unfussy traveller, with a gracious appreciation of any country's efforts at hospitality, Margaret found Chicago almost intolerable. Her resistance was broken down by the heat, while wind off Lake Michigan gave the whole party chest colds, the only illness even mentioned in all the long voyage home. Some years later, Rowley Leigh married Mabel Gordon, a girl from Savannah, Georgia, but with a grandfather who had owned land on the shore of Lake Michigan. Mabel Leigh, admittedly something of a myth-maker, assured her sister-in-law that her grandfather had sold this land, part of the site of the future city of Chicago, to buy his wife a pony. Margaret, when she heard the story, could only deplore a sale that had encouraged the growth of such an abrasive city. In fact she would probably have applauded the action, twenty years before, of Mother O'Leary's cow, who was said to have kicked over a lantern, and reduced many acres of Chicago to a heap of ashes.

As it happened the path of Henry Adams again ran parallel to that of Lady Jersey, for the historian arrived to inspect the Exposition in the same month that the Jerseys paid their visit. To Adams 'the Exposition defied philosophy'. It asked the question, he wrote, as to whether the American people knew what they were driving at. He, for one, did not know, but would try to find out. Probably the American people, he added, knew more than he, but might, on the other hand, be unconsciously drifting to some point in thought that might become fixed. To Margaret the Exposition defied not so much philosophy as description, though she admired the choice of site that allowed the white buildings to be reflected in the waters of Lake Michigan. Her main enjoyment came from a succession of social contretemps, which demonstrated that Adams' 'fixed points in thought' were still a long way off.

There had been a poor response from Royalties and other nota-
bilities, invited to view the Exposition as guests of the city of Chicago. The chief catch was the Spanish Duke of Vedagua, reputedly
a lineal descendant of Columbus himself, though as the Spaniards,
after four hundred years, were still in disagreement over the actual
tomb of Columbus, such a descent might also have had a proble-
matical element. Prominent in the early ceremonies, the position
of the Vedagua family was undermined by the arrival of a genuine
Princess, the Infanta Eulalia, aunt of the King of Spain. Remorse-
lessly the Duke was jettisoned and put on the train to New York,
with his expenses paid only from a Friday to a Monday. After
that, he was told, he was on his own.

Getting rid of the Duke was a minor problem. The Mayor of
Chicago, determinedly a man of the people, had never worn a tall
hat, and had a bush of hair that would make wearing such headgear
an impossibility. Margaret suggested that he was a Socialist Sam-
son, whose political strength lay in his unshorn locks. With an exuberance recalling the Sydney newspapers in their ragging of Parkes
and Dibbs, the Chicago papers shouted gleefully, 'Will the Mayor
cut his hair?' 'Will the Mayor wear a tall hat?' A whoop of joy
went up when, transformed, the Mayor met the Infanta at the
station. 'He has cut his hair!' 'He wore a tall hat!'

Once captured, the Infanta Eulalia was guarded by her hosts,
according to Margaret, as a real princess of romance might be
secluded by 'father, enchanter, giant or dwarf'. Mr Fearn, the
Head of the Foreign Section of the Exposition, was an old friend
of the Jerseys from their days in Athens, where he had been American Minister. He had also been *en poste* in Madrid, spoke Spanish,
and, already knowing the Infanta, not unreasonably arranged a
reception for her. This he was obliged to cancel, as the Princess's
guardians mistrusted the idea of a conversation in Spanish, which
no one else could understand. Mr Fearn was also elbowed out of
the Foreign Section, of which he was officially in charge, and it
was only by almost literally digging in his toes that he was able
to retain control of the gallery, to which he had invited the Jerseys
to review the reception. This was not an impressive ceremony.
Some little girls strewed a few small flowers at the Infanta's feet,
while she was ushered in by a group of uncomfortable-looking
dignitaries.

Her escort might well look uncomfortable for the Infanta was
both a live wire and something of a tartar. Shunning the marvels

of domestic and agricultural machinery, she insisted on patronising a kind of fair, where her cortège was obliged to sit drinking
with her in a beer garden. The Infanta had been given rooms at
the Palmer House Hotel, sumptuously rebuilt after the Great Fire
of Chicago. It was only as she was preparing to leave for a reception in her honour that she realized that her hostess, Mrs Potter
Palmer, Chairman of the Lady Managers of the Exposition, was
also the wife of the owner of the hotel. Taking the view that any
hostelry was a *posada*, the Infanta said that she preferred not to
meet this inn-keeper's wife, and had to be talked into attending.
The Jerseys had also been sent an invitation to the reception, but
so much at the last moment they did not think it necessary to
appear. From reports, however, Margaret learnt that the Infanta
had refused to unfreeze, injury being added to social insult when
a cup of coffee was split over her gown.

After a spell as a Queen overseas, and with the prospect of
returning to an established position at home, to Margaret there
was something comic in the despotism of new wealth which had
established Mrs Potter Palmer as, socially speaking, the Queen
of Chicago. Lady Jersey was, it seems, unaware that Mrs Potter
Palmer had made a stunning collection of French Impressionist
paintings, nor would the fact have raised her opinion of the
Queen of Chicago. She might perhaps, have sympathized with
the commissioning of that pantomine fairy Queen portrait, painting of Mrs Potter Palmer by her protegé, the Swedish painter
Anders Zorn. In fact, when Zorn had yet to make his name, the
Jerseys had shown initiative by commissioning him to paint their
infant daughter Beatrice. French Impressionists were another matter, and their paintings remained, for Margaret, objects of un-
concealed derision.

The intransigence of the Infanta passed into legend in the social
history of Chicago. Rancour remained with Mrs Potter Palmer,
both on personal grounds and for the embarrassment caused by
the Infanta's insistence on refreshing herself at the beer garden.
When the Exposition was long over, Mrs Potter Palmer, in Paris,
was invited to yet another reception in honour of the Infanta
Eulalia. She hit back hard by refusing to meet what she called, with
feeling, 'this bibulous representative of degenerate monarchy'.

It may have been tourist combat-fatigue that made Margaret
unusually waspish on the subject of Chicago. She was, however,
grateful for a 'noble luncheon' given by Mrs McCormick, head

of that clan, even though there was the ordeal of shaking hands with upwards of thirty McCormicks. One of the family took the Jerseys to a spectacle called 'America'. Margaret called its historical scenes eclectic, particularly the discovery of America, heralded by a page in white satin, and backed by men-at-arms whose golden helmets were untarnished by sea-spray. The Pilgrim Fathers, in Puritan dress, were then entertained by a ballet, and the finale was a tribute to the supremacy of the McCormick family in the manufacture of agricultural machinery.

In Japan, the Jerseys had admired many spectacular waterfalls, so they approached Niagara in a mood that was dutiful but apprehensive of disappointment. All such fears were dispelled in the foam of Niagara, ever after to be, for both Jerseys, a wonder of the world. New York, in a June heat wave, was empty of the friends they had hoped to see, and sailing was nothing but a relief. England was also heat-stricken, but when the train had run through the dried-up countryside and stopped under the black vault of Euston Station the family were gathered in an abundant welcome. The Australian adventure was over.

17

The Children Grow Up

WITH NO ABATEMENT of the energy with which she conducted her life, Margaret at once assumed the position she had left two years before. One of the changes she found, which she remarked on to her daughter Beatrice, was that people now went in to dinner, on formal occasions, arm-in-arm instead of hand-in-hand, a custom that can still be seen at Royal weddings. Plenty of opportunity was offered to observe social change, for welcoming friends at once sent invitations, and not only to Lord and Lady Jersey. Indeed the greatest change was in Margaret's own family, for she had sailed to Australia with children in the schoolroom, and now she returned to the tail end of the London Season with a débutante daughter to be introduced to the grown-up world.

Lady Margaret Villiers made her first appearance as a 'come-out' young lady in London at a ball at Bridgewater House. There was a certain rather scandalous appropriateness about this background for her début. Bridgewater House had once been Cleveland House, a present from Charles II to one of Markie's most flamboyant ancestresses, Barbara Villiers, Duchess of Cleveland. Although the débutante's attractiveness had been demonstrated in the Far East, her mother warned her that she must not expect to dance more than once or twice in the evening. Immediately surrounded by eager partners, Markie was puzzled by the gloomy picture her mother had painted, until she realized that Lady Leigh had frequently passed on the task of chaperoning Cordelia to her eldest married daughter. Consequently Lady Jersey's previous experience had been that of a chaperone to a wallflower chronically uninterested in social life.

Strangely enough, among the trivialities of the past that could still arouse passion in the nineteen-fifties was argument over the system, prevailing in the eighteen-nineties, by which engagements to dance were made in London ballrooms. A correspondence took place in a Sunday newspaper, which involved Somerset Maugham's recollection of balls in high-society when he was a young man. It may have been he who made the original rash statement that each dancer on arriving was handed a *carnet de ball* with pencil attached. In any case this was denied by one indignant letter-writer, affirmed by another, whose argument was supposedly clinched by being in possession of a dance-programme for a ball given at Devonshire House. In reality this was a confusion of two different types of entertainment. On most nights of the London Season there might be two, or even three balls, with largely overlapping guest lists. It was therefore impossible for more than a few dances to be booked ahead with a floating company going on from house to house.

On the other hand the Devonshire House ball, a famous fancy-dress affair with a cotillon, required a programme as partners had to be booked in advance. At this ball Markie made a splendid appearance as Madame, sister of Charles II and wife of the unpleasant Duke of Orleans, brother of Louis XIV. She was a princess famous for her charm and Markie looked not unworthy of her model, in spite of a Victorian dressmaker's anachronistic idea of what French princesses wore in the sixteen-seventies, Sir Anthony Van Dyck having set the pattern once for all.

Not only did she waste no time in launching her daughter, but Margaret fitted in a garden party as something of a flourish to celebrate her return to what Augustus Hare called 'the radiant gardens' of Osterley. There were also house-parties from Saturday to Monday, and it was now that Lord and Lady Northcote became even closer friends than they had been before the Jerseys left for Australia. Cordiality between Lord Jersey and Lord Northcote made the friendship between their wives more of a family matter than that between Margaret and Lady Galloway. Childless, and separated from her husband, Lady G. was thought by the younger generation to feel that she was in danger of being separated from her twin.

The Northcotes were also childless, Lady Northcote, adopted as Aunt Alice, becoming godmother and benefactress by will to some of Margaret's grandchildren. Herself, as already mentioned, the niece and adopted daughter of Lord Mountstephen, the chief promoter of the Canadian Pacific Railway, Lady Northcote could afford to rent Brocket, the home of the Melbourne family in the days when Lady Caroline Lamb was its *belle dame sans merci*. It was at Brocket that her laughter had been interrupted with the stern injunction to behave herself, news having come of Lord Byron's death. But this precaution against hysteria did not prevent the accident that brought Byron's funeral cortège, feathered and coroneted, past the gates of Brocket just as Lady Caroline and William Lamb were riding by. When Markie, Mary, Beatrice and Arthur stayed with the Northcotes these sad histories cast no shadow. The bicycles which carried the Villiers family on expeditions were remote as transport from the stormy days of Caroline Lamb as the demeanour of their riders was from her behaviour.

Arthur was now a preparatory-schoolboy. He was found to be clever, but somewhat lacking in grounding. This may have been the result of the family's English governess marrying in Sydney, leaving education only in the hands of the charming Helène Witzell, soon herself to marry an Englishman. Ten years separated the brothers, Villiers having passed into a smart sporting world at Christ Church, Oxford, a world never to be wholly sympathetic to his junior.

With only twenty months between them, Mary, treading hard on her sisters heels, came out in the summer of 1895. She was popular with her partners, but she had lost the forwardness with which, at the age of three, she had amused her mother by flirting with Mr Bourke (Lord Connemara). Markie's habit of encouraging simultaneous admirers both fascinated and appalled her younger sister. Mary would take a turn or two on the ballroom floor, but already, in the cloakroom, Markie would be champing to join the emotional excitement of the dance. Beatrice was still in the schoolroom, her dark hair hanging down her back under hats less highly decorated than those chosen by or for her sisters. Mary's hats, in particular, were apt to be trimmed with high-rising feathers or bunches of flowers, which concoctions, perched on her thick pillow of ash-blonde hair, added half a cubit to her not inconsiderable stature.

It has been mentioned that *The Lesson of the Master* begins with a young literary disciple arriving at Summersoft (Osterley), and that, impressed with the warm beauty of the house, he found irreverent the patronising attitude of an elder fellow guest 'It's a nice little place ... but there is nothing much to do!' If the occupations of the guests on Sunday were as James described they were indeed sedate, church for those who felt the obligation, conversational walks for those who did not. However, after the return from Australia, Sundays at Osterley were less formal and more active. Lawn tennis was now permitted in the afternoons, which was still banned on strictly Sabbatarian English lawns. Violet Leigh, contemporary of Markie Villiers, triumphantly reported to her mother that Lady Jersey had bidden the girls to partner members of the Cabinet who happened to be among the guests. Mrs Chandos Leigh accepted resignedly that anything allowed by her husband's socially powerful niece must be considered as no breach of keeping the Sabbath holy.

Sunday tennis was the centre of an incident at Osterley in the summer of 1895. It was the year that saw the birth of the British motor industry, but means of political communication were still, as will be seen, in the bicycle age. On the grass court a game of tennis was being played between Arthur Balfour (nephew of Lord Salisbury and his eventual successor as leader of the Conservative party) and Lord George Hamilton, a Conservative M.P. Suddenly the hostess and her other guests, from their seats in the shade, saw a hot, dusty figure coming through the gate into the garden. He was recognized as Schomberg (Pom) McDonnell, Private Secretary to Lord Salisbury, but when offered every kind of hospitality by Lady Jersey all he would say was, 'Give me an egg beaten up in brandy and find me Arthur Balfour.'

The mixture was produced. McDonnell downed it, and, after a conference with Balfour, the game of tennis was resumed, the messenger, without more words, at once pedalling away on his bicycle. Only to his opponent did Balfour mention that the Government had resigned, Lord Rosebery's Liberal administration having recently been defeated on the cordite vote in the House of Commons. Secrecy, obliging him to finish the game in the manner of Sir Francis Drake, had been forced on Balfour by his leader's secretary. He, personally, thought it absurd that the house party had to wait for Monday's papers to give an explanation of the drama. (Balfour's aside to his opponent over the tennis net may have come from a wish not to be handicapped by the exciting knowledge of their party's return to power.)

Next morning Lord Rosebery's resignation became generally known, and with it the circumstances of McDonnell's ride. Sent by his chief to find Balfour, McDonnell had bicycled the eighteen miles from Hatfield to London, and, drawing a blank, had ridden a further eight miles to Osterley. Politicians may still be found playing tennis on Sunday afternoons, but the Leader of an Opposition no longer has the necessity, or indeed the nerve, to alert a supporter that the Leader will be forming a government by sending a Private Secretary across London on a bicycle.

Although she viewed great men from as far off as was compatible with politeness, Beatrice Villiers remembered certain of her parents' guests with special amusement or affection. There was, for example, 'greedy old Sir Donald Wallace who liked to read the menu aloud', a contrast to Miss Flora Shaw whose charm captivated the young daughter of the house. Sir Donald Wallace had been Private Secretary to two Viceroys and had come to rest as Director of the Foreign Department of *The Times*. Flora Shaw had led a more adventurous life, being one of the first women to make a name as a foreign correspondent. She was a formidable expert on Africa, and also on Australia, where she had made friends with the Jerseys. Married to Sir Frederick Lugard, she came to a dinner at Osterley given for foreign Colonial Delegates. Sitting between a Belgian, interested in the Congo, and a Dutchman, Lady Lugard gave her dinner neighbours such a rough ride that they afterwards appealed to their hostess. Who, the unhappy men asked, was this lady, 'si forte dans l'Afrique'? 'Elle vous a bien roulé, mon cher,' one added to the other. Knowledge of Lady Lugard's true identity produced an awe-struck comment, 'Quoi – la grande Miss Shaw! Alors cela s'explique.'

Putting a girdle round the world had done nothing to quench the Jerseys' thirst for travel. Since their first visit to Egypt when they had met Kitchener, then adjutant to the Sirdar, he had become increasingly a friend and a constant visitor to Osterley. He had also become Sirdar in his turn, which added to the interest of their next Egyptian expedition. In January 1896, taking their two eldest daughters with them, the Jerseys sailed from Marseilles to join Lady Galloway in Cairo. The Messageries boat, the *Sénégal*, was so decayed that Margaret thought it a mystery and a tribute to the Captain's skill that she weathered a storm and reached Alexandria. The inevitably bizarre fellow-passenger was, on this occasion, a woman who, hearing Columbus mentioned, remarked that he was the man who went to sea in a sack.

In those days there was a saying that the Nile was like Piccadilly, with Cairo as the Bachelors' Club, as far as meeting friends was concerned. Lord Jersey had hired a dahabyah charmingly called the *Herodotus*, which proved worthy to be named after the first historian of Egypt, for while others, dependent on sail, were becalmed in the Egyptian Piccadilly, the dahabyah *Herodotus* was steadily pulled up to Assouan by a steam tug. Over all was the shadow of Kitchener, the Sirdar, under whom the death of Gordon at Khartoum was to be avenged two years later at Omdurman.

Eager as the officers stationed at Assouan were to move against the dervishes, they were even more antagonistic towards the French. Margaret was told of a tall English officer in a café in Cairo, who had put up with various insults from three or four Frenchmen, until an attempt to trip him up drove him to retaliate. He picked up the offender and used him to hit the others. The Englishman would have been overwhelmed in the subsequent scuffle, if the girl behind the bar had not come in on his side, driving off the French attack with a well-aimed shower of empty bottles.

It was at Assouan also that the Jerseys heard of the arrival of Slatin Pasha, escaped after eleven years of slavery as the Mahdi's prisoner. Sir Herbert Jackson, who told the story, had doubts about the identity of the dirty Arab trader claiming to be Slatin. 'However,' [said Jackson] 'I put him into a bedroom and gave him some clothes and a cake of Sunlight Soap, and there came out a neat little Austrian gentleman.' Margaret thought Jackson had missed the opportunity of making a profit, by selling the story to the soap makers of the sort of transformation Sunlight Soap could effect.

Transferred to a bumpy stern-wheeler, the party set off towards Wadi Halfa and the Egyptian frontier with the Sudan. The fervour of the Holy War being unabated, the stern-wheelers were ordered to travel in a fleet of four, Sudanese soldiers being stationed on board. The boats anchored at night in mid-stream, where far from a barracks, as Margaret realistically wrote, there would have been little that could have been done had the dervishes attacked.

As it happened the only contretemps occurred in the supposed safety of Assouan, among the Bradley Martins from New York, who had also hired a stern-wheeler. Besides their daughter and her husband, Lord Craven, the American party included Mrs Sherman, mother of Mrs Bradley Martin. This kind old lady developed a sudden panic that dervishes had captured the boat and that the fact was being concealed from her. Implored by the

Bradley Martins to come and reassure her, Jersey was able to do so. It remained a mystery as to why she thought the dervishes had respected her cabin, and why she believed Lord Jersey, rather than her own family, which even included an earl among them in the shape of Lord Craven. Margaret's view, given with sardonic reserve, was that 'it is not uncommon for people to attach more weight to the opinion of an outsider that to that of the relatives whom they see every day'.

There had been some doubt as to whether the flotilla of stern-wheelers would be allowed to pass through Nubia, but, unimpeded, they chugged in moonlight past the glory of Abu Simbel, arriving, unchallenged by dervishes, at Wadi Halfa. Here the beasts of the Camel Corps were lying in rows, so well prepared for an advance that only water-bottles needed to be filled. A two hours' journey on a military railway line took the travellers to Sarras, the Egyptian frontier and the Fort that marked it. Out beyond the arid sandy hills held the threat of violent death. This was the Mahdi's country, from whence the dervishes pressed their attack on Egypt, caring nothing for losses, as fatal casualties would find themselves immediately in Paradise.

Eighteen months later, Margaret was able to write to congratulate her friend the Sirdar on the victory of Omdurman. She was always incensed when Kitchener was accused, as he was in the newspapers, of inhumanity towards the defeated. In refutation, in her memoirs, she quoted his reply to her letter of congratulation. Kitchener wrote that he had read a report that the wounded had been killed after the battle. On the contrary, when he left Omdurman there were six thousand dervishes in hospital, the over-worked army doctors being helped by Egyptian doctors released from the Mahdi's prisons. Bandages having given out, even first field-dressings had been requisitioned.

Both Kitchener and Margaret valued their friendship, he finding in her a confidante for his feelings of depression that, after Omdurman, there were no worlds left for him to conquer. Margaret's assurance that there would soon be work for this Alexander to do came true only too soon, for the South African War loomed almost immediately.

Great as was her admiration for Kitchener, having seen how he had dominated the Egyptian scene, Margaret could not resist feeling some pleasure when natural forces, on a purely frivolous occasion, went against him. Having spent a May afternoon at

Osterley sorting the Chinese china from the Japanese, which he despised, Kitchener felt the need of refreshment. After the arbitrary rejection of what may well have been valuable ceramics, he announced that it was time to go into the garden and pick strawberries, which he regarded as permanently ripe at Osterley. Although she was able to placate Kitchener with the hot-house strawberries that appeared at tea-time, Margaret enjoyed pointing out that not even a general of his distinction could command English strawberries to ripen out of doors in May.

18

The Victorian Finale

BY HER OWN account Margaret's engagement to marry had arranged itself with practical good sense, emotional disturbance being, it seems, limited to her grief at leaving home. Consequently, when dealing with the love affairs of others, she seldom saw why good sense, rather than passion, should not prevail. As has been seen, her sisters turned out to be incapable of following their elder's brilliant example, but Margaret did not, for many years, entirely give up hope for Agnes, less of an enemy to worldly pleasures than Cordelia. The story of Margaret's final attempt to transform her sister Aggie, then in her forties, into a married woman became a family legend passed on by her children to their children.

One cool summer evening at Osterley, Arthur, a schoolboy who had left the dining-room with the ladies, was told by his mother to sit beside his Aunt Aggie. She had been strategically placed in a chair beside the door which opened from the gallery onto the curving staircase. This descended to the garden, where many an engagement to marry had been clinched. When the gentlemen had finished sampling Lord Jersey's excellent cellar, they joined the ladies and Arthur was sent to bed, leaving the chair beside his aunt vacant, as his mother had planned. It was a natural sequence for the seat to be taken by a gentleman who, in Lady Jersey's opinion, needed only slight encouragement to propose to Miss Agnes Leigh.

In meek furtherance of this scheme, Agnes suggested a stroll in the garden. The couple passed through the double doors, which were promptly closed behind them by their hostess, in the determination that no third party should intervene. With the satisfaction that her friend Kitchener might have felt in a well-executed manœuvre, she turned to face the company, the look of triumph on her face making a lasting impression on her eldest daughter. Perhaps sunshine and strawberries were needed to bring a suitor up to scratch at Osterley. In any case the plot failed, the inclement evening being said to have induced colds, if not pneumonia, in the chief actors.

It was at about this date that Margaret conceived a practical joke, a throwback to the days when she had been a star in her Uncle Chandos's 'businesses' at Stoneleigh. The planning of the joke also showed how little, after twenty years of marriage, she had been impressed by her husband's touchiness. A caller, a lady, was announced one day to Lord Jersey. She wished particularly to discuss with him the success of his service in Australia, a success which had earned the lady's admiration. Pleased and flattered, Lord Jersey, rather touchingly, accepted this tribute without question. When it was revealed to him that the caller had been his brother-in-law, Dudley Leigh, in what would now be called drag, it became apparent that the joke had fallen catastrophically flat. Only the quick summons of his son Arthur from the children's wing, and the replay of the joke on him, enabled Lord Jersey to regain his composure.

Plays continued to be produced at Middleton, though Margaret's children lacked the uninhibited pleasure in performing that the Leighs and Cholmondeleys had enjoyed. Mary and Arthur suffered peculiar agonies from stage fright. Eventually it was Arthur's humiliation on the boards which caused his father to ban further theatrical productions. Tempers among the company were already frayed by an argument between the male leads as to the most effective way of dying on the stage, in a fine frenzy or with the dignity of pathos. At the actual performance the clash of personality was still absorbing the actors, so much so that Arthur, entering to deliver his solitary line, was waved off the stage with the words unspoken. In the manner of Sir Thomas Bertram in *Mansfield Park*, Lord Jersey then permanently disbanded the company of players, and, though his wife may have had regrets, his family were more solidly behind him than that of Jane Austen's baronet.

Margaret's own diary-keeping was an intermittent affair, but her daughter Mary had more regular habits. Her journal often reflected aspects of her mother which contrasted with Lady Jersey's public character. Details were sometimes difficult to decipher, partly from a handwriting of weirdly Gothic convolution and partly from an attempt at code, different, and sometimes inconsistent, forms of the letter 'M' standing for either her mother or her sister Markie. Much as the Villiers children admired their mother, their confidence was given among themselves rather than to her. When Fräulein Witzell married an English doctor, her pupils were her bridesmaids and their father gave her away. The family still loved her, but Mary wrote in her diary that 'Frl', or Ina as she now wished to be called, would be lost to her as a confidante, and that Mary herself must now seek for another.

Villiers, it seems, hardly even gave his confidence to his sisters, though he would play billiards with Mary. She once noted that their 'relations', presumably meaning parents, might well be surprised at the opinions that she and her brother shared on family matters. The awe with which his parents treated him could sometimes shield a sister from their father's temper. Lord Jersey would show annoyance if, on hunting days, his daughter Beatrice came home later than he did, but would accept meekly her persistence in staying out if she could say she had come home with Villiers.

Among Villiers' correct assessments of the power of his own position, was his request to the station-master of Bletchley that the Scotch express might be specially halted on a night that Villiers wished to go North. The station-master obliged, and set a family standard for wresting railways to an individual purpose that was put to even more dramatic use by Markie Villiers. She, accidentally finding herself in a express that was not due to stop at Oxford, her destination, invoked her friendship with the Oxford station-master to such effect that the guard was persuaded to throw out a message at Reading. This resulted in an unscheduled halt at Oxford in the middle of the tracks. There she was helped down by the station-master, who said, reproachfully, 'My lady, my lady, you didn't ought to have done it.'

Less successful was the Jerseys' attempt to establish Villiers in a local constituency, to his mother a natural first step on the path of political distinction for a clever eldest son. The Conservative party of Banbury, conveniently near to Middleton, needed to adopt a candidate, and Lord Villiers was among the aspirants. According to his sister Mary, while expressing his willingness to campaign at election time, he made it clear that he was not prepared to nurse the constituency beforehand. Understandably, the local Conservatives adopted a candidate with more accommodating views. For a while the Jerseys, affronted, put Banbury into disgrace.

Besides the entries in her diary concerning gardening and bicycling at Middleton, tennis and boating at Osterley, Mary noted the public works which occupied so much of her mother's time. At Middleton afternoon drives were frequently directed to dealing with village problems. Lord Jersey's moral boundaries were rigid in their geographical application. On his estate he condemned the Sunday opening of public houses, and the actual birth of children conceived out of wedlock. He achieved success on the former point by only granting leases which prohibited alcoholic consumption on Sunday. Over the question of illegitimate children his attitude, possibly a reaction from the gallantries of his ancestresses, was no deterrent. 'Another scandal in the village,' his daughter Mary wrote, 'the second this year. Why don't people *think*?'

At Osterley, where there was no village for which Lord Jersey could lay down moral regulations, the summer was marked by tea-parties for the schoolchildren of the neighbourhood and for the many charities, such as the Arethusa Homes, founded by the philanthropic Lord Shaftesbury, and the children's Happy Evenings, in which Lady Jersey interested herself. The daughters of the house rowed relays of these guests on the lake. This proved inadequate training, when one of them ventured onto the Thames with a boatload of girls from the East End of London. Ignorant of the rules of the river, the oarswoman and her passengers were threatened with swamping by a pleasure steamer. As she said herself, Lady Jersey was perennially in demand as a prize-giver, and she seems to have been adept at making bricks without straw. Her daughter Mary wrote sardonically, 'Mama made an excellent speech, all about nothing.'

Since 1872, the year of his marriage, Lord Jersey had been Senior Partner of Child's Bank. This gave his family a ringside seat whenever the Sovereign drove into the City, for at Temple Bar, exactly opposite the Bank, it was the Lord Mayor's duty to offer the Pearl Sword to the reigning Monarch. When Queen Elizabeth I had presented this beautiful weapon to the City, the Lord Mayor had been Lady Jersey's ancestor, Sir Thomas Leigh. Two of Jersey's forebears, in the eighteenth century, had been Lord Mayors. These Childs, a father and son both called Francis, had been painted with the Pearl Sword in their hands. Princess Lieven and Lady Palmerston might exchange sneers about the banking blood of Sarah Lady Jersey, but at the Diamond Jubilee the advantage of such an ancestry was obvious.

Soon to celebrate their Golden Wedding, Lord and Lady Leigh joined their daughter and son-in-law on the balcony of Child's Bank. From there they watched the Lord Mayor, Sir George Faudel-Phillips, offer the Pearl Sword to Her Majesty, receive it back, then, in his mayoral robes, leap onto his horse. Having accomplished this feat, one, alas, no longer required of Lord Mayors, he rode before the Queen to St Paul's, bearing the sword. Although the Lord Mayor comported himself perfectly, to the watchers on the bacony the mantle flying in the air irresistibly recalled John Gilpin.

It was, however, Lady Northcote, another guest, who scored the most spectacular tribute. Meeting three Field-Marshals shortly before the celebrations, she complained, in joke, of the futility of knowing such senior soldiers, if they did not salute her on public occasions. This, at Temple Bar, they all three obligingly did, but the most splendidly exotic homage came from Lord Roberts, the Jerseys' friend from their days in Lucknow. He was riding at the head of the Colonial and Asiatic troops on a white Arab horse which had carried him throughout the Afghan War, and during his command in India. The horse was wearing the Afghan medal and the Kandahar Star, conferred by Queen Victoria. With his much decorated rider, they made a magnificent pair when Lord Roberts wheeled round to salute Lady Northcote on the balcony of Child's Bank. An evening paper, under the impression that the Field-Marshal was saluting the City, even congratulated him on a 'fine thing finely done'.

The Jerseys were invited to Windsor in the May of the following year, when Margaret, talking to Queen Victoria of the Jubilee celebrations, hoped that their fervour had not unduly exhausted the object to whom they were addressed. With some pathos, the Queen said that she had not been tired on the day when she had driven to give thanks at St Paul's, but by the end of a month of loyal junketing she had begun to wilt. As it happened the year 1898 was to see celebrations, accompanied by some drama, in two generations of Margaret's own family.

To their parents the Villiers girls had grown up to be all that could be desired. The eldest wrote her father's letters every

morning. All the daughters filled in the invitations to the Osterley
garden parties from a list which, though many, commoners came
between, began with the Duke of Abercorn, his name beginning
with AB and leading all the rest like Abou Ben Adhem's. The list
ended with Lord Zouche, last on the register as he was last in the
Peerage. The girls also shielded their mother from the necessity
of playing picquet with their father. The fairy at her christening,
who had withheld the gift of a musical ear, had also failed to be-
stow even an elementary card sense.

It would, however, be unfair to say that Lord Jersey could not,
at moments, reveal a smiling face behind a frowning countenance,
as Cowper wrote of the Almighty in one of the Olney hymns.
Mary Villiers' hands might tremble so much from terror of her
parent at picquet that she had difficulty in picking up her cards,
but her diary records generous gifts of jewellery on her birthdays.
When a waiter had ruined her ball gown by spilling sauce over
it, her father, happening to overhear of the disaster, bade her buy
a new one at his expense.

It would also be unfair to say of Lady Jersey, as Jane Austen
wrote of Mrs Bennet in *Pride and Prejudice,* that the business of
her life was to get her daughters married. As has been seen, she
had a thousand other businesses on her mind, but when the date
for Beatrice's coming-out drew inexorably nearer, she began to
look with a sharper eye on the admirers of her eldest daughter.
The eye was not, on all occasions, as sharp as its owner imagined.
Writing of a ball where a ban on Markie Villiers dancing with
one particular young man was supposed to be in force, her
younger sister noted, '——never noticed that——danced three
times with——'. 'Mama' and 'Markie' can be filled in the first two
blanks, but the hero of the episode remains for ever mysterious,
with a wide range from which to choose.

House parties were generally considered to be a more fruitful
scene for making matches than the chances of the ballroom. Convention dictated that an unmarried girl could not stay in a house
of other than her near kindred, unless accompanied by at least one
parent, or a brother who would be accepted as a chaperon. A
Christ Church friend of Villiers, Walter Rice, was therefore
allowed to entertain Villiers and his two sisters at Dynevor Castle
in Carmarthenshire, where the Rice family had lived for five
hundred years. Their surname had been anglicized in spelling and
pronunciation from the Welsh Rhys. Walter Rice (when Lord

Dynevor) restored the original spelling, and in due course his grandson reverted to the Welsh pronunciation.

Lady Dynevor was dead, so a cousin was imported to act as hostess for the bearded Lord Dynevor. With one exception the rest of the male guests were contemporaries of Walter Rice, including Lord Jedburgh, the brother of Lord Ancram accidentally shot in New South Wales. The exception was Sir Everard Doyle, who belonged to an earlier generation. He was thought to have placed too much confidence in Markie's attractive manner, to the extent of beginning to collect household goods with an eye to setting up a conjugal home. Smitten by Markie's charm, Sir Everard was physically bowled over by her sister Beatrice, when he made a facetious attempt to halt her bicycle and the brakes failed to respond.

In the group photograph of this house party Markie leans somewhat aloofly against a pillar of the verandah, on which, had she known it, she was to preside over the tea-pot for nearly sixty years. Several romances were to bloom and wither, and two years were to pass before she accepted Walter Rice as her future husband, his proposal being made on the roof at Osterley. In the interval Mrs Bourne, retired to Bicester from her position as nurse at Middleton, had cross-examined Mary on the prospect of an engagement, leaving her former charge with the feeling that she and her sisters were hanging fire. Lady Jersey herself claimed that she had had to point out to her daughter that it was only possible to marry one among a number of admirers.

Unabashed by her failure to arrange a marriage for her sister Agnes, Margaret turned her attention to the prospects of her second daughter. Much shaken by the abrupt solution of her elder sister's complicated affairs of the heart, Mary was careful to keep her own fancies to herself, particularly after an experience of the way her parents could jump to unwarranted conclusions.

In the face of all the evidence, Lord Jedburgh had asked Mary, as daughter of the former Governor-General, whether it was possible that the shooting accident which had killed his elder brother might have been not entirely accidental. (After this tragedy, the family decided to leave the name of Ancram sacred to the memory of the eldest son, Jedburgh being another title in the Lothian peerage.) Acting, as she thought, sympathetically, Mary suggested that Lord Jedburgh should come down to Osterley to see her father, who could assure him that such idea about his brother's death was preposterous. The Jersey's immediately deduced that to ask such a question suggested a degree of confidence between their daughter and this eligible young man greater than that of mere acquaintance, and Mary had the embarrassment of disabusing them.

Mary was also conscious that her mother thought that Lord Beauchamp was showing a gratifying amount of interest in her second daughter. The Jerseys took Mary with them to stay at Madresfield Court, Lord Beauchamp's moated home, but though she found the house charming, her friendship with the host did not become a courtship. Neither did Lord Jedburgh, who was also present, show signs of warmer feelings. However Lord Beauchamp's second cousin, Lord Longford, an officer in the Life Guards, was at once impressed by Mary Villiers' liveliness, and the fair good looks which suggested Greek goddesses to his classic-loving mind. Lord Longford was also a third cousin of Walter Rice, so he was able to improve his acquaintance with Mary Villiers at her sister's wedding.

Between the engagement of the Jerseys' eldest daughter and her wedding, there was a gathering at Stoneleigh to celebrate the Golden Wedding of Lord and Lady Leigh. The family group brought together a fine array of kindred, many of whom have been heard of in the course of Margaret's life story. She herself was seated beside her father, with a more lively expression of happiness on her face than she usually showed when being photographed with her husband and children. On the other side of Lord Leigh sat Hélène, daughter of his heir, her profile slightly turned as she preferred it to be, and her dress of a studied richness, worthy of the Court of Napoleon III where she had been a young beauty. The sadness of her childlessness was emphasized by her neighbour Mrs Cholmondeley, her husband's aunt, who had, at that date, nine living sons and daughters.

At the end of the row behind stood Rowland Leigh, the youngest Leigh son and the favourite of his mother. His response to this partiality was enigmatic. If she asked him where he was going, he would reply 'not far'. If she asked to where his letters should be forwarded, he would say that he had told the butler. His chief interest was in racing, and in later life he would sometimes expand to tell the story of being summoned by telegraph from the Goodwood Meeting to represent his father at a relation's funeral. The telegram promised him five pounds for performing this duty. At the church he was met by a gardener from Stoneleigh with a wreath, a five pound note in an envelope and instructions from Lord Leigh to see that Mr Rowland signed the accompanying receipt. ('Papa knew you, Rowley', his sisters would say at this point in the story.) Regarding his duty as discharged, he then approached the chief mourner and inquired as to the time of the first train that would carry him back to Goodwood. He was told, curtly, that the business of interment must be finished before consulting the time-table.

At the time of his parents' Golden Wedding, Rowland Leigh had been engaged for seven years to a charming American girl. To choose an American bride was almost a habit in the Leigh family, but Mabel Gordon, unlike Fanny Butler or Helène Beckwith, came from a family impoverished by the Civil War. Although constant in love, Rowland seemed unable or unwilling to desert the comforts of Stoneleigh in order to earn what his sister Margaret once called 'sufficient provision for matrimony'. Meeting him in New York, Henry James called Rowland, 'Lady Jersey in trousers', but the resemblance was physical, his inward fires being banked while hers blazed. However, in the glow of the Golden Wedding, the long engagement was brought to a happy ending. Someone had the inspiration of turning Rowland's knowledge of the form of every horse in training to professional use. He was said never to bet, which qualified him to be appointed a handicapper to the Jockey Club. Here he dictated the weights that horses should carry for thirty years, only when he retired was he at last able to back his fancy.

Next to Rowland in the group, stood one of Mrs Cholmondeley's daughters, and next to her Alice Leigh, called by Henry James 'that handsome and natural Alice'. Almost concealed behind another Cholmondeley daughter stood Mrs Chandos Leigh, who had consulted planchette before accepting her husband. On this occasion Mary Villiers' hat was well up to her eccentric standard, though it was a close-run thing between her and the cousin beside her, one of the fifteen children of Lady Leigh's sister Lady Macclesfield. In the centre of the group, Lord Jersey peered out from an open glass door, over-topping his small sister-in-law, Cordelia, whose muslin and ostrich plumes were only too clearly temperamentally unsympathetic to her. Typically obscured, Agnes Leigh could only just be seen, peering round a Cholmondeley granddaughter, whose father had died nearly a year before but

for whom she was still in mourning, a black crow among the pea-
cocks.

Margaret Villiers, newly engaged, showed that, put on with the
right dash, ostrich plumes could enhance the wearer. Beside her
the rubicund Chandos Leigh had such an air of hearty extroversion
that it is easy to believe that, as his niece wrote, he was innocently
convinced that his affairs were of as much interest to others as to
himself. Lord Norton, aged eighty-four, stood at the end of the
line. His wife, Lord Leigh's sister, had passed on her family's
histrionic talents, particularly to a son, Father Adderley, whose
High Church practice was of an exoticism that frequently left his
congregation floundering in confusion. Two clergymen were
actually present, seated on the ground. James Leigh, Dean of Here-
ford and father of Alice, still wore the white tie that was by then
going out of fashion for parsons. One look at his mobile face
would suggest that his rendering of *Alonzo the Brave and the Fair
Imogene* would hardly need a white sheet to make its dramatic
impact. He had cast an arm round the shoulders of yet another
Cholmondeley, Lionel, who devoted much of his life to tilling
the stony mission field in Japan.

In the centre of the group sat Lord Leigh, handsome and
benign, but his loved and loving wife was not beside him. Lady
Leigh's absence from the scene of which she was the heroine might
be considered startling, if her habit of ruling her dominions in-
directly is not remembered. Accustomed to her fifty years of un-
challenged supremacy, none of her subjects would have
questioned her decision to leave her husband alone as the centre
piece of the group. Actually, as well as charm and generosity, he
had a modesty about his own position which embarrassed his
granddaughter Markie. He took every opportunity to deflect congratulations to Markie and her fiancé, who were starting on the
course which he had, himself, so happily run. It was a golden sun-
set, the Abbey's vicissitudes of the past forgotten, when through
a double rank of powdered footmen the family of the patriarch
entered the home that had seen the birth of so many of them.

Lady Northcote showed practical friendship, by giving the
reception for the wedding of Markie Villiers', and putting up the
whole family as well. Hardly had Lady Margaret Rice made her
appearance in her own neighbourhood as a married woman, wearing the tiara that had been her father's wedding present, when
Lady Northcote had reason to make the same gesture on behalf

of Mary Villiers. This second daughter, on moving up in the family, had not found the advantages undiluted. She had inherited her sister's duty of writing her father's letters, a task made onerous by his habit of making false starts, 'Dear Mr Smith,' 'Dear Sir', 'Lord Jersey presents his compliments,' Mary's handwriting was both spidery and emphatic, so perhaps it was as well that matrimony freed her after only a year of secretarial duties.

Years of work and travel seem to have blotted out Lady Jersey's recollection of the days when she herself was considered to be delicate. She totally failed to notice that sitting on the back seat of a carriage made her second daughter feel queasy. Mary's hopes that she would be promoted to sit facing the horses when her sister married were dashed. It was not considered that the young couple could afford a carriage, although Walter Rice was heir to a castle and an estate. Consequently, missing her eldest daughter more than she might have been prepared to admit, Margaret invited Markie to drive with her on most afternoons, the carriage-sick Mary being again relegated to the back seat.

Besides feeling sick when driving, Mary also suffered from what would now be recognized as an allergy, but was then called simply 'spots'. She was distressed enough to appeal to her mother, and to ask for medical advice. This did little to help her, her mother treating a consultation as a social call, a complaint to be mentioned apologetically when more interesting topics had been exhausted. A diet was, indeed, recommended, but this was not an idea that appealed to Lady Jersey in her housekeeping capacity, and the diet remained theoretical.

If there had been maternal interference over Markie's love affairs, Mary's were unobserved by her mother. Her most favoured partner was far from being an eldest son and, though she drove to meets of the Bicester Hounds where she knew she would meet him, she havered as to the amount of encouragement she felt inclined to give. A sudden crisis took place when Lord Longford appeared, uninvited, on a Sunday afternoon at Osterley. Unlike 'Pom' McDonnell, he was in search of a wife rather than a statesman. To Lord and Lady Jersey he was such a vague acquaintance that Lord Jersey could not even remember his name. When Mary told her parents of the offer she had received which she contemplated accepting, they made something of a fuss about Lord Longford's character and resources, subjects on which they were totally uninformed. Then it was remembered that he was a third cousin of Walter Rice, Longford's mother having been one of a family of heiresses, from whom the Dynevor peerage and Castle had passed to Walter's grandfather.

Walter was able to assure his parents-in-law that Longford was a man much respected and financially sound, his mother's branch of the Rice family having taken from Dynevor a fortune of a size to cause complaint to later generations. The engagement was announced, and the fiancés made their first appearance together at an Osterley garden party. On this occasion a fashion-writer reported that Lady Jersey was dressed in a gown of electric blue, which must have been helpful to guests in search of their hostess. The wedding, for which Lady Northcote was to repeat her hospitality of the year before, was postponed till November to allow for the recovery of Margaret Rice from the birth of her first child. Certainly delighted by the prospect of a grandchild for herself and a great-grandchild for her own parents, Margaret had displayed less than her usual forthright good sense at the time of her daughter's wedding. The prospect of children was only alluded to obliquely, by saying that it would be wise to choose a house with two spare bedrooms.

In the months before Mary's wedding, which would take her to live in an Irish castle she had not yet seen, Beatrice and Arthur made no attempt to conceal their despondency. They felt, acutely, the loss of a sister whose devotion had been a buffer between them and the mysterious whims of the grown-ups. It is not recorded if Margaret gave her daughters the sensible advice of her own mother, not to think that one way of doing things was the only right one. If she passed on this counsel, it had little effect on Mary Longford, who, even in widely different circumstances, never thought things done rightly if they varied to any great degree from the manners and customs of her father's house.

Easily stirred to writing verse on private and public events, Margaret composed a hymn that was printed in gold on a card for the christening of her grandson Charles Arthur Uryan Rice at St George's, Hanover Square. The hymn admonished the baby to grow up to be a soldier of the Lord, but when, a few weeks later, the family reassembled in the same church for the wedding of Mary Villiers and Captain Lord Longford to be a soldier had taken on a sombre meaning. A black shadow, the South African War, had fallen across the evening of Queen Victoria's reign, and no one could pretend that the bridegroom would not soon be in its penumbra. By the following March, at the desire of Margaret's old friend, Lord Roberts, Longford had raised the Irish Horse. Having seen her husband sail from Cork on a troopship bound for Cape Town, Mary returned to Middleton for a long visit. Her mother tried to make this comfortingly homelike by giving her daughter the bedroom that had been her maiden bower. Mary appreciated this gesture, but she later admitted that she had only really believed in herself as a married woman when she and her husband were installed in the most imposing of visitor's bedrooms.

The South African War, harrowing as it was, in no way affected ordinary travel. Sir Stafford Northcote's appointment as Governor of Bombay gave the Jerseys another splendid excuse for a visit to India, taking their daughter Beatrice with them. It was on this journey that Beatrice noticed her father's sensible approach to the problem of shopping when travelling. He put his dressing-case inside an empty suitcase, so that he could fill it with objects that took his fancy.

Following her policy of not reproducing guide-book material, Margaret only mentioned in passing the new experience of visiting the rock temples of Ellora, making no mention of the five-hundred-year-old avenue of banyan trees that leads to them or the great fortress of Daulatabad that towers above. However, a return to Hyderabad led to such an extraordinary visit that she could not help describing it, remote as it was from the ordinary material of guide-books.

Always getting on well with Prime Ministers, Margaret was invited by the Vikar (Prime Minister) of Hyderabad to call on his wife, the sister of the Nizam. This call was made when the sudden Indian night had fallen, and the caller was welcomed by women in red saris bearing torches, as it might be beldames guarding the Gate of Tartarus, the gate itself leading into a chamber resembling the Hall of Eblis. In these hellish surroundings the Princess sat on a chair, her bare feet uncomfortably extended before her, her rich gold and green sari and her jewels glowing in the uncertain light of the torches. What went on in the recesses of the unearthly hall, Margaret could not clearly see, and felt it was perhaps better not to look. A prospective daughter-in-law crouched at the Princess's feet, but her son and a stepson standing by were incongruously dressed in smart English evening clothes. In fact, with their perfect command of English, Margaret thought that they might have stepped out of the Bachelors' Club, had it not been for their mitre shaped head-dresses, a sign of belonging to the family of the Nizam.

After this visit to the infernal regions, the Jerseys spent the happiest of Christmases with the Northcotes in Bombay. There was none of the sourness of Kipling's *Christmas in India*, but the party sailed for home in a mood of foreboding. News had come of the illness of the Queen and Empress, and though few could bring themselves to admit aloud that this might well be the end of her reign and her life, the thought was inescapably present. At Aden, Margaret awoke in her cabin to hear the voice of someone on deck announcing the end of an age, 'She went off very quietly,' the voice said, and the hearer had no need to ask who was meant.

Middleton Park, Christmas 1904. *Back row*; Viscount Villiers, Honble Arthur Villiers, Honble Walter Rice with Imogen Rice, Lord Dunsany, Earl of Jersey. *Front row*; Earl of Longford, Lord Silchester, Countess of Longford with Lady Pansy Pakenham, Elwyn Rice, Lady Margaret Rice, Lady Dunsany, Countess of Jersey, Charles Rice

The Library at Middleton
Park

Margaret, Countess of Jersey,
on her 90th birthday, October
29th, 1939

My 90th Birthday
October 29th 1939
M. E. Jersey

19

The New Century

CONTRARY TO WHAT is often promulgated, the death of Queen
Victoria did not immediately create a void in London society that
was filled by an Edwardian bacchanalia. The Court was, naturally,
transformed, now that a Queen, who had mourned for almost
half her life, had been succeeded by a King who had spent much
of his in revelry. On the other hand Lady Jersey and her contemporaries continued to carry out public duties unaffected by
the new reign. Although he was only a few years her senior,
Margaret does not seem to have had any close acquaintance
with King Edward. There was, however, one episode in which
she had had experience of the unpleasant manners of one of his
friends.

This incident took place at a dinner party at which Margaret,
by her own account a comparatively young woman, happened
to be seated near Sir William Gordon-Cumming, a baronet and
an officer in the Scots Guards, a man about the same age as herself.
For reasons that were not clear, Sir William settled down to shock
Lady Jersey by sniping at her with remarks that he mistakenly imagined would discompose her. Naturally she resented the idea that
she would give voice to her horror when Sir William announced
that he had broken all the commandments except 'Thou shalt do
no murder,' and that, he said, he had broken in his heart. Her dislike of Sir William Gordon-Cumming, self-confessed idolator,
adulterer and thief, might be said to have been vindicated when,
in 1891, the Tranby Croft card scandal became public knowledge.
Accused of cheating at baccarat, Sir William declared he was innocent, but also gave an unwise undertaking never to play cards
again. Consequently he found himself obliged to bring a libel suit,
in which the Prince of Wales, a fellow guest at Tranby Croft, was

called as a witness. Queen Victoria's distress was great and anti-monarchists had a day on the moors.

Her experience with Sir William was only a footnote of social life to Margaret. She was in no way prejudiced against the King. Indeed when she came to sum up her life in the twentieth century she firmly linked King Edward VII and his son King George V as 'two great Kings' and their wives as 'gracious Queens'. It was, however, to keeping alive the memory of the Queen Empress as the mother of her Empire that Margaret's attention was immediately turned.

On April 2nd 1901, when the Queen had been dead for three months, a meeting was convened of distinguished ladies with the object of founding a society to draw British subjects throughout the world more closely together. The ladies met at 10 Downing Street, at the invitation of Arthur Balfour's sister, he being now Prime Minister. Like the other ladies Margaret was still wearing deep mourning for the Queen, but of this sable company she was the one asked to take the chair and told that it was proposed to make her the first President. She had been given no chance to refuse, and modestly wrote that, as the plan was to keep the society free from party politics, she was chosen as one whose husband had no ministerial pretensions. In addition there was her wide experience of the peoples whom the Victoria League, as it was christened, wished to bind with the bonds of friendship and hospitality.

It was at this point that Margaret Jersey brought *Fifty-One Years of Victorian Life* to an end, but her own life continued to expand. Her appointment as first President of the Victoria League was the happiest of inspirations. A member of the committee, experienced in many meetings, described its first President as the best chairman under whom she had ever sat, but the President also knew well that it is hospitality that warms the heart of visitors.

At long range from the Antipodes, she had promoted the English tour of an Australian politician, watching his supposed Republicanism dissolve in the warmth of his welcome. Besides this lesson, she had learnt that no party is a success into which the hostess does not throw her heart. Her heart was completely thrown into the setting up of the new league, the executive committee meeting fourteen times in the first eight months after its formation. With an impeccable record as chairman, she steered a skilful course among rival organizations, set up with equal good will towards the Empire but with less sense of direction, the fledgling

Victoria League growing in weight while other societies eva-
porated.

News of the birth of Mary Longford's eldest son was tele-
graphed triumphantly to Delhi where, in the winter of 1902 the
Jerseys had gone yet again to visit the Northcotes. Mary had been
handicapped in the race to produce grandchildren by her husband's absence in South Africa, but after his return she made up
for lost time, giving birth to three children in less than three years.
The object of the visit to Delhi was to see the Durbar of King
Edward VII, at which the camp of the Governor of Bombay lay
next to that of the Commander-in-Chief, Lord Kitchener. He was
not on the happiest terms with the Viceroy, Lord Curzon, another
frequenter of Osterley. Possibly wishing to assert his superiority
over all, including the Viceroy, Kitchener tried vainly to persuade
Lady Jersey that his camp, in which there was a rich display of
presentation plate, was more imposing than Lord Northcote's.
When Kitchener claimed that he had a fender seat which Lady
Northcote had not, Margaret retorted that the Northcotes had a
billiards table. Having a London house big enough to include a
billiards room, Lord Northcote seems to have regarded the game
as a necessity of life, even among the splendours of a Durbar.

The summer of 1902 had seen the end of Arthur Villiers' Eton
career. It should have ended in a blaze of glory, playing in the
Eton XI against Harrow at Lords, a match that was an event of
the London Season as well as a sporting contest. In his first innings
Arthur was out for a duck, and his parents showed a lack of intelli-
gence by sitting gloomily at home, instead of seeking to cheer
their son by taking him out to a theatre. Next day Arthur was
again out for a duck. His comment to his anguished father, 'But,
Papa, its only a game,' showed commendable balance in trying
circumstances. His mother fled from Lord's Cricket Ground in
disgust, but her daughter Mary loyally remained and was rewarded by seeing her brother make a catch. She was never afterwards separated from a miniature of Arthur in the pale blue cap
of the Eton XI.

Going up to Oxford, Arthur showed that he had inherited his
father's turn of speed, getting a half-blue for the three-mile. His
Oxford friends naturally came to Middleton, as his brother's had
done in earlier years. One in particular, Gerald Wellesley, was to
have an immense influence on Arthur's life. He also had an impression of the Jerseys as a couple at variance with those who saw a

benign matriarch and a stormy male parent. Lady Jersey was to him an object of awe, rather than liking. He supported his view of her by quoting John Hugh Smith, who, as one of the American novelist Edith Wharton's court, was qualified to judge forceful women. Lady Jersey's complete assurance of her own social position, John Hugh Smith said, was only equalled by that of senior non-commissioned officers in the Brigade of Guards.

On the other hand Gerald Wellesley found Lord Jersey the most charming of hosts, kind and generous to his son's friend. This affectionate feeling survived a visit when Arthur's relations with his father were strained by a financial crisis, which must have had baleful implications to those aware of past family history. Many fortunes have been lost at roulette by those who persistently double their losses on the same number. Arthur had adopted this principle with his racing bets, and in consequence had the choice of asking his father for funds or facing his creditors with empty pockets. A report of this incident may have inspired Hilaire Belloc's verses on Lord Hippo, who in the same straits approached his father with the words,

'Dread Sire – to-day, at Ascot, I . . .'
His genial parent made reply:
'Come! Come! Come! Come! don't look so glum!
Trust your Papa and name the sum . . .
. . . Fifteen hundred-thousand, . . . Hum!'

These verses were illustrated by Basil Blackwood, Lord Hippo bearing a striking likeness to Arthur's brother Villiers, which seems to show a connection with the Villiers family, though Villiers was famous for his good luck with his bets.

If the actual scene between Arthur and his father was less dramatic than Lord Hippo's with 'his Sire the Earl of Potamus', it gave Gerald Wellesley the first hint that Arthur might develop into a financial genius. The racing debts presented to Lord Jersey added up, his son said, to some thousands of pounds. Gloom lay over the house throughout Sunday, neither of the young men being, presumably, aware that Lord Jersey was not in a strong position for making a fuss about a *débâcle* on the race-course. On Sunday evening Arthur faced his father for the second time. He had cast up his debts again, he said, and found that they were half what he had first supposed. Lord Jersey, in relief, handed over a cheque. Arthur settled his debts on the Monday, and went on to

become what an immensely experienced broker described as the
wisest investor on the stockmarket that he had ever known.

Lord Jersey's temper towards his younger children was notoriously light on the trigger, but it was unusual for Margaret to lose
her self-control. However this occurred when Beatrice revealed
her attachment to a young man whose prospects were unpromising. The gentle Beatrice was swept by a storm of wrath from both
her parents, her mother's anger being more frightening for its in-
frequency. It may have been Margaret's time of life which made
her nerves less easy to control, and she may also have been
affected by the illness of Lady Galloway. This ended in death in
August 1903. On receiving the news by telegram, as most news
was received in Ireland, Mary Longford wrote in her diary of her
godmother's generosity, adding, 'So that is the last of Lady G.'
Some consolation for Margaret came a week later when her first
granddaughter, to be called Imogen, was born at Middleton. The
telegram to Mary Longford said the baby looked as if she might
be pretty, a better prediction than many made over the cradles
of the new-born.

In the summer of 1904 Beatrice Villiers was twenty-three years
old. Her previous suitor had faded from the scene, but she was
admired by a brother of John Hugh Smith. This was something
of a family habit, as yet another brother had been the favourite
dancing partner of her sister Mary. Beatrice's own eyes, however,
were now set on young Lord Dunsany, who drove one of the
earliest motor-cars. When motoring was still a heady, new
adventure chauffeurs were not, perhaps, easily to be found. Dunsany solved the problem by ordering one from the firm that
supplied his motor-car. The unorthodox transaction was a brilliant
success. The two families remained united, one of the chauffeur's
many daughters being with Beatrice Dunsany when she died in
her ninetieth year. Dunsany and Beatrice were married in the
church at Middleton. Among the presents was a writing desk
equipped with a china slate on which the week's engagements
could be written. Dunsany wrote in the space for Thursday, 'To
be married – weather permitting'.

Weather permitted, and Margaret now found herself with three
sons-in-law who lived in Celtic castles, staging posts in the summer tours that became part of her life when a widow. Walter,
her host at Dynevor Castle, proceeded to make a useful, if
unspectacular niche for himself, first as Conservative M.P. for

Brighton and then, after his father's death, in the House of
Lords. To his mother-in-law his career may have lacked the
glamour of high office, but it was one that she recognized as
honourably useful.

Although Longford, husband of Mary Villiers, was the holder
of an Irish earldom, he also sat assiduously in the House of Lords
as Baron Silchester in the Peerage of the United Kingdom. A more
serious professional soldier than Rupert Leigh, 'the Captain of
Hussars', Longford had no settled English home until he retired
from the Household Cavalry. Margaret, however, regularly
crossed the Irish Sea to visit Pakenham Hall in Co. Westmeath.
Here she found her daughter installed in a Gothic Revival castle,
in which Mary Longford lived by the domestic standards she had
learnt in her mother's house. Outside Margaret found differences
from the phlegmatic habits of the English Midlands. Gates and
their posts, she learnt, had to be made respectively of iron and
stone to prevent appropriation for firewood. Strolling with her
pregnant daughter, she was startled to see a man concealed behind
a tree near the path. Undaunted, she went to inquire the reason
for this furtive behaviour, to be assured that it only came from
a wish not to cause offence.

Strange behaviour might take place outside the walls of Pakenham, but through the interior of Dunsany Castle blew the gale
of its owner's capricious personality. From holding only an Irish
peerage, Dunsany was qualified to stand for Parliament, which
he did as a Conservative for a Wiltshire constituency in 1906. He
was among the casualties of the Liberal landslide, but his mother-
in-law, a veteran in politics, considered an additional factor in his
defeat had been speeches too clever for the comprehension of his
audience. At the time she did not know that, in marrying Beatrice,
Dunsany had acquired an audience for the writing he had begun
to practise, an audience full of the appreciation lacking among
the Wiltshire electors.

As Dunsany developed as a writer, his mother-in-law appreciated the poetry and fantasy of his work, but she never, it seemed,
entirely distinguished him from the cultivated, but essentially
amateur, writers as she was herself, and her mother had been
before her. On his side, Dunsany was galled by this attitude,
as well as by his mother-in-law's frequent suggestion that ideas
based on imaginative supposition should be checked by reference
to history book or classical dictionary. He called this desire for

facts a bludgeoning of the conversation. Finally, and literally, it was Dunsany who had the last word, for it was he who composed Lady Jersey's entry in the *Dictionary of National Biography*.

With a flourish the first of a new generation had been commemorated when Lord and Lady Leigh, Lord and Lady Jersey and Walter and Margaret Rice had been photographed with Charles Rice, a curly-headed baby, on his mother's knee. Age had not eroded Lady Leigh's position as the dominant force in her family. When her granddaughters married she did not hesitate to demote her unmarried daughters to a position where they could be arbitarily silenced should she wish to hear the opinion these girls, still in their twenties but with the status of matrons, might have to offer. Death was one force that even Lady Leigh could not control, but when, in 1905, it came to her husband she behaved with her customary determination. Long after, herself in her nineties, Margaret wrote that her mother had only survived her father for a few months.

'. . . they remained lovers to the end . . . I shall never forget the gleam on her face when I said, "Give Papa our love" with that gleam she died. Six of us standing round her bed.' The closeness of mother and daughter was thus ended by death, but the message of love to the next world was given and received in perfect confidence that it would be delivered.

With Lord Leigh's death the title and the Abbey of Stoneleigh passed to his son Dudley, husband of Hélène, the beauty of the Second Empire. Dudley, Duddy or Duds, according to the speaker's familiarity, had inherited his father's charm, but the unpracticality of his nature made for business difficulties. In his travels he had collected a fine heap of odds and ends, souvenirs from the Rockies, examples of native crafts from Bombay, pink satin slippers suggesting champagne suppers in private rooms. His social round was equally all-embracing, for besides his visits to the midgets and dwarfs of the Christmas circus, already mentioned, he was said to attend faithfully every function set out in To-Day's Events in *The Times*.

Her brother's succession to the family honours did nothing to change Margaret's attitude of affectionate tolerance towards him. There was also pity mixed with amusement at Hélène Leigh's determination to keep pace with her husband's remorseless activity. Hélène, thought to be somewhat older than it was polite to mention, shared a faith in fortune-tellers with her friend the Empress

Eugénie, and clung to belief in one who had promised her that she would bear a child. Dudley's well-known kindness of heart did not include apprehension of physical frailty. It was thought that the rigours of Hélène's life might have shortened it, for she died less than four years after becoming Lady Leigh. Consequently Agnes Leigh returned to Stoneleigh, after this brief absence, to housekeep for her brother, and continue her life's work of giving way to the convenience of others.

Meanwhile young Lord Villiers had become famous on the race-course, after an Oxford career in which he had not troubled to read for a degree. In his early thirties he was elected to the Jockey Club, where he became such a strong influence that the 1914 Act, restricting admission to the stud-book until 1949, was known as the Jersey Act.

If his pattern of life did not have his mother's entire sympathy (or, indeed, his father's) no mention of the fact was ever made. There were even those who thought that if Margaret was afraid of anyone she might have had some slight awe of her eldest son. When she wished to ask him for a favour she would begin 'Villiers, my dear boy' on a note of propitiation. His marriage in 1908 to Lady Cynthia Needham was the occasion of general rejoicing, enhanced by the golden-haired prettiness of the eighteen-year-old bride. She was escorted, as pages, by Charles Rice and his brother Elwyn, boys of such angelic beauty that one of the guests, Prince Francis of Teck, said that now he knew what the Seraphim looked like.

Prince Francis of Teck was the brother of the then Princess of Wales, afterwards Queen Mary. His obstreperous habits had long been the despair of the Royal family. He was said, also, to have shunned a grand marriage to King Edward's daughter Princess Maud on account of his devotion to Lady Kilmorey, mother of the new Lady Villiers. As it happened, Prince Francis died only two years after the Villiers wedding, but his sister, the Princess of Wales, having frequently had to rescue him from financial difficulties, may well have doubted if he would have the immediate opportunity of verifying that the Rice brothers did actually resemble the Seraphim.

At the foundation of the Victoria League the new Princess of Wales had been asked if she would agree to be the League's Patron. Her refusal was only on the grounds that she wished an organization to be well established before she lent her patronage. By 1906 the League had got into its stride, and the Princess, again approached agreed to give the imprimatur of her patronage. Although Margaret was always on friendly terms with the Princess when she became Queen Mary and also with Queen Alexandra, she never felt the same romantic devotion for either that she had felt for Queen Victoria.

Queen Alexandra carried something of an atmosphere of the nursery into later life, cocooning her children in a woolly haze of love. This was not Lady Jersey's attitude, and she was able to boast to the Queen that she dressed with eight grandchildren squabbling on the floor of her bedroom, and enjoyed the Queen's admission that she had never made such a display of grandmotherly affection. Margaret herself had to own that she had been defeated by the wildness of her daughter Beatrice's only child Randal Plunkett, who was banned from the morning levée. The child's father was also found to be such a trying fellow-guest by some of his wife's family that the great Middleton Christmas parties, inspired by those of Stoneleigh, were found to be happier if the Dunsanys and their son were excluded. Watching their mother's mellow approach to their offspring, Margaret's daughters spoke wryly among themselves of the days when they were not allowed to sit on the embroidered chairs over which the next generation romped unrebuked.

A new field of public activity opened for Margaret with the growth of the movement to promote Votes for Women, its outrages being to her intensely unsympathetic. From experience it seemed to her that any woman who deserved to influence political events succeeded in doing so. Consequently she became a moving spirit in the Anti-Suffrage movement. Among her co-workers was Gertrude Bell, who had also found the lack of a vote no handicap to a career as a scholar, and a traveller, in lands where women were shrouded in veils and confined in seraglios. A public meeting in favour of Anti-Suffrage remained a matter of some disgust to Margaret in after years. Lord Curzon, a friend from his earliest days in politics, had promised his support which was not, in the end, forthcoming. Considering her long acquaintance with politicians, it was strange that she had not recognized their incurable habit of hedging their bets.

Lord Jersey's health had been unreliable throughout his grown-up life, and in 1909 a stroke turned him into an invalidish figure. Hospitality continued unabated at Middleton and Osterley, but,

pulled in a bath chair or immobilized in his sitting-room, affairs
came ever more under his wife's control. When she happened to
notice a lady at an Osterley garden party, a former guest but for
reasons unrecorded omitted from that year's list of guests, Margaret, on her own initiative, sent one of her brothers to ask if this
gate-crasher could send her hostess the invitation. This was a trap,
for that year's invitations, owing to the increase in motoring,
omitted the times of the trains to Osterley Station. One of Mrs
Hauksbee's successful social exploits concerned a forged invitation
card, but this unhappy woman was less adroit. The card that she
sent, with a stiff letter, was blatantly one belonging to an earlier
season.

As opposed to this buccaneering deed, risking humiliation and
permanent exile to appear at Osterley, there stands Sir Walter
Raleigh's misanthropic poem *Thoughts of An Elderly Gentleman at
a Garden Party*. Sir Walter, a famous figure in literary circles, was
a frequenter of Osterley parties, where he made friends among
the flock of grandchildren. His poem beginning, 'I wish I liked
the human race . . .' and ending, 'And when I'm introduced to
one, I wish I thought what jolly fun,' has a melancholy not usually
associated with the place that was the joy of Margaret's life.

Villiers' own children were now added to the flock of grandchildren; brought up, like their parents, on Margaret's children's
books. Her earliest published work, *Poems and Hymns for Very
Little Children*, dated from before her marriage. It was dedicated
to her little sister Cordelia, who presumably was obliged to learn
the simple rhymed renderings of bible stories. When the count
of grandchildren had risen to fourteen, their grandmother produced *John Alexander*, a moral tale of an unruly boy, whose mentor
was a singularly unpleasant gnome, and whose adventures included disasters in that modern phenomenon a motor-car. This
book was dedicated to Charles, Elwyn, Silchester, Imogen, Pansy,
Frank, Randal, David, Mary, George, Joan, Violet, Mansel and
Julia, grandchildren ranged in order of seniority. She published
nothing more until after the 1914 war, by the end of which the
circumstances of Margaret, her family and her fellow countrymen
had suffered changes unforeseen and arbitrary.

20

The End of an Old Song

IF AUGUST 1914 was the beginning of a cataclysm, it was also, as Lord Seafield said when he signed the Act of Union between England and Scotland, the end of an old song. Particularly this was to apply to Margaret's own life. Less than a year was to pass before her circumstances had entirely changed, the homes where she had reigned since her marriage becoming houses where she would now be a visitor.

From September 1914, Arthur Villiers, a lieutenant in the Queen's Own Oxfordshire Hussars, was serving in France. His gifts as a financier, early spotted by Gerald Wellesley, had already begun to show themselves. Under the influence of this same friend, Arthur had also become one of the chief organisers of the Eton Manor Club in Hackney Wick. This club for the boys of the East End of London was to become a monument to his philanthropy, his life's chief interest and, finally, his home.

As in the moment before light dies on entering a tunnel, Margaret gathered her family round her at Middleton for what was to be her last Christmas party. The Christmas tree still yielded presents of Edwardian opulence, but perpetual anxiety for Arthur hung like a black shadow over the minds of his family. Arthur himself, when he came on leave, wrote to an American friend of the courage of the wives, mothers and sisters of the fallen, the number of whom was growing with a grisly inexorability.

The Anti-Suffrage movement disappeared under the sterner pressures of war, the Victoria League, on the other hand, grew ever more valuable. Indefatigably, its President promoted new efforts of hospitality, for the troops who came largely, as Kipling wrote in his epitaph for the Canadian Fallen, 'from little towns in a far land'. In France the front line had been stabilized, but as more attacks were certainly expected it is surprising to find the Jerseys following the normal pattern of their lives, and setting out for their winter visit to the South of France.

Their daughter Mary wrote in her diary; 'January 5th (1915) M and P (Mama and Papa) leave to-day for Cannes. January 9th. Heard from M. reached Paris safely taking 12 hrs from Folkestone Hotel to Paris Hotel'. No mention was made of the sounds of war, but it cannot have been an easy journey with an invalid. The Jerseys seem to have returned home little the worse, after what was to be Lord Jersey's last visit to Cannes, where as a young man he had sat in the sunshine working at his crochet.

On May 28th Lord Jersey had another stroke, a massive haemorrhage, which caused the doctors to set a limit of hours to his life. By this time Mary Longford's husband had sailed with his Yeomanry brigade to the Middle East. On her own she went down to Osterley, moved by its loveliness, and by the sight of the trees that her father had planted and loved. Her mother poured out tea for a family party with the utmost calm, but she may well have shared her daughter's sadness '. . . all the time felt the minutes slipping by during which it's still one's home'.

Lord Jersey died on May 31st. His widow took her daughters to see him in a repose that was comforting after his troubled spell of unconsciousness. 'It *does* make one believe,' Margaret said to Mary and Beatrice, though doubt had played little part in her own life. At the Front Arthur received a telegram, which he passed to a brother officer with words that reflected his enigmatic approach to family relationships. 'You see [he said] Jersey's dead.' When Arthur arrived on leave for the funeral, the continuous Zeppelin raids allowed him no escape from the war. To the funeral at Middleton Stoney there came five of his father's old friends who, between them, had already lost seven sons, a tribute the family found intensely moving. It was to be thirty years before Jersey's widow was to join him under the Celtic cross that she chose to set up over his grave. Now a Dowager, she was faced with building a new life.

Packing-up took place with Margaret's customary lack of fuss. By the end of June she had said good-bye to Osterley, and moved on to Middleton to remove belongings accumulated in the forty years since her marriage. Possibly because it was in the square parallel to Bryanston Square where the Longfords had a house, the lease of 18 Montagu Square was bought. This house became what Charlotte M. Yonge, in her book *The Young Stepmother*, called 'the Family Office'. It remained so until World War II drove its owner back to Oxfordshire.

Reorganizing domestic matters, on the reduced scale appropriate to a dowager, was complicated by wartime shortages of labour. A butler, engaged rather rashly, turned out to be an unsuccessful gambler and embezzler, suspicions being aroused by his inability to produce even the smallest of change. Hardly less reliable was the brougham, hired to drive the Dowager about to her public engagements. For such a keen observer when sight-seeing, Margaret's lack of sense of direction on ordinary occasions was remarkable. The hired cab-driver seems to have been only acquainted with the seamier side of London life, and, bidden to drive to the Ritz, halted his brougham very far from Piccadilly. The hotel was, indeed, labelled Ritz, but it was one of a notorious row opposite Paddington Station. Now all demolished, the grandeur of the names of these hotels contrasted with the squalor of their façades, and the disreputability of their fly-by-night clientèle. Their reputation remained unknown to Margaret, who complained of the cabman's ignorance of the West End, rather than of his attempt, without apparent surprise, to deposit her in a seedy *maison de passe*.

Towards the end of August, only three months after her father's death, news came to Mary Longford that her husband was wounded and missing in the Dardanelles. He had led his brigade of Yeomanry in the final attempt to take the heights above Suvla Bay, in that campaign over which bitter argument has never ceased. His eldest child was twelve years old, his sixth and youngest only eighteen months. For nearly a year their mother lived in a limbo, struggling to find out if he had survived, clinging to uncertainty as better than accepting the finality of loss.

Throughout the winter Mary Longford nursed a hope that her husband might be a prisoner, wounded and unidentified, though even her devoted sister, Beatrice, had come to see that for an officer of his rank this was increasingly unlikely. Margaret must have realized that her daughter was most probably as widowed as herself, but her attempts to keep up Mary's spirits with everyday gossip were felt to be incongruous by their object. It was in this continued state of receding hope that Mary Longford took her six children to Ireland for the Easter holidays of 1916.

Communications were suddenly interrupted by the Easter

Week Rising, which marooned Margaret's two youngest daughters in their Irish castles. Dunsany, on leave, drove into Dublin to find out what was happening, was shot in the face and taken prisoner by rebel forces (his chauffeur, the one ordered with his motor car, losing a finger in the same incident). Throughout her life Margaret had travelled undaunted by discomfort or danger. Fortunately her daughters had inherited her composure, a quality valuable during the years between Easter 1916 and the end of the Irish Civil War in 1922. While the Pakenham grandchildren were still cut off in Co. Westmeath by the aftermath of the fighting Margaret had the joy of welcoming her last grandchild, Ann Villiers. In the years that followed she sometimes showed her wish that so many of her descendants were not spending their holidays in places where perils seemed endemic, but she understood and respected the principles which made the journeys necessary.

At last, in June 1916, the War Office told Lady Longford that it must now be assumed that her husband had died in the attack on Hill 70 on August 21st, 1915. A memorial service was held for him at St Mary's, Bryanston Square, where three of his children had been christened, and where the horror of the casualty lists was apparent from the number of war widows in the congregation. Of her son-in-law Margaret wrote that he was 'one of the best and bravest of men'.

It has been mentioned that the children of Margaret's Leigh uncles were more the contemporaries of her own children than of herself. Consequently the two sons of Chandos Leigh were of military age, and both were killed in the first year of the war. Twice wounded and decorated with the D.S.O. and bar, Arthur Villiers survived. The thankfulness of his family was intense, his sister Mary being particularly grateful that she had not been asked to bear the additional blow of his loss. In theory Arthur returned to his mother's house, but, though he made a habit of dining with her on Sunday night, he had other quarters where he was more likely to be found.

To quote again from Charlotte M. Yonge 'no one knows what it is to lose a father except those who have the care of his children'. Margaret found herself frequently accommodating Pakenham grandchildren, either gathered to face the rigours of the night journey across the Irish Channel or recovering at breakfast after a rough crossing. Gradually the pressure of grandchildren seeking beds made it permissible for nephews to be insinuated into what was still called Uncle Arthur's room. It had been many a year since he had slept in the bed, but the myth persisted that he might suddenly claim his right to do so.

After its exotic beginnings, Margaret's household had settled down. At ten minutes to nine every morning the servants paraded in the dining-room where their employer read prayers, as she had been brought up to do. The only absentee was the parlour maid, who had replaced the gambling butler. Being a Plymouth Sister, she was excused from joining the rank of cook, kitchen maid, upper and under housemaid, the lady's maid, daughter of a Middleton butler, and a page boy, the solitary male element. Together this company gave thanks for being safely brought to the beginning of the day, and asked for protection from falling into sin or running into any kind of danger.

Through the Eyes of a Granddaughter

THE FIFTH CHILD of Mary Longford, I took my place in the dedication of *John Alexander*, between two cousins, like a puppy newly entered in a pack of hounds. It was not, however, till some-time in the summer of 1920, when I was eight years old, that I began to sort my grandmother out from among a misty crowd of relations, and to realize that she had not always inhabited the plateau of honoured old age across which I saw her so briskly moving.

Uncle Jimmy, I was told, was coming to luncheon, the only meal which my sister Julia and I shared with the grown-ups. He was a clergyman, and, something mysterious, a 'teatotaler'. Not only that, he was actually Grandmama's uncle, an enormously ancient relationship. Brown as a nut and lively as a cricket, he carried my mother and her sister Beatrice back into a state of girlish gaiety, which gave me an idea of how much they must have enjoyed the fun and high spirits at Stoneleigh. His hands were cripply, and he asked the butler's help with the potato dish, but he showed his standing as a famous temperance lecturer by waving away the wine the same butler offered. Not to have offered any wine to a noted abstainer would have seemed a better idea, but in my mother's family there were so many conflicting attitudes towards wine that to discriminate would have led to infinite confusion.

Grandmama herself, perhaps from supposed delicacy, had been accustomed to drink wine from her girlhood, her palate being said by my grandfather to have been almost too good. Wine was not given to her own daughters, the eldest growing up to be a temperance campaigner like the Revd James Leigh, though neither her husband nor her children rallied to this cause. Mary, my mother, never tasted wine, regarding it as an expense only justified by the presence of guests. My Aunt Beatrice behaved rationally, drinking a glass with her meals, without making it a moral issue. Her brother Arthur's attitude was more peculiar. He only cared to drink champagne, except on Sunday evenings in his mother's house, when he drank water so consistently that she considered him to be as much of an abstainer as her Uncle Jimmy. I cannot help speculating as to whether, when Mrs Kemble took Henry James to spend Christmas with her daughter and son-in-law, the host's principles allowed him to offer his famous guests any drink stronger than water.

It was in this summer of 1920 that I first noticed a peculiarity of my grandmother's house. Unlike its neighbours no curtains of net or lace concealed the interior from passers-by, from those living opposite, and particularly from those ringing the bell on the doorstep. My brother Frank, my sisters and I were eating the lavish tea that was to give us support on the journey to Holyhead, if not on the sea crossing. Grandmama was absent, and a feeling of Saturnalia prevailed, interrupted by a taxi stopping outside the house. Up the steps came the sable figure of my father's widowed sister, Lady Gough. Aunt Georgie's charitable works were wholly admirable, but she also cultivated lugubriousness as though it was a plant in her carefully tended London garden. Amid cries of dismay, Frank, forgetting that if we could see out Aunt Georgie might see in, disappeared under the table with his tea-cup. Distressed by the idea of her dead brother's children leaving for the dangers of Ireland, Aunt Georgie had called to say good-bye, and had witnessed only too clearly the disarray her appearance had caused. 'Where's Frank?' she inquired, 'Under the table, I suppose,' and, picking up the table cloth, revealed that that indeed was where he was.

This all-too-visible dining-room was furnished with a sideboard with an unusual number of cupboards, out of which came the chocolates, which were the reward to greedy grandchildren for the tedium of grown-up conversation. After my eldest sister married the painter Henry Lamb, my grandmother bought one of his landscapes, a painting of an olive grove. It must have brought back the days when she had roamed with her parents through the South of France, with no greater cares than keeping Lady Leigh in good health. This painting joined landscapes by Lady Leigh herself, and the conversation piece of the Grosvenor family, already referred to, which hung over the fireplace. Only much later did I learn that the most attractive of the men in this group was Lord Wilton, of such bad reputation that Lord Clarendon habitually wrote of him as 'The Wicked'.

When my grandmother was approaching ninety, her eldest daughter made a tentative suggestion that the steep stairs of 18 Montagu Square might be a reason for exchanging the expiring lease for a convenient apartment on one floor. Even from this devoted and loved daughter such a suggestion was presuming. Her mother liked her house. She was quite prepared to renew the lease, and wrote to say so with much firmness.

I am glad to think that Grandmama liked her house, because, though often grateful for its shelter, I never found it easy to make the kind of nest there at which my mother's habit of parking me on her relations had made me an adept. Sitting on the rock-like sofa I would listen to my grandmother as she wrote her letters, for she spoke tantalizingly half-complete sentences, 'I don't want to be catty, but . . .' leaving both her correspondent and her subject forever unknown.

The prettiest object in the drawing-room was the painting by Zorn, the artist subsequently taken up by Mrs Potter Palmer of Chicago. This charming work showed Beatrice Villiers as a small child in a froth of white frills and red ribbons. My sister Mary once remarked to my grandmother's maid that the sitter's chair was out of perspective and got the surrealist reply that, on the contrary, it was out of his lordship's study. This sister has also pointed out that not only did Grandmama say that Zorn, 'poor man', had died of drink at a time when he was prosperously alive, but insisted that another artist who painted Beatrice had met the same fate.

It is never exactly clear what intake of alcohol qualifies as being known 'to drink', in any generation. There was one occasion when Dunsany and my grandmother were harmoniously excoriating Lytton Strachey's *Eminent Victorians*, and Dunsany added, as a coping stone on Strachey's crimes, that the saintly General Gordon had been described as drinking to excess. Unprecedentedly, my grandmother found herself defending Strachey. 'Nonsense,' she said, 'Of course Gordon was a saint, but we all knew that he drank.' She also gave some realistic advice to Pansy on the subject, urging her to marry an atheist rather than a drunkard. Wives sometimes converted atheists, she said, but never cured drunkards. Here my mother intervened, taking the opposite line. She practically told her daughter that it was all right to marry a man with a brandy bottle in one hand if, like General Gordon, he had a Bible in the other.

Pansy was a favourite visitor to 18 Montagu Square. Family loyalty left many of my mother's proceedings uncriticized by my grandmother, but looking back it seems obvious that she was consciously rescuing her granddaughter from a home that was bleak and sometimes unfairly repressive. Consequently, Pansy happened to be present when Aunt Aggie, with all the delicacy of her spinsterhood, came to inquire if their brother Dudley's remarriage to another American lady, this time many years younger than himself, might result in the birth of a direct heir to the head of the family.

Grandmama's reaction was characteristically robust. Duddy was, indisputably, seventy years of age, but she well remembered another peer who fathered several children in his seventies. Marie, the new Lady Leigh, won the affection of her husband's family by the charming naiveté of her disposition. She brought perfectionist American standards to the management of Stoneleigh, while the elaborate floral offerings she made to her sister-in-law added an air of unexpected luxury to the latter's drawing-room. The position of Robin Leigh, heir presumptive and orphan son of the marriage, late in life, of the Captain of Hussars, was, however, never usurped.

When *Fifty-One Years of Victorian Life* appeared in 1922, I was not of an age for it to be considered suitable reading. Indeed it was never quite clear if Grandmama's own children thought it a suitable book for her to have written. Accepting children's books as desirable works for her mother to produce, my own mother gave the impression that even discreet memoirs were a threat to the privacy of the family. Herself a buyer of every book she wished to read, an admirable practice, she spoke with some disparagement of Grandmama's taste for the society of authors. It took me long to learn how many of the writers I knew between boards had been to Grandmama friendly acquaintances and correspondents, even in the time of my own childhood.

I had no idea that my grandmother corresponded with Kipling, to me the magical exponent of the life of Mowgli and his furred and feathered friends. She sent, apparently as the result of some discussion, a copy of Spenser's *Faerie Queene* to Kipling, and kept his letter of thanks, which speculated on the influence of Tasso on Spenser, and Spenser on Bunyan. His writing paper was headed by a telegraph pole and a railway engine, and conveyed the now practically useless information that telegrams for Bateman's, Kipling's house, should be addressed to Burwash, and that guests should travel by train to Etchingham Station. Kipling wrote:

Nov. 17. 1920.

Dear Lady Jersey,

Thank you a hundred times for the Faerie Queene in its solid mid-Victorian dress that is so full of memories. I hold to it that John Bunyan, who was always hearing things (he got conscience you remember through voices) must have heard his Spencer [*sic*] quoted-as you suggest. I will now get a Tasso and compare notes. (By the way, do you notice how thoroughly Sir Walter Scott is saturated with Tasso? It comes, I think, almost next to Shakespeare in his references and allusions.)

Very gratefully yours
Rudyard Kipling.

Another exchange took place with E. F. Benson, apparently about some printing blunder in connection with Swinburne. Benson wrote in extenuation, 'I did the best I could and murdered the printer'. A letter Grandmama preserved from Wilfred Meynell might almost be called skittish, 'My wardrobe actual and symbolical is of the scantiest [but] I hope you will let me feel that there is one jersey I shall always keep near to a grateful heart'.

Although the Victoria League remained very much in the foreground of my grandmother's life, the secretary, Miss Drayton, becoming a close friend, there was nothing of Mrs Jellyby in Grandmama's nature. (Mrs Jellyby, it will be remembered, is the archetypal do-gooder in Dickens' *Bleak House*, devoted to far-flung causes while her family slide into confusion, dirt and finally bankruptcy.) For many years a magistrate in the Juvenile Courts, she mostly talked of things that had caught her imagination as comic. One family fracas reached such a pitch that she reported herself as suggesting to her neighbour on the bench that the court should be cleared and the contestants allowed to fight it out. Eventually it was deafness which brought her to feel obliged to resign, an affliction she found more trying than failing sight.

Unable to read to herself, a middle-aged lady was found who read *The Times* to my grandmother, but supplied also some lurid gossip of goings-on in fast London society. From whence the reader got her information was mysterious. It mostly concerned a group supposedly designated by the police as The Black Four Hundred of Mayfair. When I suggested that there was obviously some confusion over a rather sedate *boîte de nuit* called simply The 400, Grandmama definitely preferred to stick to the reader's version. The vices of the Black Four Hundred were not, I think, particularized.

As an epigraph to *Fifty-One Years of Victorian Life*, my grandmother quoted lines by her son-in-law Dunsany,

> 'Who is this child of man that conquers
> Time and that is braver than Love?
> Even memory.'

She echoed the thought in three stanzas of her own, which ended,

> 'But we will not, cannot, banish
> Bygone pleasure from our side,
> Nor will doubt, beyond the storm cloud,
> Shall be Light at Eventide.'

The book was dedicated to her children and grandchildren, the latter, she wrote, 'as delightful as their parents.' Two years later another storm cloud came out of a clear sky. In January 1924 Villiers, her admired eldest son died suddenly, leaving four children. Grandison, the eldest was only thirteen and had always had a particular place in his grandmother's affections, augmented by a long illness that followed his father's death.

It had been Villiers' wish that his mother should make a compilation of the *Records of the Family of Villiers, Earls of Jersey*, which she proceeded to do, dedicating the privately printed book to the memory of her son, George Henry Robert Child Villiers, 8th Earl of Jersey. It is enjoyable rather than reliable reading, the author facing the moral lapses by which her husband's family rose in the world with unblenching calm. She also accepted without question the legend of the highwayman bishop, and the demonstrably untrue story that Matthew Arnold had written *Requiescat* on the death of Clementina Villiers. When Grandmama had to deal with the career of Francis Villiers, she admittedly 'handled the truth a bit carelessly'. Francis, his niece by marriage wrote, was 'handsome and extravagant . . . He had no idea of the value of money, and in the end left the country.'

This was a smooth handling of a rough subject, but there was sly enjoyment in my grandmother's record of a famous scandal of the early 19th century, perhaps because the pay-off line was so remote from her own way of life. Caroline, wife of the Lord Anglesey who lost his leg at Waterloo and daughter of Frances Lady Jersey, divorced her husband and married the Duke of Argyll. Lord Anglesey also remarried to another divorcée. The change of partners was amiably accepted by the large number of children involved, but the next generation was more critical. To the second Lady Anglesey one of her grandchildren remarked, 'Grandmama, I know what you did – you committed adultery.'

There was not, I believe, any special family celebration when the Countess of Jersey (no longer a dowager as her daughter-in-law had remarried) was made a Dame Commander of the Most Excellent Order of the British Empire. No one could have been more worthy of such a distinction, for to her the British Empire was an ideal to be served with devotion. The only two occasions, to my knowledge, on which she wrote letters of rebuke to grand-sons on political matters, were both concerned with what she regarded as a flouting of this ideal. The D.B.E. itself she wore one day for a family dinner party, together with the assorted medals she had accumulated in her public career, with a cheerful lack of discrimination for their widely varied merits.

By this time the Plymouth Sister had been replaced in the Montagu Square household. She was known to have been courted by an attendant from Burlington House, who came in to help at dinner parties, but my grandmother's apprehension of losing her was fulfilled in another way. For many months the Plymouth Sister's name had been on a waiting list to sail as a stewardess. Suddenly the call had come and she sailed out of our lives. After an unhappy stop-gap, who was swindled out of her savings under promise of marriage by a man she met on the top of an omnibus, the household settled down with a chubby newcomer. It was odd, said Grandmama, that this new parlourmaid should look like a cabbage, and that Cabbage should be her name. The parlourmaid always laughed when so addressed, which was put down to her jolly nature, until it transpired that her name was actually Cubbage.

It was Cubbage who showed the fiancés of grandchildren into the drawing-room when they were brought to meet their new grandmother. In my own case she made little attempt to conceal that she was well aware that I was making no casual call, having taken my telephone message asking if my grandmother would be at home. The latter barely greeted me before asking what was the matter on which I wished to see her. She was wishing me well when, after an interval carefully arranged, Cubbage announced 'Mr Powell', in a voice vibrant with interest and congratulation.

My mother had died a year previously, and so it was my grandmother who signed the register and walked out of the church on the arm of my father-in-law. In the vestry, she had embraced me with her blessing, adding, with unselfconscious conviction, that she was sure my father and mother knew and were blessing me also.

I shall have given a feeble portrait of my grandmother if I have not conveyed her *sang froid* in painful circumstances, which was tested not infrequently in later years. She might disapprove of marriages breaking-up, but grandchildren remained grandchildren, to be loved, fed and housed, whatever the complications of their private lives. The fourth generation were welcomed to tea-parties and to digging presents out of what they called a 'Gran Pie'. The noise could be heard from afar, particularly when all the presents had been discovered and the company devoted themselves to throwing handfuls of bran into the lint-white curls of my cousin Joan Colville's daughter Sally.

As she advanced into her eighties, my grandmother saw no reason to cease to entertain on a generous scale, even after one of her dinner parties had been wrecked by a practical joke of perverted maliciousness. The party was in honour of Princess Alice, and her husband the Earl of Athlone, the youngest brother of Queen Mary and Prince Francis of Teck. In the deGermanisation of the British Royal Family during World War I Lord Athlone had surrendered his German rank, and, in compensation, had been made an Earl in the Peerage of the United Kingdom. Princess Alice, granddaughter of Queen Victoria, remained a Royal Highness, while her husband, as Grandmama pointed out, had only the precedence of a relatively newly created earl. It was for this reason, she explained afterwards, that she had not asked her grandson, Jersey, to the dinner party, for, as an earl of a much earlier creation, he, instead of Lord Athlone, should have sat on her right.

Hardly had the guests been seated, Princess Alice on the right of the host, Arthur Villiers, when a telephone message was brought in. It purported to come from the City Police and announced that Lord Jersey had met with a fatal accident, news

causing extreme consternation. Arthur left his seat by Princess
Alice to make further inquiries, while his mother remained at her
end of the table, awaiting with fortitude whatever might be the
truth. To add to the tension, Dunsany, on the other side of Princess
Alice, was held in the conversational grip of a cousin of famous
volubility. Afterwards Dunsany said he should have at once
strangled his neighbour, but Princess Alice, left stranded, turned
a cold shoulder on him for the rest of the meal.

This proceeded through several agonized courses before the
supposed victim was traced to a friend's house, and could reassure
his grandmother of his continued and unharmed existence. Complimented on her calm, Grandmama said she had not seen what
else she could have usefully done except await developments. If
the cruel sender of the message did it for the enjoyment of causing
chaos as well as pain, in this, at least, he or she was thwarted.

By the nineteen-thirties Time had removed most of the literary
figures whom Grandmama liked to entertain, but she enjoyed one
opportunity to excavate memories of earlier days, and, incidentally, to contradict posthumously the by then late Lytton Strachey.
Hector Bolitho came to consult her when writing *Albert the Good*,
his life of the Prince Consort. Though she had found the Prince
unduly brusque on his visit to Stoneleigh, it was a pleasure to dwell
on that glowing moment in the past.

If her older literary friends had faded away, my own family
were doing their best to fill the gap with novels, plays and assorted
journalism. When my husband Anthony Powell's last pre-war
novel, *What's Become of Waring*, appeared Grandmama took a sub-
jective view of this story of a literary fraud. She had enjoyed the
book, she wrote, 'but I do not think Browning would have
approved of Tony making Waring such a scoundrel'. She spoke
as someone who had known Browning, but she did not seem
to have reflected on what Browning may have thought of the real
career of Waring's original, Alfred Domett. The poem ends with
a moment's glimpse of Waring, sailing, with a bronzed young
boy to cry his wares, around the port of Trieste, purveying goods
that sound contraband to incoming ships. Domett chose to sail
another course, and achieved the position of Chief Justice of New
Zealand.

A world upheaval shortly before her ninetieth birthday removed my grandmother from her house more effectively than
any suggestions of her daughter. Some years before, Middleton

Park had been demolished and rebuilt with staff cottages in the grounds. One of which was offered to the Dowager when World War II was obviously imminent. On the day on which she was preparing to leave her house, as it turned out forever, I ate what I suppose was the last luncheon to be given to a grandchild under that intensely hospitable roof.

I had sometimes argued with my grandmother on questions of behaviour or points of history, but I had never found her anything but easy to get on with. If I did things of which she disapproved she did not hesitate to say so, but no ill-feeling remained. Compared with my mother's attitude of ignoring bodily functions as far as was possible, my grandmother's straightforwardness was refreshing. She had consulted me if it was necessary to wear her false teeth, uncomfortable and superfluous, to consume the light diet that had sustained her for ninety years. I had assured her, truthfully, that her appearance was perfectly reasonable without them.

She had also displayed the appalling bruise that had been inflicted on her by a fierce black swan, which had attacked her when she was strolling by the lake at Hallyburton, the Scottish home of a niece of her husband. Beating off the swan had bent her silver-handled umbrella into a curve like a new moon, but it was the attitude of her husband's niece that Grandmama really resented. Her hostess agreed that it might be wise to give the swan away, particularly when my grandmother pointed out that little Princess Elizabeth and her sister, often visitors to Hallyburton, might be the next victims. The swan's owner was, however, troubled by the idea that change of lake might make the black swan unhappy.

At this last luncheon we passed into the dining-room through a hall stacked with the paraphernalia of departure. Much of my growing-up had taken place in that dining-room, but my grandmother seemed to me not to have altered vastly since the days of my childhood. Her bracing attitude had often been tempered by sympathy. 'Poor Violet,' she had said, on learning that I had been in hospital, adding, with a throwback to the age before anaesthesia, 'did the surgeon hurt much?'

My grandmother showed no more signs of discomposure at being driven from her home than she had shown regrets for the glories of the other homes she had been obliged to leave. I might wonder, she said, at the various hampers in the hall. They were filled with bottles from her cellar, for she did not know what resources she might find at Middleton. Accustomed to drink wine twice a day, she saw no reason why a flight from possible bombings should force her to change her habits. Since that day I have never again been inside 18 Montagu Square, but should there be ghosts in the house they can only be those of love and friendship.

Uprooting did not have the extinguishing effect on Grandmama that often overcomes the aged with a change of house. Her expression when photographed, to celebrate her ninetieth birthday on October 29th 1939, was positively cheerful. Hardly had her birthday passed when she joined in a correspondence in *The Times* on the heinousness of using nouns substantive as adjectives. How, she inquired, would these purists describe such objects as a corner cupboard, a sofa cushion or a ration book should nouns be banned from adjectival use? From someone who had been known to declare the study of English grammar to be superfluous, this was an invasion of enemy territory, and it was a deft stroke to cite 'ration book' as a contemporary example, little truck as she probably had with her own.

When our eldest son, Tristram, was born in Oxford in April 1940 Grandmama welcomed her twenty-first great grandchild with enthusiasm unabated by the gloom of the war news. Her congratulations were positively exuberant. No birth of any boy, she assured me, short perhaps of a Royal Prince, had given more general satisfaction than the arrival of Tristram. When I took him to Middleton, a bundle of three weeks old, she asked permission to kiss him, and so linked him with a past when his great grandmother had met the Duke of Wellington.

When Germany invaded Russia, my grandmother's interest was primarily that of someone remembering the Crimean War, with Russia as the enemy. At ninety-one her memory for the apt quotation still held good, with a bull's-eye from Samuel Johnson's poem on *Charles XII of Sweden*.

'Think nothing gained,' he cries, 'till nought remains,
On Moscow's walls till Gothic standards fly,'
And all be mine beneath the polar sky.'

Lines which were, indeed, a startling prevision of Hitler's plans for his Russian campaign.

Although the ills of old age increased their grip, the power of the Dowager's personality still held awe for those around her. To her daughter Beatrice, on a visit, it was reported that Her Ladyship was distressed by breathlessness, but her maid said she herself would not dare to send for the doctor without permission. My Aunt Beatrice realized that neither would she, and nervously applied to her mother for leave, to be saddened, though relieved, at being told, 'I don't mind what you do.'

Sometimes the past came creeping back so vividly that my grandmother would ask when the young ladies, her daughters, would be coming downstairs. On one occasion she even ordered a telegram to be sent to book rooms at a French hotel. This order she later cancelled, not because she recollected that France was cut off by war, but because it had come to her that the travelling companions she had in mind were dead.

Throughout the War her Villiers granddaughters, and their increasing families, lived nearby, providing for her last days a family group as lively as she had always felt family life should be. In London my sister Mary had been in the habit of devotedly dining with Grandmama, and playing the simple game of Patience with which the time after dinner was filled. Now, married to a great-grandson of the Mrs Archer Clive who had known Lord Leigh before his marriage, she delighted Grandmama by extracts from the Clive diaries. Mary also earned the gratitude of the whole family by arranging that, on the death of my father's eldest sister, her maid should take on the care of my grandmother. As reality became more remote this care became more onerous, Joan Colville, from constant observation, thought that, though Grandmama boasted that she would outlast Hitler and Mussolini, her strongest interest was in the prospect of seeing again the many people she had loved long ago.

On her ninety-third birthday, I saw her for the last time, smiling at a bevy of great granddaughters, ravishingly pretty in bridesmaid's dresses from assorted family weddings. On that day she talked of the evening long ago in Bhownugger, when the Maharajah had said that God was a light and different religions the prisms through which God shines.

The end of Margaret Jersey's long life came on May 22nd 1945, in her ninety-sixth year. She herself might have deprecated the idea that the Victoria League, which still keeps alive its ideal of Commonwealth hospitality, was more of a memorial to her than to the many others concerned in its work, but it is hard to feel that she is not commemorated in its continued existence. In her memoirs she wrote that she had counted herself fortunate to have been brought up among an elder generation of which each member strove to act up to a standard of right, an example which she followed unflinchingly on her own account.

Her youngest sister, her surviving son, her eldest daughter, her daughter-in-law, her brother Dudley's widow and eight of her grandchildren followed her coffin down the avenue to the Church of All Saints, where she had worshipped for so many years, and where so many of her family awaited her in the churchyard. Her daughter Beatrice wrote from Ireland, 'It was no life for one of her spirit, but I feel very forlorn.' Her grandchildren mourned her, as one whose letters to them had been signed,

'Ever your loving Grandmama

M. E. Jersey.'

Index

Abdul the Damned, Sultan, 101–3
Adam, Robert, 58
Adams, Henry, 23, 128–9
Aga Khan, 86
Albert, Prince Consort, 10, 108, 188
Alexandra, Queen, wife of Edward VII, 19, 20, 173
Ancram, Earl of, 109, 119–20, 127
Arnold, Sir Edwin, 60, 92, 93
Arnold, Matthew, 39, 61, 185
Ashley, Lionel, 63–4, 67, 72
Athlone, 1st Earl of, 187
Athlone, Princess Alice, Countess of, 187
Aubrey, John, 26
Augusta, German Empress, 65
Austen, Cassandra (widow of Revd George), 1
Austen, Revd George, 1, 2
Austen, Jane, 1–6, 13, 22, 32

Baker, Sir Samuel and Lady, 84
Bakhméteff, Russian diplomat, 69–70
Balfour, Arthur, statesman, 144, 166
Balfour, Gerald, 124
Beatrice, Princess, 21
Beauchamp, 7th Earl, 158
Beckwith, Hélène see Leigh
Bedford, Anne, Duchess of, see Jersey
Bell, Gertrude, 173
Belloc, Hilaire, 111, 168
Benson, E. F., 184
Berwick, Duke of, 34
Bhownugger, Maharajah of, 92–3, 191
Bismarck, Prince, 66
Blavatsky, Madame, 85
Bligh, Captain, 116
Boldrewood, Rolf, (Thomas Browne, author of *Robbery Under Arms*), 115
Bolitho, Hector, 188
Boulanger, General, 100
Bourget, Paul, 79
Bourke, Robert, see Connemara
Bourne, Mrs, nurse, 54, 83, 110, 111, 151
Bradley Martin, Mr and Mrs, 148
Brandling, Charles, 47
Brougham, 1st Baron, statesman, 19
Brown, John, 97
Browning, Elizabeth Barrett, 60

Browning, Robert, 59–60, 188
Buckingham, George Villiers, 1st Duke of, 34
Bute, 3rd Marquess of, and Gwendolen, Marchioness of (née Howard), 27
Butler, Alice, Lady Butler (née Leigh), 77, 79
Butler, Frances, see Leigh
Butler, Pierce, 23
Byron, 6th Baron, the poet, 4, 38

Cairns, 1st Earl, 85
Campbell, Sir Archibald (of Garscube), 45
Campbell, Marie, see Leigh
Camperdown, 3rd Earl of, 28, 31
Cardigan, 7th Earl and Adeline Countess of (née de Horsey), 41
Caroline, Queen, 19 Princess of Wales, 37
Carr, Robert, 34
Cecil, Beatrice, see Harlech
Cecil, Mary, see Devonshire
Cecil, Mary, see Galloway
Chalon, A. E., painter, 38
Chamberlain, Beatrice, 75
Chamberlain, Joseph, 59, 74–5, 99, 119
Chandos, 2nd Duke of, 4
Charles I, 34
Charles II, 35
Charlotte, Queen, 36
Chiffinch, Barbara, see Jersey
Chiffinch, William, 35
Child, Robert, 37
Child, Sarah, see Westmorland
Cholmondeley, Harry, 109, 113
Cholmondeley, Revd Lionel, 138
Christian, Princess, 21
Churchill, Arabella, 34
Churchill, Lord Randolph, 109
Clarence, Victor Albert, Duke of, 108, 120
Clarendon, 4th Earl of, 40, 41, 182
Cleveland, Barbara Villiers, Duchess of, 34, 143
Cleveland, Grace, Duchess of, 51
Clive, Caroline, (wife of Revd Archer Clive), 6, 7, 191
Colville, Joan (née Villiers), 187, 191
Colville, Sally, 187
Compton-Burnett, I, 16
Connemara, Robert Bourke, 1st Baron, 83, 88–9, 145

Connemara, Susan, Lady Connemara, (née Broun-Ramsay), 88–9
Conyngham, 1st Marquess of, 36
Cook, Sir Francis, 106
Craven, 4th Earl and Countess of, 148
Crawford, Countess of (née Bootle-Wilbraham), 106
Curzon, 1st Marquess of, 75, 167, 173
Custarde, Miss, governess, 16–17

D'Abernon, 1st Viscount, 102–4
Darke, Charles and Rebecca (née Gyles), 88
Darke, Julia Rebecca, 88
Darley, Sir Frederick and Lady, 115, 119
Daudet, Alphonse and family, 81–2
Davis, Jefferson, 23
Derby, 15th Earl of, 50, 68, 73, 74
Derby, Mary Countess of (née Sackville, formerly Marchioness of Salisbury), 50
Desborough, William, 1st Baron, 59
Des Voeux, Sir William, 74
Devonshire, Mary, Duchess of (née Cecil), 98
Dibbs, Sir George, 114–15, 132
Disraeli, Benjamin, 38, 39, 40, 50
Dommet, Alfred, 188
Doyle, Sir Everard, 157
Draper family, 49
Drayton, Gertrude, 184
Dryden, John, 18
Dunsany, Beatrice, Lady Dunsany (née Villiers), 47, 53–4, 105, 119, 145, 147, 182, 191–2
Dunsany, 18th Baron, 169–71, 173, 182, 188
Dynevor, Margaret, Lady Dynevor (née Villiers), 54, 105, 109–10, 119–29, 134–6, 160
Dynevor, Walter Rice, 7th Baron, 156, 160, 162

Edel, Professor Leon, 77, 129
Edmonds, Mrs, 40
Edward VII, 19, 165
Elphinstone, Sir Howard, 97
Esterhazy, Prince Louis, 75
Esterhazy, Prince and Princess Nicholas (née Sarah Villiers), 39
Eugénie, Empress, 109
Eulalia, Infanta, 140–41

Fane, Charles, 42
Faudel-Phillips, Sir George, 155
Fearn, Mr, American diplomat, 140
Ferdinand, Tsar of Bulgaria, 103
Fitzgerald, Edward, 24, 63
Fitzherbert, Mrs, 36–7
Floyd, General Sir John, 33, 88
Floyd, Rebecca (née Darke), 33
Francis, Prince, of Teck, 172
Frank, Doctor, 45
Frank, Lady Agnes (née Grosvenor, formerly Campbell), 45

Gailey, Mrs, 11, 60
Galloway, 10th Earl of, 50, 55, 73
Galloway, Mary Countess of (née Cecil), 50–4, 59, 64–7, 73, 94, 99–103, 106, 108, 110, 120, 144, 147, 169
George V, 20, 165
George IV, as Prince of Wales, 36–7

George, King of Greece, 68
Gladstone, William, Ewart, 13, 59, 74
Gordon, General, C. G., 182
Gordon-Cumming, Sir William, 165
Gordon, Mabel, see Leigh
Goschen, George, 109, 117, 119
Gough, Georgiana, Viscountess, 181
Grant, Captain James, explorer, 84
Greek Royal family, 94
Grenfell, Field Marshal, 1st Baron, 94–5, 99–100
Grenfell, William, see Desborough
Greville, Charles, diarist, 40
Grosvenor, Agnes, see Frank
Grosvenor, Caroline, see Leigh
Grosvenor, Theodora, 9
Gyles, Rebecca, see Darke

Haggard, Michael Bazzet, 68, 121–31
Haggard, Rider, 68
Haggard, William, 68
Hamilton, Lord George, M.P., 146
Hardy, Violet (née Leigh, wife of Sir Bertram Hardy) 15–16, 18, 106
Hare, Augustus, 105–7
Harlech, Beatrice, Lady Harlech (née Cecil), 64
Henry, footman, 117
Hertford, 3rd Marquess of, 36
Howard, Gwendolen, see Bute
Hughes, Thomas, 55, 62
Hunt, Revd Isaac, 4
Hunt, James Leigh, 4
Huxley, Aldous, 94

Ibbetson, Captain Charles and Lady Adela (née Villiers), 39, 41

Jackson, Sir Herbert, 148
James I, 34
James II, 34
James, 'the Old Pretender', 35
James, Alice, 79
James, Henry, 24, 76–82, 181
Jeacock, Job, 113
Jedburgh, Lord, 157
Jenkins, William and Lady Caroline (née Villiers), 45–6, 101
Jersey, Countesses of, 33–42
Jersey, Cynthia, Countess of (née Needham, later Slessor)
Jersey, Earls of, 33–42
Jersey, George Francis, 9th Earl of, 187
Jersey, George Henry Robert, 8th Earl of, 46, 54, 84, 91–2, 109, 132, 145, 156, 172, 185
Jersey, Julia, Countess of (née Peel), 47, 88, 110
Jersey, Margaret Elizabeth, Countess of (née Leigh): birth, 4; education, 11–17; marriage, 29–32; birth of her children, 45–7; politics and friendship with Lady Galloway, 50–3; at Osterley, 57–64; in Berlin, 65–7; in Greece, 67–71; in India, 83–95; at Windsor, 96–8; typhoid fever, 108; in New South Wales; 113–18; in Samoa, 121–8; returns home by China, Japan and United States, 133–42; in Egypt, 147–9; her children's marriages, 155–8; in India, 163; death of Queen Victoria, 164; first President of the Victoria League,

166; widowhood, 176–9; made DBE, 186; old age at Middleton Park, 189–92

Jersey, Sarah, Countess of (née Fane), 43–4, 46, 48, 68

Jersey, Victor Albert George, 7th Earl of, 45–7, 50–3, 57, 73, 78, 86, 93, 96–9, 106, 112–19, 133–42, 149, 152–4, 161–4, 168, 173, 176

Jeune, see St Helier

Johnson, Samuel, 190

Jowett, Benjamin, 51

Kelly, Ned, 115

Kemble, Charles, 23

Kemble, Fanny, 23–4, 29, 77, 181

Kerim, Abdul, The Munshi, 97, 100

Keynes, Maynard, 34

Kilmorey, Ellen, Countess of, 172

Kipling, Rudyard, 92, 176, 184

Kitchener, Field Marshal, 1st Earl, 94, 99, 147–50, 167

Laffon, M., Governor of New Caledonia, 117–18

Lamb, Lady Caroline, 21, 145

Lamb, Henry, 184

Lamb, William, see Melbourne

Lawley, Caroline, 27

Leigh, Agnes, 17, 31, 58, 151, 172, 183

Leigh, Caroline, Lady Leigh (née Grosvenor), 4, 6–8, 12–24, 28, 38, 58–9, 72, 83, 126, 171

Leigh, Chandos, 1st Baron, 4–6, 8, 14

Leigh, Cordelia, 8, 17, 30–1, 91, 134, 143

Leigh, Dudley, 3rd Baron, 17, 24, 58, 109, 171

Leigh, Edward Chandos, 14–15

Leigh, Mrs Edward Chandos (née Katherine Rigby), 146

Leigh, Gilbert, 17, 22, 26, 56–9

Leigh, Golden Wedding, 158–60

Leigh, Hélène, Lady Leigh (née Beckwith), 109, 171–2

Leigh, Henry, 2nd Baron, 4, 6–9, 12–24, 28, 45, 58, 79, 83

Leigh, James, 2–6

Leigh, Mrs James (née Julia Judith Twisleton), 2, 5

Leigh, Revd James, 23–4, 32, 180

Leigh, Mrs James (née Fanny Butler), 23–4, 29–32, 77

Leigh, Margaret Elizabeth, see Jersey

Leigh, Marie, Lady Leigh (née Campbell), 183

Leigh, Honble Mary, 1

Leigh, Robin, 4th Baron, 183

Leigh, Rowland, 17, 58, 159

Leigh, Mrs Rowland (née Mabel Gordon), 139, 159

Leigh, Rupert, 17, 58, 105, 109, 119–21

Leigh, Revd Thomas, 1–2

Leigh, Violet, see Hardy

Leigh-Perrot, Mr and Mrs James, 2–3

Leighton, 1st Baron, 64

Leopold, Prince, 21

Lieven, Princess, 38

Longfellow, Henry Wadsworth, 24

Longford, 5th Earl, 158, 161, 170, 176–7

Longford, Mary, Countess of (née Villiers), 47–9, 54, 83, 111–12, 133–4, 145, 156, 158, 161, 167, 176–8, 181

Longford, Elizabeth, Countess of (née Harman), 97

Lowell, James Russell, 55, 62–4, 77

Lugard, Sir Frederick and Lady Lugard, (née Flora Shaw), 147

Macauley, Thomas Babington, 24

Macclesfield, Mary, Countess of (née Grosvenor), 20

McCormick family, 142

McDonnell, Schomberg, 146

Malet, Lady Ermyntrude, 65

Manchester, Louise, Duchess of, 40

Marlborough, 1st Duke of, 34, 36

Marlborough, Frances, Duchess of (wife of 7th Duke), 42

Marlborough, Sarah, Duchess of (wife of 1st Duke), 36

Mary, Queen (wife of George V), 172

Mary, Queen, (wife of William III), 35

Mason, Ada, 83, 110

Mata'afa, 124, 126, 131

Maugham, Somerset, 144

Melbourne, 2nd Viscount, 4, 145

Meredith, George, 81

Milman, Henry, 14

Milton, John, 18

Mitford, Mary Russell, 6

Mitford, Nancy, 26

Molyneux, Caryl, 27

Mortimer, Roger, *History of the Derby Stakes*, 42

Mountstephen, 1st Baron, 108

Muncaster, 5th Baron and Lady Muncaster (née Constance L'Estrange), 67

Napier, 1st Baron Napier of Magdala, 46

Napoleon III, 39, 109

Newman, John Henry, Cardinal, 61

Nicholas, dragoman, 101

Nizam of Hyderabad, 86

Norfolk, 14th Duke of, 11

Norfolk, 15th Duke of, 11–12, 61

Norfolk, Augusta, Duchess of (née Lyons), 11

Northcote, Sir Stafford, 1st Baron, and Alice, Lady Northcote (née Stephen), 108, 144, 160, 167

Northumberland, Eleanor, Duchess of (née Grosvenor), 29

Olcutt, Colonel, theosophist, 84–5, 89–90, 133

Orkney, Elizabeth Villiers, Countess of, 35

Osbourne, Lloyd, 123

Otho, King of Greece, 68

Pakenham, Frank, Julia, Mary, Pansy, Violet, 180 *passim*

Palmer, Mrs Potter, 141

Parker, Mr and Mrs Frank, 106

Parkes, Sir Henry, 113–14

Peel, Arthur, 1st Viscount, 96

Peel, Julia, see Jersey

Peel, Sir Robert and Lady Peel (née Julia Floyd), 33

Peel, William, 1st Earl, 88

Pender, Sir John, 73

Pigot, 1st Baron, 88

Plunkett, Randal, 173
Ponsonby, Sir Henry, 96
Ponsonby, Sir Frederick, 97
Powell, Anthony, 187–8
Powell, Mr and Mrs, 46
Powell, Mr, balloonist, 46, 101
Powell, Tristram, 190

Raleigh, Sir Walter, Professor of English, 174
Reay, 11th Baron, 86
Rice, Charles, 162; Elwyn, 172
Rice, Walter, see Dynevor
Roberts, Field Marshal, 1st Earl, 92, 155, 163
Rogers, Samuel, 24
Rosebery, 5th Earl, statesman, 146
Rous, Admiral, 40
Rudolf, Crown Prince of Austria-Hungary, 95

St Helier, Susan, Lady St Helier (née Mackenzie, formerly Jeune), 74
Salar Jang, Sir, 87
Salisbury, 3rd Marquess of, 50, 56, 65–6, 107, 146
Schmieche, painter, 89
Schwartz, missionary in India, 33
Shaw, Flora, see Lugard
Shaw-Stewart, Sir Michael, Lady Octavia (née Grosvenor) and Hugh (son), 26–8
Sherman, Mrs, 148
Slatin Pasha, Baron Sir Rudolf, 148
Smith, Francis, of Warwick, 1
Smith, Sydney, 24
Soest, Gerard, 35
Somerville, E. Œ and Martin Ross, 51
Speke, J. H., explorer, 84
Spurgeon, Charles, 11
Stael, M. de, Russian Ambassador, 106
Stanley, H. M., explorer, 100–1
Stendhal, 17
Stevenson, Fanny (formerly Osbourne), 123–131
Stevenson, Robert Louis, 20, 121–31
Strachey, Lytton, 10, 182
Strong, Belle (née Osbourne), 123, 125–6, 128

Theodoki, Greek Minister of Marine, 69
Theodore, King of Abyssinia, 46
Thomas, Edward, 5
Thompson, Flora, *Larkrise to Candleford*, 44
Tricoupi, Prime Minister of Greece, and his sister, 68–70
Twisleton, Revd Charles, 13
Twisleton, Julia Judith, see Leigh, James
Twisleton, Miss, 2, 5
Twisleton, Thomas, Archdeacon of Colombo, 5, 13

Twysden, Philip, Bishop of Raphoe, 36
Tyler, Sir John, 97–8

Vedagua, Duke of, 140
Vetsera, Baroness Mary, 95
Victoria, Princess Royal, Crown Princess of Prussia, Empress Frederick, 20, 66
Victoria, Queen, 9–10, 33–4, 50, 52, 96, 107, 134, 155, 164
Villiers, Ann, 178
Villiers, Arthur, 47, 56, 91, 105, 109, 111, 119, 145, 167–8, 175 *passim*, 188
Villiers, Beatrice, see Dunsany
Villiers, Clementina, 28, 39, 185
Villiers, Francis, 40, 185
Villiers, Frederick, 40
Villiers, George Henry Robert (Viscount Villiers), see Jersey
Villiers, Margaret, see Dynevor
Villiers, Mary, see Longford
Villiers, Reginald, 105
Villiers, Sarah, see Esterhazy
Vyner, Frederick, 67

Wallace, Sir Donald, 147
Wallace, Mrs, housekeeper, 17
Wallace, Sir Richard, 64
Walpole, Horace, 38, 58
Ward, Mrs Humphry (née Mary Arnold), 123
Webb, Augusta, 60
Wellesley, Gerald, 167–8, 175
Wellington, 1st Duke of, 9, 56
Westminster, 1st Duke of, 31 and Duchess of (née Constance Leveson-Gower), 61
Westminster, 2nd Marquess of, 6, 8, 21
Westminster, Elizabeth, Marchioness of (née Sutherland-Leveson-Gower), 9, 12, 65
Westmorland, 10th Earl of and Sarah Countess of (née Child), 37–8
Wharton, Edith, 168
Wilde, Oscar, 72
Willes, Charles, 22; his wife (née Polly Wise), 22, 31
William I, German Emperor, 65–6
William II, German Emperor, 20, 66–7
William III, King of England and Prince of Orange, 34
Wister, Owen, 30, his mother, (née Sarah Butler), 77
Wolseley, Field Marshal, 1st Viscount, 74
Wombwell, Sir George and Lady Julia (née Villiers), 41
Wombwell, George, 92

Yonge, Charlotte M., 13, 178

Zaimes, John, 38
Zorn, Anders, 141, 182